26206

D0759337

STUDIES IN EVANGELICALISM
edited by
Kenneth E. Rowe &
Donald W. Dayton

THE LANE REBELS:

Evangelicalism and Antislavery in Antebellum America

by
Lawrence Thomas Lesick

Studies in Evangelicalism, No. 2

The Scarecrow Press, Inc.
Metuchen, N·J., & London
1980
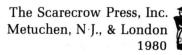

A portion of this work was published in the
Cincinnati Historical Society Bulletin, Volume
37, Winter 1979, Number 4, pages 237-248.
It has been reprinted here by permission.

Library of Congress Cataloging in Publication Data

Lesick, Lawrence Thomas, 1950-
    The Lane rebels.

    (Studies in evangelicalism ; no. 2)
    Bibliography: p.
    Includes index.
    1.   Church and slavery--Presbyterian Church.
2.   Slavery in the United States--Anti-slavery movements.
3.   Evangelicalism--United States--History--19th century.
4.   Abolitionists--United States.   5.   Lane Theological Seminary, Cincinnati.   I.   Title.   II.   Series.
E449. L64   326   80-24123
ISBN 0-8108-1372-6

ACKNOWLEDGMENTS

This work could not have been completed without the aid of numerous individuals and institutions. I would like to thank Professor Herman A. Norton and Professor Richard C. Wolf for their encouragement and patience throughout my tenure as a graduate student, and for their helpful criticisms of this work.

I am most appreciative of the assistance given to me by the staffs of the following institutions: Joint University Libraries, Nashville (particularly Mrs. Lois Griest, Interlibrary Loan Librarian, and Miss Dorothy Parks, Reference Librarian of the Divinity Library); the Boston Public Library; the Cincinnati Historical Society; the William L. Clements Library, University of Michigan, Ann Arbor; the Illinois State Historical Society Library, Springfield; the Trustees of Lane Theological Seminary, Cincinnati (particularly Mrs. M. E. Hagemann, Secretary-Treasurer); the Library of Congress; McCormick Theological Seminary, Chicago; the New York Historical Society; Mudd Learning Center of Oberlin College, and the Oberlin College Archives (particularly Mr. William E. Bigglestone, Archivist); the Ohio Historical Society, Columbus; the Presbyterian Historical Society, Philadelphia; and the Western Reserve Historical Society, Cleveland.

In addition, I am grateful for the help which the following individuals contributed to this project: Mr. Richard A. G. Dupuis, London, U. K.; Miss Gertrude Jacob, Oberlin, Ohio; Mrs. Betty Lehocka and Mrs. Nell Cannell, Cleveland; Mr. John R. Lesick II, Cincinnati; and Ms. Penelope Rohrbach, Boston. Mrs. Rebecca Smith did an excellent job of typing the manuscript.

Finally, I owe a debt of gratitude for moral and financial support to my parents, Mr. and Mrs. John R. Lesick; and to my wife, Linda, who also corrected my errors of grammar and style.

CONTENTS

EDITORS' NOTE

The current resurgence of Evangelical religion has highlighted the important role of this force in the formation of American culture. This series will explore its roots in the Evangelical Revival and Awakenings of the 18th century, its 19th-century blossoming in revivalism and social reform, and its 20th-century developments in both sect and "mainline" churches. We will be particularly concerned with emphasizing the diversity within Evangelicalism--the search for holiness, the Millennial traditions, Fundamentalism, Pentecostalism and so forth. We are pleased to publish Lawrence T. Lesick's study of Evangelicalism and antislavery in antebellum America as number two in the series.

Following undergraduate studies at Ohio Wesleyan University, Mr. Lesick took the doctorate in Church History at Vanderbilt University. He has published an article on the founding of the Lane Seminary in the Bulletin of the Cincinnati Historical Society and has taught at the University of Tennessee at Nashville. He currently resides in Cincinnati.

Donald W. Dayton
Northern Baptist Theological
   Seminary
Lombard, Illinois

Kenneth E. Rowe
Drew University
Madison, New Jersey

PREFACE

What follows is an attempt to delineate some of the ways in which evangelicalism--in this case that espoused by Charles G. Finney--influenced the American antislavery movement. Gilbert H. Barnes was the first to delineate specifically the ties between evangelical revivalism and the antislavery movement in terms of personnel, techniques, and thought. His negative attitude about Garrison should not lessen his extraordinary contributions to the history of the antislavery movement. More recently, Anne C. Loveland has shown how the techniques of revivalism were appropriated by the antislavery movement, and Donald M. Scott has demonstrated convincingly that antislavery became a religious "vocation" for many of those who joined the movement.

Despite the fine work of Loveland and Scott, and others, comparatively little attention has been given to the theological bases of evangelicalism which undergirded the antislavery movement. We know, for example, that William Lloyd Garrison derived the idea of immediatism from listening to the sermons of Lyman Beecher. There has not been a great deal of work seeking to uncover the theological premises that led evangelicals to antislavery.

I hope to indicate that evangelical theology must be regarded as a very real part of the evangelical contribution to antislavery. To ignore the fact that evangelicals were self-conscious theologians who based nearly all of what they did and said on their theology--however unsystematic or even simplistic--is to ignore vital sources which aid our understanding of both evangelicalism and the antislavery movement. More important, I hope that a study of the theological bases of antislavery can give us some insight into the ways in which ideas can (or cannot) influence the actions of people in society.

Obviously, my grasp is farther than my reach, and the scope of this book is much more restricted than my reasons for writing it in the first place. It is my intention here to increase the knowledge we have of the relationship between evangelicalism and antislavery by examining how a small number of evangelicals became abolitionists, the forms that their antislavery took over time, and the changes that occurred in both their evangelicalism and abolitionism because of the relationship.

Lawrence T. Lesick
Forest Park, Ohio
April 1980

CHAPTER I

INTRODUCTION

The Lane Affair in Brief

During the winter of 1834, in response to the national excitement caused by the new controversy over slavery in the United States, the students of the Lane Seminary, located near Cincinnati, Ohio, held a debate to consider two questions. The first was whether or not the people of the South should abolish slavery immediately. The second was whether or not the Christian community should support the efforts of the American Colonization Society.

At that time debates were common activities in colleges and seminaries. They provided information on current topics of interest, aided in the sharpening of the rhetorical skills required by educated men, and were a source of entertainment for participants and observers. This debate, however, was different. First, the questions presented for discussion were extremely controversial, given both the times, and the location of the Seminary near the border of a slave state, Kentucky, and near Cincinnati, which considered itself pro-Southern in character. Second, the decisions of the students in regard to the questions--favoring immediate emancipation and condemning colonization--caused consternation among the faculty and fear and anger among the trustees. Third, and most important, many of the students felt impelled to become directly involved in antislavery activities, and in benevolent projects to aid blacks in the Cincinnati community.

When the school year ended in July, members of the faculty and most of the trustees undoubtedly were relieved that no untoward incidents had occurred involving students' antislavery activities which might reflect on the good name of the Seminary. Some of the trustees may have hoped that the two-mile trek down the hills into the black sections of Cincinnati would become tiresome for the students during the

1

oppressive heat, humidity, and dust of an August in Cincinnati.

However, in August the benevolent projects of the students in the black areas of the city were still in operation. By then the trustees had decided that national as well as local events had combined to threaten the very existence of Lane. Acting on their perceptions, and encouraged by the one faculty member remaining in town, the trustees adopted measures to insure their complete control over every aspect of Seminary life, including the extra-curricular activities of the students. They announced a ban on all antislavery labor and discussion.

When the faculty stated at the beginning of the fall term that it would accept and enforce the trustees' newly adopted regulations, most of the students requested honorable dismissions and left the Seminary. This exodus of students created a national sensation and was exploited by the antislavery press. With the issuance of the students' Statement of the Reasons Which Have Induced the Students of Lane Seminary, to Dissolve Their Connection with That Institution, the Lane rebellion was assured a place in the history of the antislavery movement.

The subsequent antislavery activities of the Lane "rebels" (as the students have been traditionally labelled) are not well known, with the exceptions of those of Theodore Dwight Weld and Henry Brewster Stanton. Some of the "rebels" became advocates of abolition as agents and propagandists for the American Anti-Slavery Society. Others became missionaries to blacks in places such as Canada, Jamaica, British Guiana, and Sierra Leone. Others worked at various times as home missionaries, and spread the "gospel" of abolition as a recognized part of their regular ministerial duties. A number of them engaged in politics, or made other reforms or revivalism their primary focus. Some withdrew from any connection with reform. Almost all of the "rebels" have been ignored by historians of both the antislavery movement and evangelicalism.

Evangelicalism and Social Reform

American society in the nineteenth century was greatly influenced by evangelical Christianity. Supported by limitless resources, buoyed by optimistic ideas of perfectionism and natural ability, and having discovered the utility of voluntary societies, evangelicals set out to Christianize and civilize America. This reform activity was especially noticeable during the second quarter of the century.

The many reform movements that evangelicalism helped to spawn during this period have been given considerable attention, and studies have been made of movements as exotic as the Oneida Community and as current as feminism. Comparatively little, however, has been written on the relationship between evangelicalism and the antislavery movement. Although it was generally recognized that the antislavery movement was a "religious enterprise,"[1]* it was not until the publication of Gilbert Hobbs Barnes's The Antislavery Impulse, 1830-1844 that this religious aspect was investigated. Barnes's major contribution to antislavery history was a corrective to the overemphasis that had been placed on the role of William Lloyd Garrison. Barnes located the basis for the antislavery movement in revivalism, and pointed out that both were similar in "leadership, in method, and in objective."[2] Notably absent in his discussion, however, was an examination of the ideas of revivalism, and, in the larger context, of the evangelicalism which produced revivalism and supported antislavery.

Only fairly recently have there been any serious attempts made to understand the relationship between the ideas of evangelicalism and antislavery. William G. McLoughlin's Modern Revivalism: From Charles Grandison Finney to Billy Graham noted that Finney's doctrines of benevolence, perfectionism, and post-millennialism could be combined to form an impulse for reform. However, McLoughlin ended his discussion with an examination of Finney's own refusal to endorse whole-heartedly the antislavery movement.[3] Dwight L. Dumond's Antislavery: The Crusade for Freedom in America examined some of the ideological bases of antislavery, but Dumond's bias against Garrison was so great as to make his whole account unbalanced.[4] Bertram Wyatt-Brown's Lewis Tappan and the Evangelical War against Slavery was a masterful biography of one of the leaders of the movement, but it contained little information with regard to the relationship between evangelicalism and antislavery. Possibly the reticent character of its subject made such a discussion impossible.[5]

---

*Notes to Chapter I begin on page 13.

Anne C. Loveland's article, "Evangelicalism and 'Immediate Emancipation' in American Antislavery Thought," was the first attempt to develop the idea that the abolitionists "derived the doctrines and methods of immediatism from evangelicalism and ... prosecuted the antislavery movement as a religious and moral enterprise." Limited in that it was primarily an introduction to the relationship between evangelicalism and antislavery, Loveland's article noted the ways in which evangelical ideas provided the antislavery movement with the justification, vocabulary, and method of immediatism. [6]

After the publication of Loveland's work, there remained the task of going beyond the delineation of those aspects of evangelicalism appropriated by antislavery to an investigation of evangelicalism's basis for opposing slavery. This shift of focus from evangelical antislavery to antislavery evangelicalism was begun in Donald Moore Scott's "Watchmen on the Walls of Zion: Evangelicals and American Society, 1800-1860," an analytic study "of changes in the way personal religious experience defined a Christian's public responsibility" during the first half of the nineteenth century. Scott recognized that the relationship between evangelicalism and antislavery was central to illuminating the tensions between different conceptions of a Christian's public responsibility, of ministerial styles, and of institutional authority. However, his major concern was not antislavery evangelicalism so much as it was the whole of "evangelical benevolence." [7]

One of the purposes of this book is to investigate the role of evangelicalism in the formation of the antislavery ideas and actions of those students of the Lane Seminary who were later designated "rebels." An examination of the foundation of Lane can help to place the antislavery conflict within the context of evangelicalism and American life. An examination of the antecedents of the Lane students and a close study of the Lane debate can illuminate the major evangelical source, the revivalism of Charles G. Finney, which provided a foundation and impetus for the antislavery of the students. Further, an examination of the debate can help to explain how, within the context of a number of circumstances (such as the pro-Southern character of Cincinnati), Finney's type of evangelicalism provided the framework and impulse for the students' antislavery ideas and actions. A study of the Lane rebellion can help settle certain questions of a purely historical nature, such as the number and identities of the Lane "rebels." Moreover, a study of the Lane rebellion can provide a major example of the conflict which evangelically-grounded antislavery helped to precipitate.

All of this leads necessarily to a re-evaluation of the Lane debate and rebellion and of the influence of Finney in the antislavery movement. More importantly it leads to a more accurate estimation of the role of evangelicalism in the formation and expression of antislavery in America.

A second major purpose of this work concerns the Lane "rebels" themselves, and the different ways in which their antislavery activities reveal the changing nature of the relationship between evangelicalism and antislavery. Charles C. Cole noted, in The Social Ideas of the Northern Evangelists, 1826-1860, the importance of "those lesser known individuals who ... contributed in no small way to the crystallization of a nation-wide sentiment concerning slavery and its place in American society."[8] While this point of view has been endorsed by scholars, for the most part only the more prominent leaders of the antislavery movement have been studied. Relatively little attention has been given to those people who were less publicized--ordinary people made extraordinary by the dedication of significant portions of their lives to a worthy cause. A study of some of the lesser known rank and file antislavery activists can illuminate the different forms of the relationship between evangelicalism and antislavery, and thus show how evangelicalism contributed to the complexity of the antislavery movement. In addition, such a study can reveal the various ways in which people responded to an evangelical demand for antislavery, and can help disclose why people joined, and sometimes left, the movement.

In short, this book presents a specific example of the way in which evangelicalism furnished the framework, motivation and theological rationale for antislavery, and shows some of the ways in which the relationship between evangelicalism and antislavery changed over a period of time.

Some Definitions of Terms

The boundaries of this work need to be made clear at the outset. The book is not an examination of the institutions and major events of the antislavery movement, except insofar as these relate directly to the Lane rebels. Nor is this an investigation of the evangelical wing of the antislavery movement, although most of the rebels remained evangelicals all of their lives. The goals are more modest: to examine the antislavery events that occurred at Lane Seminary and the antislavery impulse which was expressed therein; and to examine the relationship between evangelicalism and antislavery expressed in the later antislavery activities of the Lane rebels.

Some of the terms used in succeeding chapters require definition to avoid confusion. The phrase "Lane rebels" was not widely used in 1834 and 1835 to describe the students who left Lane because of the trustees' regulations. Some supporters of the students referred to them as "rebels," and Theodore D. Weld was once denounced as a "rebel" by an irate minister, but usually the students were simply called "students" by the press. 9 For our purposes, "Lane rebels" and "rebels" will be used to identify those students of Lane Seminary who, in the fall of 1834, chose to leave the Seminary rather than accept the restrictive measures adopted by the trustees and endorsed by the faculty. The term will not refer to those who were not considered students of the Seminary at the time, nor to those new students who refused, upon learning of the new regulations, to enter the school. The "Lane rebellion" will refer to the voluntary withdrawal of the students from the Seminary in the fall of 1834.

Another term which requires definition is "evangelicalism." By the 1840's, Robert Baird, historian of religion in America, divided Christianity in the United States into the "evangelical" and "unevangelical" denominations. The evangelical ones, he wrote, were those which "hold the great doctrines of the Reformation."10 "Evangelicalism" was clearly the dominant form of Protestantism in the United States. It was made up of a number of assumptions, ideas, and beliefs which many Americans shared in the early nineteenth century. A typical "evangelical" statement of belief would have included the acceptance of the following:

> a belief in the guilty and lost condition of all men without a Saviour; the Supreme Deity, incarnation and atoning sacrifice of Jesus Christ, the only Saviour of the world; the necessity of regeneration by the Holy Spirit; repentance, faith and holy obedience, in order to [achieve] salvation; the immortality of the soul; and the retributions of the judgment in the eternal punishment of the wicked, and salvation of the righteous. 11

Within this broad characterization of evangelicalism, there were differing types or expressions. Each would have formulated the above statement of beliefs in different ways, and would have understood it from the perspectives of different theological traditions. This study is concerned with only one kind of evangelicalism: the kind which was adhered to by the Lane rebels. An indication of this particular kind of evangelicalism is apparent from a study of the origins of Lane Seminary.

Presbyterians founded Lane to prepare ministers for Presbyterian and (because of the Plan of Union which allowed cooperation between denominations which differed only in polity) Congregational churches. Its theological basis was Calvinist rather than Arminian. Further, Lane espoused the New School theology, which emphasized man's ability and responsibility in his response to God, and the moral government theory of the atonement, which preserved God's justice while allowing for His mercy through Christ's sacrifice. [12] This particular kind of evangelicalism is significant because it became dominant among northern Presbyterians and influential within much of American Protestantism by the Civil War. [13]

Explicit in this evangelicalism was a social content to go along with its theology emphasizing man's ability. According to Lyman Beecher, a leading churchman and first President of Lane, evangelicals were common people of "sound morality," and "piety of great solemnity, and ardor, and decision," who had "an unwavering confidence" in the truth of their Gospel. They were social activists who favored the "reformation" of "vicious habits" such as intemperance, "voluntary associations of the wise and the good, to aid the civil magistrate in the execution of the laws," and "a spirit of missions" to convert the world. [14] Thus, the evangelicalism at Lane contained a social element as well as a theological framework and content. Ironically, it was not Lyman Beecher but his disaffected students who, influenced by Finney, recognized the applicability of evangelicalism's theological and social aspects to the problem of slavery.

It must be understood that the evangelicalism which condemned slavery at Lane was only one kind of evangelicalism, albeit an influential one. It is questionable whether or not there was a "united evangelical front" regarding slavery, and no attempt will be made in this study to establish that there was such a consensus. That evangelicalism contained within itself the theological rationale and moral impulse which, under particular conditions and in certain forms, did lead to antislavery advocacy is argued in this study.

Another term which must be defined is "antislavery."

Simply stated, "antislavery" will be used here to refer to that movement which favored the immediate emancipation of black slavery in the United States. This is a departure, somewhat, from other definitions of "antislavery," which have used it as the genus under which different species, most notably "abolition" have been placed. "Antislavery" will be used synonymously with "abolition" to coincide with the usage of the period (e. g. America) Anti-Slavery Society), and to avoid unnecessary categorization.[15]

"Colonization" will refer to that movement which believed that slavery was an evil, that slaves should be freed over a period of time, that blacks and whites were unable to live as equals in a free society, and therefore free blacks should be transported out of the United States.[16]

"Evangelical antislavery" will refer to those elements of evangelicalism (e. g. immediate repentance from sin) which were incorporated into the antislavery movement, while "antislavery evangelicalism" will refer to those theological and social aspects of evangelicalism which led directly to antislavery advocacy.

The Lane Rebels in American History

Participants in the antislavery movement, usually writing after the Civil War had ended slavery, considered the Lane debate and rebellion significant, but certainly not central, events in the cause. Parker Pillsbury, in Acts of the Anti-Slavery Apostles, considered the Lane rebels to have been "conscientious and high-minded." However, he merely noted the rebellion in connection with a similar exodus of students from Andover Latin Academy, both of which were the results of "downright pro-slavery intolerance."[17] Henry Wilson, in History of the Rise and Fall of the Slave Power in America, characterized the Lane rebels as among the first of the "new" antislavery groups to attract unfavorable public attention, but he erred in placing the Lane debate in the winter of 1834-1835, a year after it occurred.[18] Samuel J. May, in Some Recollections of Our Antislavery Conflict, ended his brief account of the events at Lane with a statement of relief that the faculty and trustees had acted to forbid antislavery discussion, and thus forced the students to leave, for otherwise, "What a loss it would have been to the cause of liberty...."[19]

Oliver Johnson, in William Lloyd Garrison and His Times, presented one of the most informative accounts of the

Lane debate and rebellion. Although he wrote over forty
years after the events had taken place, he had the advantage
of having known many of the participants. In fact, he based
much of his account of the Lane rebellion on information supplied to him by a "friend," i. e. someone who probably took
part. [20] This first-person character of Johnson's presentation
of the Lane incidents was probably responsible for his giving
them twenty-six pages in a book devoted to Garrison, even
though Garrison played no role at Lane.

An account by a participant, Huntington Lyman, appeared in the Oberlin Jubilee, a book commemorating the
semi-centennial celebration of Oberlin College in 1883. Lyman added to the previous accounts of the rebellion in noting
that the term "rebellion" "applies in a way of metaphorical
accomodation [sic] only." While the term was remembered,
the events it conveyed had been forgotten, and Lyman wanted
to insure that it was known that relations between students
and faculty always remained respectful. Ignoring whatever
reasons the trustees might have had for their actions, Lyman
likened them to Herod, Torquemada of the Inquisition, and
the Lords of the Star Chamber, images hardly calculated to
insure historical accuracy--but then, that was not his purpose. [21]

Lyman Beecher's Autobiography contained his version
of the "Anti-Slavery Imbroglio" at Lane Seminary. Although
not concerned with the relationship between the Lane debate
and rebellion and the antislavery movement, Beecher did present the obvious negative effect which the rebellion had upon
the Seminary's welfare, which was an example of the frac-
tious nature of the slavery controversy. Beecher's account
reflected his view that he was blameless in the entire affair,
and had supported the cause of principle and right. His son,
Charles, wrote that, if the students, like the trustees, had
in the end "consented to adopt Dr. Beecher for their leader,
... trusting [him] to bring things right again," then the students could have maintained their principles (he said nothing
about restrictions on their activities) and the Seminary would
have prospered. [22]

None of the earlier accounts of the Lane debate, rebellion, or of the rebels themselves provided an indication of
their significance within the antislavery movement. The contemporary accounts, as long as forty years after the events,
were postbellum antislavery tracts, with the obvious exception
of Beecher's. The debate was viewed as one of the first

efforts of the new antislavery movement which originated in
the 1830's, but little of its actual content was discussed.
The rebellion was presented as an incident in the conflict between the clearly distinguished adversaries of right and wrong
and freedom and oppression. In accordance with this moral-
istic style, the rebels were portrayed uniformly as selfless,
righteous, "earnest," "devoted," and "fervent" saints,[23] all
of whom had dedicated themselves to the eradication of slavery, or any other sin that needed fighting. These early por-
trayals suffered because they were one-dimensional and they
tended to vaporize the rebels into the mists of antislavery
obscurity.

Antislavery histories, written later by non-contempor-
aries, did little to improve the earlier versions. In some
cases these histories compounded the problem regarding the
historical significance of the Lane episodes and participants
by a disregard of the facts. Albert Bushnell Hart placed the
debate in 1832, the rebellion in May, 1833, and identified the
student leader as Theodore F. Weld.[24] Jesse Macy included
among the rebels "many" of their professors.[25]

The publication of Gilbert Hobbs Barnes's The Antislavery Impulse, 1830-1844 in 1933 completely revised the
history of antislavery. Even now, forty-seven years later,
studies must deal with Barnes's conclusions. He made two
major contributions to antislavery history. The first was a
reassertion of the importance of the moral aspect in bringing
about the Civil War, an assessment still accepted. Second,
as previously noted, Barnes provided a corrective to the (then)
current interpretation of the role of William Lloyd Garrison
in the antislavery movement. The influence of Garrison and
his followers was minimal, insisted Barnes, while that of the
Western, revivalistic abolitionists was much more significant.[26]

In refuting Garrison's dominant antislavery role, Barnes
raised the Lane debate, rebellion and rebels out of obscurity
to a position of major importance. Barnes believed that the
antislavery movement which originated in the West in the
1830's was based on a "religious impulse" provided by the
revivalism of Charles G. Finney. Lane Seminary was the
place where this religious impulse was transformed into an
antislavery impulse. The debate was the occasion of the
transformation, the rebellion one of its first results, and the
rebels among its first apostles.[27]

Since the 1930's, and until fairly recently, studies

which dealt with aspects of the Lane imbroglio generally have
been of two kinds. The first has accepted and promulgated
Barnes's thesis of the connection between Finney's revivalism
and antislavery, a connection prominently formed at Lane.
The most prominent advocate of this thesis was Dwight L.
Dumond, who wrote that the revivals of Finney provided the
antislavery movement with "an unprecedented number of devoted apostles," the first group of which came from Lane
Seminary. [28]

   The second kind of study which has dealt with Lane
has been one which treated it within the context of the development of Oberlin College. The major representative of
this emphasis was Robert Samuel Fletcher's A History of
Oberlin College: From Its Foundation Through the Civil War.
Fletcher demonstrated the Finney-connected, revivalistic character of the first theological class at Lane by tracing many
of its members' antecedents back to Oneida Institute and the
Finney revivals.   In showing this relationship, he proved the
continuity of Oberlin with the eastern, Yankee, reform impulse and thus proved that the acquisition of Lane students
did not materially change Oberlin's original character.   In
addition, Fletcher presented the Lane debate and rebellion
from the perspective of those who later went to Oberlin: the
students, Asa Mahan (a Lane trustee), and John Morgan (a
Lane professor); and demonstrated the importance of the issue
of freedom of speech in the Lane affair. [29]

   Neither type of these studies of Lane--those that began
with Barnes and those that viewed Lane from Oberlin--has
dealt with the Lane debate, rebellion, and rebels themselves.
This occurred in the first case because Barnes presented such
a compelling story, and in the second because Fletcher and
other historians of Oberlin were not concerned with Lane
per se.

   During the turmoil of the 1960's and 1970's, the Lane
rebels were rediscovered by a new group of historians with
a new set of priorities.   Colleges and universities were ex-
periencing student unrest, and historians searched for precedents which could explain this phenomenon.   Lewis S. Feuer,
in The Conflict of Generations: The Character and Significance of Student Movements, cited the Lane rebellion as the
only "episode in the prehistory of the American Civil War
[which] partook of the characteristics of a student movement."
For Feuer, the Lane debate provided an example of the generational conflict which defines the character of student move-

ments. The Lane students, in discussing the moral evil of
slavery, engaged in "a collective experience of guilt in which
the sons tried to thrust from themselves the evil of their
fathers." Their benevolent work with blacks in Cincinnati
demonstrated "that missionary, self-sacrificing quality of the
back-to-the-people spirit, which is the high calling of student
movements."[30]

In 1971, Lois W. Banner wrote an article which dealt
with the idea of generational conflict, and she, too, used the
Lane rebels as examples. She concluded that reformers of
the very early nineteenth century, such as those at Andover
in 1810, had combined the idealism of the Revolutionary generation with benevolent projects which they had believed would
reform the world. Twenty years later the Lane rebels adhered to this idealism of the Revolution, but they differed
from the Andover reformers in that they did not have the institutional and emotional connections with the reform institutions of the older generation. The Lane students found themselves alienated from "respectable" causes, and, fueled with
the idealism of their fathers, they rejected the means of the
fathers and became activists in radical causes.[31]

Where Feuer's account found precedents for the student activists of the 1960's in the Lane rebellion, and Banner'
description of the rebels read like one of more recent radicals, Stuart C. Henry explored the major differences between
the Lane rebels and the new radicals. He wrote that "there
is a despair which separates the new radicals from the Lane
Rebels--a despair which arising from a sense of destiny de-
void of any mercy has thus forced its devotees to displace
providence with fate." While the new radicals became activists because of their alienation and loss of faith in the dominant moral order, the Lane rebels had become alienated because of their activism which was based on faith.[32]

Unlike Feuer and Henry (and indirectly Banner), Donald
W. Dayton studied the Lane rebellion, not in relation to the
new radicals (or even the older reformers), but in relation to
the "Evangelical currents" which "had over the course of a
century fallen into a form of decadence." Dayton set his task
as that of Discovering an Evangelical Heritage of reform which
would help to offset the "[c]ultural insularity and reactionary
social perspectives" of present day evangelicalism. The Lane
rebellion had formed a part of this heritage which Dayton obviously wanted renewed.[33]

Finally, Donald M. Scott, in "Watchmen on the Walls of Zion: Evangelicals and American Society, 1800-1860," studied the changes in the ideas of evangelical benevolence and ministerial roles which occurred during the Middle Period. The Lane rebellion was a major incident illustrating the culmination of these changes. [34]

None of the authors mentioned made any systematic attempt to determine the impact of the Lane debate and rebellion on those who took part. Biographies exist for Theodore Dwight Weld, Marius Racine Robinson, Henry Brewster Stanton, Robert Livingston Stanton, and Hiram Wilson. [35] Barnes and Dumond gave brief notices, sometimes inaccurate, of the lives of some of the rebels. [36] Dumond gave way to enthusiasm or wishful thinking when he wrote that all of the rebels "without any known exception" continued as "courageous and outspoken opponents of slavery." [37] Fletcher presented biographical data on some of the rebels who attended Oberlin, and references to these and others are scattered throughout other works. [38] There has been no consensus as to who the individual Lane rebels were, and this has compounded the problem of deciding the significance of the debate and rebellion. [39] In addition, there have been great differences regarding even the number of Lane rebels. Estimates have ranged from "three dozen" to "hundreds." [40]

Thus, even with so many accounts of the Lane debate, rebellion, and rebels, the addition of yet one more is defensible. The lack of primary investigation since Barnes, the Oberlin-oriented studies following Fletcher, the comparative approach of more recent studies, and the lack of any systematic discussion of the Lane rebels themselves make another study desirable, and potentially useful.

Notes

1. Noted in Charles C. Cole, The Social Ideas of the Northern Evangelists, 1826-1860 (New York: Columbia University Press, 1954), p. 194.

2. With a new Introduction by William G. McLoughlin (New York: D. Appleton-Century Co., 1933; reprint ed., Gloucester, Mass.: Peter Smith, 1973), p. 107.

3. (New York: Ronald Press Co., 1959), pp. 104-111.

4. (Ann Arbor: University of Michigan Press, 1961).

5. (Cleveland: Press of Case Western Reserve University, 1969).

6. Journal of Southern History, 32 (May 1966): 172-88; quotation from p. 174.

7. (Ph. D. dissertation, University of Wisconsin, 1968), p. vii.

8. Cole, Northern Evangelists, p. 193.

9. George A. Avery to Franklin Y. Vail, 15 August 1835, Lane Theological Seminary Papers, Folder 5, McCormick Theological Seminary, Chicago (hereafter cited as Lane Papers, MTS); Theodore D. Weld to Elizur Wright, Jr. , 2 March 1835, in Gilbert H. Barnes and Dwight L. Dumond, eds. , Letters of Theodore Dwight Weld, Angelina Grimké Weld, and Sarah Grimké, 1822-1844, 2 vols. (New York: D. Appleton-Century Co. , 1934; reprint ed. , Gloucester, Mass. : Peter Smith, 1965), 1:206; and Emancipator, 11 November 1834.

10. Robert Baird, Religion in America; or, an Account of the Origin, Relation to the State, and Present Condition of the Evangelical Churches in the United States. With Notices of the Unevangelical Denominations, new ed. (New York: Harper & Bros. , 1856), p. viii.

11. This statement is from the "Constitution of the American Missionary Association," in Proceedings of the Second Convention for Bible Missions, Held in Albany September Second and Third, MDCCCXLI: With the Address of the Executive Committee of the American Missionary Association (New York: American Missionary Association, 1846), pp. 4-5.

12. The New School wing of Presbyterianism favored interdenominational benevolent societies, the Plan of Union, a theology similar to the New Haven theology of Nathaniel W. Taylor, and "new measures" revivalism. The Old School desired denominational control of benevolent projects, favored a strict presbyterian polity, distrusted theological innovation, and was suspicious

of "new measures" revivalism. These issues, plus slavery, led to a denominational schism in 1837. Sydney E. Ahlstrom, A Religious History of the American People (New Haven: Yale University Press, 1972), pp. 466-68. A detailed discussion of the issues which led to the schism is in George M. Marsden, The Evangelical Mind and the New School Presbyterian Experience: A Case Study of Thought and Theology in Nineteenth-Century America (New Haven: Yale University Press, 1970), pp. 66-87.

13. See William G. McLoughlin, "Introduction: The American Evangelicals: 1800-1900," in The American Evangelicals, 1800-1900: An Anthology, ed. William G. McLoughlin (New York: Harper Torchbooks, 1968), pp. 1-14.

14. Quotations are from Lyman Beecher, "The Faith Once Delivered to the Saints," and "A Reformation of Morals Practicable and Indispensable," in Beecher's Works, 3 vols., vol. 2: Sermons, Delivered on Various Occasions (Boston: John P. Jewett & Co., 1852; Cleveland: Jewett, Proctor & Worthington, 1852), pp. 263, 268, 270, 265, 95, 267. See also James Luther Adams, "The Voluntary Principle in the Forming of American Religion," in The Religion of the Republic, ed. Elwyn A. Smith (Philadelphia: Fortress, 1971), pp. 229-31.

15. See David Brion Davis, The Problem of Slavery in the Age of Revolution, 1770-1823 (Ithaca: Cornell University Press, 1975), pp. 21-22.

16. A modern study of the colonization movement is P. J. Staudenraus, The African Colonization Movement, 1816-1865 (New York: Columbia University Press, 1961).

17. (Boston: Cupples, Upham & Co., 1884), p. 217.

18. 3 vols. (Boston: Houghton Mifflin & Co., 1872, 1877; reprint ed., New York: Negro Universities Press, 1969), 1:264.

19. (Boston: Fields, Osgood, & Co., 1869; reprint ed., New York: Arno Press and the New York Times, 1969), p. 108.

20.   Johnson's book was subtitled Sketches of the Antislavery
      Movement in America, and of the Man Who Was Its
      Founder and Moral Leader, new, rev. and enl. ed.,
      with an Introduction by John G. Whittier (Boston:
      Houghton Mifflin & Co., 1881), p. 170.

21.   "Lane Seminary Rebels," in Oberlin Jubilee, 1833-1883,
      ed. William Gay Ballantine (Oberlin: E. J. Good-
      rich, 1884), pp. 60-61, 65-66.

22.   Barbara M. Cross, ed., The Autobiography of Lyman
      Beecher, 2 vols.   (Cambridge: Harvard University
      Press, the Belknap Press, 1961), 2:240-49; quotation
      from p. 248.   Asa Mahan presented his account of
      the Lane rebellion in his Autobiography: Intellectual,
      Moral, and Spiritual (London: T. Woolmer for the
      Author, 1882), pp. 172-84; and in Out of Darkness
      into Light, or the Hidden Life Made Manifest Through
      Facts of Observation and Experience: Facts Eluci-
      dated by the Word of God (New York: Willard Tract
      Repository, 1876), pp. 114-22.

23.   The adjectives describing the Lane rebels were used by
      O. Johnson, Garrison and His Times, p. 166; and
      May, Recollections, p. 205.

24.   Slavery and Abolition, 1831-1841, American Nation: A
      History, vol. 16 (New York: Harper & Bros., 1906),
      pp. 190-91.

25.   The Anti-slavery Crusade: A Chronicle of the Gathering
      Storm, Chronicles of America Series, vol. 28 (New
      Haven: Yale University Press, 1919), pp. 74-75.

26.   McLoughlin, Introduction to Antislavery Impulse, by
      Barnes, pp. xxiv-xxv.

27.   Barnes, Antislavery Impulse, pp. 64-78.

28.   Antislavery, p. 159.   See also Dumond's Antislavery
      Origins of the Civil War in the United States (Ann
      Arbor: University of Michigan Press, 1939), p. 35;
      Walter R. Keagy, "The Lane Seminary Rebellion,"
      Bulletin of the Historical and Philosophical Society
      of Ohio 9 (April 1951):   141-60; and Charles L. Zor-
      baugh, "From Lane to Oberlin--An Exodus Extraor-

dinary," Ohio Presbyterian Historical Society Proceedings 2 (June 1940): 30-47.

29. 2 vols. (Oberlin: Oberlin College, 1943), 1:150-66.
Other studies which viewed Lane from this perspective include James H. Fairchild, Oberlin: The Colony and the College, 1833-1883 (Oberlin: E. J.
Goodrich, 1883); Delavan L. Leonard, The Story of
Oberlin: The Institution, the Community, the Idea,
the Movement (Boston: Pilgrim Press, 1898); Sidney
Strong, "The Exodus of Students from Lane Seminary
to Oberlin in 1834," Papers of the Ohio Church History Society 4 (1893): 1-16; and Zorbaugh, "From
Lane to Oberlin." Russell B. Nye followed Fletcher's
account of the Lane rebellion in Fettered Freedom:
Civil Liberties and the Slavery Controversy, 1830-
1860 (East Lansing: Michigan State College Press,
1949), pp. 88-91.

30. (New York: Basic Books, 1969), pp. 321-23.

31. "Religion and Reform in the Early Republic: The Role
of Youth," American Quarterly 23 (December 1971):
677-95. See especially p. 692.

32. "The Lane Rebels: A Twentieth Century Look," Journal
of Presbyterian History 49 (Spring 1971): 1-14; quotation from p. 7.

33. (New York: Harper & Row, 1976), pp. 35-44; quotations
from p. 7.

34. "Watchmen on the Walls of Zion," pp. vii, 331-83. Dis-
sertations which have dealt with the Lane debate, rebellion, and the rebels include John Lytle Myers,
"The Agency System of the Anti-slavery Movement,
1832-1837, and its Antecedents in Other Benevolent
and Reform Societies" (Ph. D. dissertation, University
of Michigan, 1961), pp. 171-88; Vincent Harding,
"Lyman Beecher and the Transformation of American
Protestantism, 1775-1863" (Ph. D. dissertation, University of Chicago, 1965), pp. 487-525; Arthur Harry
Rice, "Henry B. Stanton as a Political Abolitionist"
(Ed. D. dissertation, Columbia University, 1968), pp.
28-57; Malcolm Lyle Warford, "Piety, Politics, and
Pedagogy: An Evangelical Protestant Tradition in
Higher Education at Lane, Oberlin, and Berea, 1834-

1904" (Ed. D. dissertation, Columbia University, 1973), pp. 1-46; and Robert Henry Abzug, "Theodore Dwight Weld: A Biography" (Ph. D. dissertation, University of California, Berkeley, 1977), pp. 83-144. Two other unpublished works have dealt with the Lane rebellion: Robert Clare Lodwick, "The Anti-Slavery Controversy in Lane Seminary" (Typewritten paper, McCormick Theological Seminary, 1951); and Thomas Bryant Corcoran, "The Lane Seminary Rebellion: Its Causes and Consequences" (M. A. thesis, University of Cincinnati, 1962).

35. Abzug, "Theodore Dwight Weld"; Russell B. Nye, "Marius Robinson, A Forgotten Abolitionist Leader," Ohio State Archeological and Historical Quarterly 55 (April-June 1946): 138-54; Rice, "Henry B. Stanton"; Timothy F. Reilly, "Robert L. Stanton, Abolitionist of the Old South," Journal of Presbyterian History 53 (Spring 1975): 33-50; and Jane H. Pease and William H. Pease, "The Clerical Do-Gooder: Hiram Wilson," in Bound with Them in Chains: A Biographical History of the Antislavery Movement, Contributions in American History, no. 18 (Westport, Conn. : Greenwood Press, 1972), pp. 115-39. Two fairly recent biographies of Lyman Beecher are Harding, "Lyman Beecher"; and Stuart C. Henry, Unvanquished Puritan: A Portrait of Lyman Beecher (Grand Rapids, Mich. : William B. Eerdmans Publishing Co. , 1973).

36. There is some biographical material on the rebels in Barnes, Antislavery Impulse, passim; Dumond, Antislavery, passim; and Barnes and Dumond, eds. , Letters of Weld, passim. An example of the inaccuracies which Barnes and Dumond sometimes made is the statement that Joseph D. Gould, in 1836, "was one of the most successful antislavery agents of the Seventy, especially in raising money for the cause," when he had died in 1835. Barnes and Dumond confused Joseph D. Gould with Samuel L. Gould, who did not attend Lane. Barnes and Dumond, eds. , Letters of Weld, 1:334, n. 5; and Lane Theological Seminary General Catalogue. 1829-1899 (Cincinnati: Elm Street Printing Works, 1899), p. 18.

37. Antislavery, p. 165.

38. Fletcher, History of Oberlin, 1:55, 165, 419-20, passim;

and Hermann R. Muelder, Fighters for Freedom: The History of Anti-Slavery Activities of Men and Women Associated with Knox College (New York: Columbia University Press, 1959), pp. 73-75, 92-99, 145-148, passim.

39. C. Duncan Rice identified James G. Birney and Elizur Wright, Jr. as Lane rebels, but neither ever attended Lane, and Wright was in New York when the debate and rebellion occurred. The Rise and Fall of Black Slavery (New York: Harper & Row, 1975), p. 321.

40. Bernard A. Weisberger, They Gathered at the River: The Story of the Great Revivalists and Their Impact upon Religion in America (Boston: Little, Brown & Co., 1958), p. 134; and An Alabama Man, "Account of Mrs. Beecher Stowe and Her Family," in Uncle Sam's Emancipation; Earthly Care; A Heavenly Discipline; and Other Sketches by Harriet Beecher Stowe. With a Sketch of Mrs. Stowe's Family, by Harriet Beecher Stowe (Philadelphia: Willis P. Hazard, 1853), p. 23.

CHAPTER II

LANE SEMINARY: 1828-1832

Cincinnati in the 1830's

Cincinnati during the 1830's was not a rough, uncivilized frontier town, nor a copy of the more established cities of the East. Located on the northern bank of a bend in the Ohio River and opposite the mouth of the Licking River, Cincinnati was characterized by extraordinary growth. From a population of almost twenty-five thousand in 1830, the city had nearly doubled in size ten years later. Much of this increase came from immigration from the Old Northwest, the Middle Atlantic States, and the South. [1]* The German element, for which Cincinnati would become known, was only beginning in the 1830's. [2] Another "foreign" element, black, had actually decreased in 1829 when local officials executed Ohio's infamous Black Laws. By the 1830's, the black population of Cincinnati was less than 3 percent of the total. [3]

Like the general growth in population, Cincinnati's industry and commerce were rapidly expanding during the 1830's. At mid-decade, the industrial output of the Cincinnati area, including the towns of Newport and Covington across the river in Kentucky, was estimated to be about $5 million. During 1835, there were over 50 steam engines producing capital goods such as 100 steam engines, 240 cotton gins, 20 sugar mills, and 22 steamboats. Cincinnati was also gaining a reputation as a packing center: in 1834-1835, 162 thousand hogs were slaughtered. In commerce, an estimated $6 million in goods was shipped out of Cincinnati in 1835, including such products as iron, wood, cotton, leather, hemp, oil, lumber, furs, flour, and whiskey (55 thousand barrels). [4] To provide financing for its industry and commerce, Cincinnati had at least ten "monied institutions" and a branch of the United States Bank. [5]

---

*Notes to Chapter II begin on page 52.

20

Although Cincinnati had commercial ties with all sections of the country, much of its trade was with the South. The 240 cotton gins and 20 sugar mills produced in 1835 were the most obvious indications of the city's Southern ties. It also shipped much of its flour and liquor to the South, and received products such as salt, coffee, molasses, and sugar from New Orleans. [6] These economic connections, added to close proximity and intermarriage, [7] reinforced the pro-Southern character of Cincinnatians.

Culturally, the city contained a theatre, Frances Trollope's bazaar (usually referred to as "Trollope's folly"), three libraries, an art school, two museums, public primary schools, and a number of "literary institutions" including the Medical College of Ohio, Woodward High School, the Mechanics Institute, and the Roman Catholic supported Atheneum. [8] At least sixteen newspapers and periodicals were published in the city. The most ambitious and best known paper was the Western Monthly Magazine, which extolled the virtues (and demonstrated the pedantry) of a native Western literature. [9]

The churches in Cincinnati provided a great number of citizens with cultural and literary outlets, as well as moral and religious training. In 1832, it was estimated that the city contained twenty-six churches: six Presbyterian, two Protestant Episcopal, four Methodist Episcopal, two Associate Methodist, two Regular Baptist, one Campbell Baptist, one Lutheran and Reformed, one African, one Christian, one Friends, one Unitarian, one Swedenborgian, one Universalist, one Roman Catholic, and one Jewish synagogue; and over twenty-five full-time clergy. [10] These churches supplied the leaders and members for most of the benevolent societies which operated in Cincinnati. These included the Miami Bible Society, the African Society, Sunday School Union Society, Western Navigators Bible and Tract Society, the Humane Society, the Hebrew Beneficent Society, and branches of such national societies as the American Temperance Society, the American Home Missionary Society, the American Education Society, and the American Colonization Society. [11]

The most influential church body in Cincinnati was the Presbyterian, which had twelve ministers and about three thousand "attendants." [12] Leading politicians, bankers, and businessmen of the city, such as Isaac G. Burnet, Cincinnati's first mayor, Jacob Burnet, jurist and board member of the United States Bank, George Neff, city councilman, and John H. Groesbeck, banker and merchant, were Presbyterian laymen. [13] Approximately one-half of the benevolent and charitable societies in the city were Presbyterian organizations or had Presbyterian men or women in positions of leadership. [14] One of the most popular local religious journals was the Presbyterian Cincinnati Journal, which at one time had a circulation of four thousand. [15]

Within Presbyterianism, however, there existed a divisive spirit based on issues of theology, church polity, and control of missions. One branch of Presbyterianism, the Old School, emphasized adherence to "strict scholastic Reformed confessional theology," believed that Presbyterian polity conformed to the law of God, and favored denominational control of missionary and educational activities. [16] The New School made allowances for theological innovation (especially with regard to the doctrine of free will), accepted mixed polity (under the Plan of Union), and favored the interdenominational character of benevolent societies. The differences between these two branches, along with the issue of slavery, would eventually lead to a Presbyterian schism in 1837. [17]

In Cincinnati, Joshua Lacy Wilson, minister of the First Presbyterian Church from 1808 until 1846, brought the issues into the open during the 1830's. Born in 1774, Wilson was largely self-educated and adhered to a strict, rigid theology which emphasized man's inability. [18] During the 1820's he engaged in moderate revival activities. In 1827, while in Kentucky, he became acquainted with two itinerant evangelists, James Gallaher and Frederick A. Ross, who had been touring the state quite successfully. Wilson convinced them to come to Cincinnati where a revival added 364 to Wilson's church. [19] About this time, he wrote, "I doubt whether the man ever lived who had more pith, point, tact and power in exhortation than James Gallaher."[20] During this revival in Cincinnati, however, some irregularities occurred, which Wilson overlooked. For the first time in Ohio, use was made of the "anxious seat," one of the new measures of modern revivalism. [21] Perhaps Wilson did not object at this time because of the great increase which had occurred in his own church, as well as the formation of the Third and Fourth Presbyterian Churches. Two years later, at camp meetings in Sharon and Montgomery, Ohio, Gallaher allowed people who believed they were converted to be admitted to communion before the close of the meeting, an irregularity brought to the attention of the General Assembly. Wilson himself was present at these camp meetings but took no offense at Gallaher's

irregularities. [22] In fact, he supported Gallaher to such an
extent that he preached the dedicatory sermon at the Third
Church, which Gallaher pastored, and which had received
over two-hundred people during the two years of revivals. [23]
However, in the early 1830's Wilson became hostile towards
Gallaher, and wrote of this man whom he had called "most
admirably qualified," "There was a time when I had ... confidence in Mr. G. in the days of my ignorance. "[24]

Wilson's change in attitude towards Gallaher was
brought about by his recognition that the revivalism Gallaher
preached was, because of its emphasis on man's ability to
respond to the work of the Holy Spirit in conversion, very
close to the theology of the growing New School party in Cincinnati. Also, Gallaher supported the American Home Missionary Society which, Wilson believed, was bringing heresy
into the church through its connection with the New England
theology or Taylorism, and because of the General Assembly's
lack of control over its missionaries. On his part, Gallaher
had arrived at an acceptance of New School doctrine through
common sense and the felt need to convert his listeners; he
was "a stranger to the 'nice points' of theology" and had had
little training. His support of the American Home Missionary Society was likewise most probably due to his desire to
convert as many as could be reached. [25]

Wilson's realization that Gallaher was moving toward
the New School was undoubtedly the result of his awareness
of the inroads which New Schoolism was making into Cincinnati. Amos Blanchard, editor of the Cincinnati Journal, was
viewed by Wilson as a heretic. In April, 1831, when Blanchard applied to the Cincinnati Presbytery for ordination, Wilson opposed on the basis of Blanchard's views on "the doctrines of Original Sin and the Atonement. " At Wilson's suggestion, Blanchard gave a trial sermon in July, and afterward
"the Presbytery engaged in very warm discussion upon the
style and sentiments of the sermon. In the course of this
discussion several things were said which had much better
have been left unsaid. " Over protest by Wilson, Blanchard
was ordained. [26]

During the same month that Wilson had originally op-
posed Blanchard's ordination, Blanchard and some other dis-
contented members of Wilson's church seceded to form the
Sixth Presbyterian Church. [27] For their pastor they called
Asa Mahan, a colleague of Charles G. Finney in New York. [28]
As disputatious as Wilson himself, Mahan quickly entered into

a conflict with Wilson over rumors, circulated in the Wilson-controlled Standard, that Mahan had not accepted the Confession of Faith when he was ordained. Mahan asked for an investigation by the Presbytery, and two of his church members charged Wilson with "unchristian conduct" in August, 1832. Although the issue was finally resolved, the lines were being drawn between the Old and New School parties. [29]

Wilson's problems with Gallaher, Blanchard and Mahan brought the theological and doctrinal issues into view in Cincinnati. Issues over polity and missions were brought forth in the conflict over the role of the American Home Missionary Society in the West.

Since the late 1820's, Presbyterians had supported both the Board of Missions of the General Assembly of the Presbyterian Church, reorganized in 1828, and the American Home Missionary Society, an interdenominational organization founded in 1826. [30] In the West, the efforts of the two bodies often overlapped, but more important was the concern felt by Old School Presbyterians that an uncontrolled voluntary society such as the American Home Missionary Society was introducing theological heresy and Congregational polity into the Presbyterian Church. [31] In 1830 an offer was made by that Society to combine its efforts with the General Board in the West under a Central Committee for Home Missions. [32] The Cincinnati Presbytery endorsed such a plan and requested the General Assembly to accept the union of the two organizations, but the request was rejected "after much discussion." A year later the "overture" was made again, and the General Assembly referred the matter to the western synods and presbyteries, which sent representatives to a convention in November, 1831, in Cincinnati. [33] The convention was unable to reach a consensus, and therefore recommended to the General Assembly a continuation of the status quo. [34]

The disagreements and factionalism within the Church at large on the issues of polity and missions were reflected within the Cincinnati Presbytery. In September, 1831, an article in the Cincinnati Journal had applauded the approaching Western Convention and had expressed the hope that it would find a solution "to prevent those collisions between our Missionary Institutions" and their supporters. [35] Arguments within the Cincinnati Presbytery had become so commonplace that the Presbytery had reduced the number of its meetings per year from four to two. Its most recent sessions in 1831 had "not been characterized for much harmony and brotherly feeling; and the remark has frequently been made that the interests of vital piety have not been much promoted.... "[36]

The October 4 meeting of the Cincinnati Presbytery most clearly reflected the growing division among local Presbyterians over polity and home missions. One participant divided the members of the Presbytery into two factions, which he termed "High Church" and "Low Church. " The "High Church" faction included Wilson, Daniel Hayden, L. G. Gaines, and James Kemper; and the "Low Church" faction included Benjamin Graves, David Root, James Gallaher, Asa Mahan, Franklin Y. Vail, Lewis D. Howell, Robert Boal, James Warren, and Amos Blanchard. All of these men were connected (or soon would be) with Lane Seminary. [37]

Two major issues were discussed at the meeting. The first was the licensing of Horace Bushnell (not the famous theologian), the first student of Lane and, significantly, a convert of one of the New York revivals of Charles G. Finney. [38] Over the opposition of the "High Church" group, Bushnell was licensed. The second issue was the approaching November convention to determine the roles of the General Board and the American Home Missionary Society in the West. "High Churchmen" favored the General Board, of which Wilson was the local chairman, and were advocates of the Old School. Members of the "Low Church" faction favored the national Society and, with a few exceptions, were New School.[39]

By 1832, issues concerned with subjects such as theology, revivalism, polity, and missions had split the Presbyterian Church in Cincinnati into two factions. The First Church, pastored by Wilson, was Old School. Wilson received support in the Presbytery mainly from churches outside the city, and, therefore, he would fight most of the battles alone. Arrayed against Wilson were the Second Church, which had drifted toward the New School under its pastor David Root; the Third Church, pastored by James Gallaher; the Fourth Church, supplied from the fall of 1831 until spring 1833 by Thomas Brainerd, a convert of Finney and later a colleague of Lyman Beecher; and the Sixth Church, under the controversial and radical Asa Mahan. [40] Any Presbyterian institution erected in Cincinnati would be fought over by these two contending parties.

Origins of Lane Seminary

The founding of Lane Seminary was accomplished after

years of sometimes disparate efforts on the part of a large
number of people. Joshua L. Wilson, Ebenezer Lane, and
Elnathan Kemper played the most prominent roles in Lane's
founding and an examination of these roles within their respective contexts indicates that the Seminary was from the
first involved in controversy: intra-denominational, interdenominational, and legal and familial. Thus, the controversy
over slavery did not represent a singular conflict within an
otherwise tranquil history, but rather one among many.

The desire to establish theological institutions for the
training of the ministry generated a great deal of activity
within the Presbyterian Church during the first third of the
nineteenth century. Many factors influenced the expansion of
theological education. First, the general rise in educational
institutions as part of a benevolent movement was fueled by
Enlightenment optimism, revivalism, and millennial expectation, and was dedicated to the eradication of all of society's
perceived ills and the completion of the Christianization of
America. [41] Although church-related colleges dominated higher
education in this period and provided ministerial training, [42]
the leadership of this benevolent movement had to be highly
trained, ministers by profession, and theologically orthodox,
and therefore required seminary training. Following the establishment of Andover Theological Seminary in 1808 to counteract the theological liberalism of Harvard, "the movement
rapidly gained momentum."[43]

Another factor in the rise of theological education in
the Presbyterian Church was that denomination's compliance
with its historic doctrinal tradition of an educated clergy.
Samuel J. Baird, in 1865, wrote that the original American
Presbytery's manuscript minutes indicated not only "the zeal
of our fathers for the apostolic order of our church," but
also that "the language in which it was written, [was] a pledge
of their sentiments as to the qualifications to be required of
those who would serve her in the ministry." This position
"has been maintained consistently from the beginning" in the
American Church. [44] Early effects of this educational position included the founding of Princeton Seminary in 1812, Auburn Seminary in 1818 (opened 1821), and Union Seminary in
Virginia in 1824. [45]

A third factor in the Presbyterian Church's expansion
of theological education was a recognition of the importance
of training and supporting home missionaries to insure the
Christianization and civilizing of the country, especially the

West.   The support given to the General Board of Missions
and the American Home Missionary Society was indicative of
the Church's desire to fill the waste places with an educated
and orthodox leadership. [46]

Although Lyman Beecher's Plea for the West (1835)
was the classic expression of this sentiment, prior statements
on the necessity of providing an educated ministry for the
West were not lacking.   In 1822, Joshua Wilson circularized
a "Letter" to encourage the united actions of the western
synods of Pittsburgh, Tennessee, Ohio, and Kentucky in bringing about the foundation of a theological seminary in and for
the West.   He wrote, "From the present state and opening
prospects of our country, and from the remoteness of our
Eastern Seminaries, it must, I think, be obvious to you that,
a 'School of the Prophets,' ... is a great desideratum in the
western section of the Presbyterian Church. "[47]   Three years
later, the Presbyterian General Assembly recognized the necessity of establishing a western theological seminary and resolved the following:

> The General Assembly, taking into consideration
> the numerous and rapidly increasing population of
> that part of the United States and their territories,
> situated in the great valley of the Mississippi; and
> believing that the interests of the Presbyterian
> Church imperiously require it, and that the Re-
> deemer's kingdom will be thereby promoted, do
> resolve, that it is expedient forthwith to establish
> a Theological Seminary in the West, under the
> supervision of the General Assembly. [48]

Franklin Y. Vail, Secretary of the Western Board of the
American Education Society, in 1829 expressed the need of
"Increasing Christian Interest and Effort for the West. "   He
noted that there were only eight thousand ministers in a total
population of twelve million and that there were two thousand
more churches than ministers.   With only about two hundred
ministers being trained every year, it was obvious that the
increase in ministers could not keep up with the immediate
need, let alone the need created by an increase in population.[49]

With so many calls for an educated ministry in the
West, Joshua Wilson strove to insure that the western seminary, if established, would be in Cincinnati.   Wilson faced
considerable competition in locating a western seminary.   Each
of the western synods desired a seminary within its own

boundaries. Those of Kentucky and probably Tennessee were eliminated from consideration fairly early because of slavery.[50] In 1826 a committee appointed by the General Assembly reported that the seminary should be located at Alleghanytown, near Pittsburgh. Most of the Westerners insisted that Alleghanytown was located too far east and would preclude cooperation of the western synods simply because of distance. The Assembly then resolved that the Seminary would be located at one of three locations: Alleghanytown, Walnut Hills (near Cincinnati), or at Charleston, Indiana; and that the issue would be decided by the Assembly in 1827. To this resolution Wilson objected. He believed that postponement of the decision was not in the best interests of the Presbyterian Church in the West; that a delay would lead to the awarding of the seminary to the highest bidder; that it "is calculated to divide the attention, distract the counsels, and cut off the hopes of those sections of the western country which most need such an institution"; and that the Assembly's postponement would discourage Cincinnati, the location which Wilson preferred, from pressing its claims.[51]

In the General Assembly of 1827, "after considerable discussion and various motions," Alleghanytown was chosen over Walnut Hills by two votes as the location for the Western Theological Seminary.[52]

The synods of the West, however, refused to cooperate with the new seminary, which opened in November, 1827. The Synods of Kentucky and Indiana made separate plans for the establishment of seminaries under their control, and in southwest Ohio, events occurred which eventually would lead to a seminary on Walnut Hills.[53]

In the summer of 1828, Ebenezer Lane, a New Orleans merchant, made known his interest in establishing a theological seminary near Cincinnati to be connected in some way with the manual labor system in which students worked to pay their fees. In response to this inquiry, a meeting was held at Wilson's First Presbyterian Church near the end of September. At that time a plan for the seminary was presented, and committees were appointed to communicate with Ebenezer and his brother William (who had agreed to supply half the donation), draft a constitution, and prepare a circular to appeal to the public.[54]

Ebenezer had originally hoped that the Baptists, of whom he was a member, and Presbyterians would jointly support the Seminary he wished to endow. When the brothers arrived in Cincinnati in October, however, Wilson stated his opinion that the Seminary should be supported by only one denomination. After discussing the matter with a prominent Regular Baptist, Isaac G. Burnet, Ebenezer decided "that the baptist [sic] were not then able or willing to establish the Institution I proposed; consequently what we had to give was offered to the Presbyterians who accepted it. "[55]

Whether or not the Baptists "were not then able or willing" is unclear. Six years later, an article appeared in the Baptist Weekly Journal of Cincinnati in reply to the question evidently being asked, "Whose Fault Was It?" that the Baptists had refused such an offer for funds for a seminary. Although some inquiry had been made by the Lane brothers, the Weekly Journal insisted that no prominent member of a Baptist church in Cincinnati was ever offered funds for the building of a Baptist seminary. [56] The appearance of the article was itself an indication of intra-Baptist squabbles in Cincinnati, as well as an indication of Baptist anger over Presbyterian good fortune and possible manipulation.

At any rate, in October, 1828, at the request (or selection) of the Lane brothers, a Board of Trustees, calling itself the Ohio Board of Education, was formed with twenty-three members. Included on this Board were Joshua L. Wilson (as president), seven other Presbyterian clergymen (a total of five of the nine members of the Cincinnati Presbytery who had full-time charges), and prominent local politicians, bankers, lawyers, and merchants. [57] The Board members accepted the offer of the Lane brothers: a total of $4,000 within four years, with a promise of continued support. In return for these funds, the Board agreed to a number of conditions, the most important being that a charter be secured from the state, that the Seminary be located in the vicinity of Cincinnati, and that the manual labor system be "a fundamental rule or principle" of the institution. [58]

Having completed their agreement, the Lane brothers returned to New Orleans and ended any control in the affairs of the Seminary which they had helped found. A year later they closed their business in New Orleans, and Ebenezer and another brother, Andrew, paid $4,000 in exchange for the bond they had given the Board. [59] Their relationship with the Seminary after this was minimal. In fact, Ebenezer would have preferred that the institution not even carry his name because he had "an aversion to any honor of a worldly nature,... "[60] By 1848 he was living in Oxford, Ohio, but evidently had little contact with the seminary that bore his name. [61] Andrew Lane at times loaned the Seminary the use of financial notes, but by 1834 he had become irritated with the Seminary's tardiness in retiring one of his notes, and that appears to have ended his relationship with Lane. [62]

The Ohio Board of Education, under the leadership of Wilson, knew that it could not depend solely on the "disinterested benevolence" of one family for the support of the institution. Thus, the Board formulated a plan to gain additional support and comply with the terms of the Lane brothers. The plan included the following: the gaining of a legal charter from the state, the procurement of land for the Seminary and for a farm to support it, the building of an endowment fund, and the appointment of a faculty. [63]

In late 1828 or early 1829, eighteen members of the Board filed a petition to the General Assembly of Ohio requesting a charter for their Seminary. This petition contained three clauses. The first noted the importance of establishing "a well regulated literary & theological Seminary in this section of the Country." The second clause enunciated "the peculiar plan of the proposed Seminary," which included the manual labor system. This would enable the "indigent young" to acquire a professional education. Third, the petition stated that financial support by the Lane brothers had been guaranteed once the institution was legally incorporated.[64]

In response to this petition, on February 11, 1829, the General Assembly of Ohio issued "An act to incorporate the Lane Seminary, in the county of Hamilton," thus making Lane the eighth institution of higher education incorporated in the state. [65] Two sections of Lane's charter were significant. Section 5 stated, in compliance with the petition and the wishes of the Lane brothers,

> that every student therein, when in good health, shall be required to spend not less than three, nor more than four hours, each day, in agricultural or mechanical labor, the avails of which shall be applied towards defraying the expenses of the institution, and the board and tuition of the students;... [66]

The importance attached to this section by the Board was indicated in an earlier manuscript draft of the Charter. This version placed the section on manual labor second (out of twelve), and stated that the manual labor system was "the" rather than "a" (as in the printed Charter) "fundamental principle of this Seminary."[67] This principle unwittingly helped insure that the students who attended Lane would be more dedicated, mature, and self-reliant than those in other seminaries.

The other important section of the Charter, the third, concerned the religious affiliations of the Board of Trustees and faculty. In the manuscript version already referred to, this section required that a "majority" of the Board and of the Executive Committee "as well as all the instructors employed in the theological department of the Seminary shall be members of the Presbyterian Church under the care of the General Assembly of the United States in good standing."[68] In contrast, the adopted version of this section stated that "all the Professors, Tutors, Teachers and Instructors in said institution" would be members of the Presbyterian Church.[69] This change reflected the Board's desire to maintain the school's denominational purity and control against possible encroachments by Congregationalists, who had cooperated with the Presbyterians since 1801 under the Plan of Union. It also indicated an awareness of the growing differences within the Presbyterian Church. These differences would finally lead to the heresy trial of Lyman Beecher (President of Lane) in 1834, the Old School-New School schism of 1837, and legal suits to determine the rightful owners of Lane.

With the granting of the Charter, some of the major conditions of the Lane brothers had been met. Lane was legally established, its fundamental principle was manual labor, and it was located (legally) in the "vicinity" of Cincinnati.

Even before securing the Charter, the Board had been searching for a location in the "vicinity" to build its Seminary. Samuel Caldwell offered to donate twenty-five to thirty acres of land near Carthage. William Cary offered to donate part of a farm between College Hill and Mt. Pleasant and to sell the rest to the Seminary for $1,650. A third site was a hundred-acre tract on Walnut Hills, two miles from Cincinnati, which Elnathan Kemper wanted to sell for $7,500. It was this land that was chosen as the site of Lane Seminary.[70]

Elnathan Kemper,[71] a farmer, was the oldest son of the Reverend James Kemper, the first Presbyterian minister appointed to settle west of the Alleghany Mountains and north of the Ohio River. In 1790, James bought one hundred and forty acres, a hilly and wooded tract of land about two miles northeast of the small settlement of Cincinnati, from John Cleves Symmes, one of the original Ohio land owners. Kemper brought his family in 1791 and fourteen years later moved them into a blockhouse, a defense against Indian attacks, which had recently been built on his property. Kemper lived on his land, which he named Walnut Hills, for the rest of his life. [72]

The Kemper family expressed an interest in education in 1819, when, at James's request, two of his sons, Elnathan and Peter H., gave him eight acres of land on Walnut Hills to support his Walnut Hills Academy. Based on the manual labor system, which was supposed to enable students to support themselves, provide them with recreation and maintain their health, Kemper's academy was the only source of education in the neighborhood. By 1825 James's health failed and the Academy, like so many others, went out of existence. [73]

Kemper still maintained his desire to aid education. At the end of April, 1827, upon hearing of the Presbyterian General Assembly's search for a location for a theological seminary in the West, he wrote to Ezra Stiles Ely, Stated Clerk of the General Assembly and Corresponding Secretary of the Board of Education of the Presbyterian Church, and offered the stone houses he had used as an academy, an adjoining frame house, and twenty acres on Walnut Hills. [74] About this time, a printed proposal was addressed to the Commissioners for locating a Western Theological Seminary for the Presbyterian Church by Kemper's church, the First Presbyterian Church and Moral Society on Walnut Hills. Presumably written by Kemper, the proposal outlined a program by which a seminary would be built on one of two sections of land on Walnut Hills. In addition, in conformance with Kemper's ideas favoring manual labor, the proposal provided for acreage which the students could farm, and for smaller lots to be occupied by "families of mechaniks," which would supply the students with board, social life, and employment. [75]

The General Assembly, as noted, did not choose Walnut Hills as the site for its western seminary, and Kemper probably gave up hope of having a school at his doorstep. However, he must have been excited by the news in the fall of 1828 that Presbyterians in Cincinnati, led by Joshua Wilson, were making plans to build a seminary in the vicinity of Cincinnati based on the manual labor system.

It was Kemper's son, Elnathan, who entered into nego-
tiations with the Board of Trustees. Possibly the elder Kemper was too old to take an active part, but Elnathan certainly
wanted to make a contribution and to be remembered as one
of the major founders. [76] On January 1, 1829, he met with
the Ohio Board of Education in the sessions room of the First
Presbyterian Church and offered to give the Board sixty acres
of his farm on Walnut Hills, and sell it an adjoining forty
acres for $4,000. The Board accepted Kemper's donation of
sixty acres the same day, and agreed to purchase the additional land eleven days later. [77] In replying to the Board's
acceptance of his offer, Elnathan wrote that once the school
received a charter and surveyed the land, he would execute
a deed. Then he wrote:

> Suffer me to assure you that this donation, (which
> has cost me, if not 'a great sum,' much labor and
> toil,) shall ever be accompanied with my sincere
> and humble prayer that it may be improved by the
> Ohio Board of Education, for the advancement of
> the Kingdom of our blessed Lord and Savior on
> earth, and the amelioration of the condition of my
> lost and ruined fellow-sinners, and to this end may
> you be preserved from all selfishness, passion or
> prejudice, but at all times, and in all circumstances,
> be under the influence of His Spirit, who seeth not
> as man, but who looketh on the heart, and at the
> motive of each action. [78]

In the spring of 1829, Elnathan agreed that his father
and five brothers, especially Peter H. and David R., would
join him in making the donation to the Seminary. Earlier
there had been some discussion of this, but nothing was done
at the time. Since the deed had not been executed, there was
still time to include them in the donation. Elnathan's reasons
for allowing this are uncertain, but he probably included his
father because of the latter's interest in education combined
with manual labor. Considerable family pressure persuaded
Elnathan to include Peter and David in the donation, while the
other brothers were not interested in being included. On
April 30, Peter, David, and James agreed to give Elnathan
a total of twenty-two and one-half acres in exchange for his
including them in his donation of sixty acres to the Seminary.[79]
This arrangement led, eventually, to family quarrels and even
legal suits, and Elnathan regretted it deeply.

Trouble in the Kemper family began in the summer

when Elnathan and Dr. James Warren, Secretary of the Board, agreed that it was not necessary to maintain the strict condition of the Lane brothers and the rest of Elnathan's family regarding the amount of time students had to devote to manual labor. Both men preferred to allow the Board to set the standard, as experience dictated. Elnathan's family disagreed. Matters were exacerbated when Elnathan and David argued over how much each should pay for the services of Jacob Lindley as agent for the Seminary, as well as over the price of a horse. [80]

The primary issue between Elnathan and his brothers, however, concerned the actual donation to the Seminary. The delay of the brothers and father in transferring land to Elnathan in exchange for a share of the donation, and the inability of all parties to determine the share of the donation contributed by each member led Elnathan to decide to donate fifty acres to the Seminary independently of any other members of the family. On the night of December 3, 1829, after Elnathan and Dr. Warren had agreed to this new donation, the Kemper sons met in their father's house in order to bring about a reconciliation between Elnathan, who had refused to "be governed by the majority" of his family, and his brothers and father, who still desired a share in the donation. Elnathan relented somewhat and agreed to allow his father and two brothers to share in a donation of an extra ten acres in exchange for signing lands of a total equal value over to Elnathan. However, an attempt "to affix comparative value to the intended donation" ended in disagreement. [81]

On December 9, Elnathan, James, Peter and David, and their wives signed the grant turning the land over to the Board of Trustees. [82] Peter gave Elnathan a note for the value of his share. Despite "considerable" efforts, the values of David's and his father's shares of the donation remained undecided and, consequently, David refused to turn over to Elnathan six acres of land in exchange for a share in the donation. [83]

By early 1830, Elnathan, thoroughly disgusted with David, and now alienated from Peter as well, [84] decided to conclude the matter. He convinced his father to deed to him a tract of land which included an area to which David also claimed title. Elnathan apparently thought that David would agree readily to give up land to which he did not have clear title in exchange for a clear share of the donation. Elnathan was mistaken; David filed suit in April, 1831, claiming the land was his. [85]

Although the suit was dismissed in 1834, the rift within the Kemper family continued. It widened when Elnathan left his father's church on Walnut Hills and joined the Lane Seminary Presbyterian Church, where he was elected an elder. [86] Lane's New School affinities did nothing to assuage the rift; James Kemper, miffed at being ignored by students, denounced the Seminary in 1833 because of "the shades of doctrine taught here being realy [sic] another Gospel. "[87]

Elnathan continued to support Lane Seminary until his death. Besides being an elder in the Seminary church, he leased another fifty-one acres to the school in 1832, subscribed $300 in 1833, and leased still more land for a cemetery in 1834. [88] He was well-liked and respected by the students and faculty. [89] In addition to his benevolent activities for Lane, he also supported an American Home Missionary Society Church in Fulton, Ohio, bought Sabbath School books for children, and collected money for the American Colonization Society, foreign missions, the American Tract Society, and the "Teachers of the African School in the City to buy books for the use in that School. "[90] On August 17, 1834, after attending services at the Seminary church, Elnathan contracted cholera and died later that night. [91] His death spared him from being involved in Lane's most famous controversy.

Early Attempts to Secure an Endowment and Faculty

While the Kempers were arguing among themselves, the Board of Trustees was making attempts to collect funds enough to insure that Lane would be more than a piece of land and a name. About the time the Charter was acquired, agents were appointed to solicit funds in the South and New England. Neither agent was successful, and the one in New England stated his belief that the Board should first concentrate its efforts in the West and establish the Seminary before soliciting in other parts of the country. [92]

Some efforts to secure local support had already been made, the first result of which had been the Kemper donation. In addition, on the day the Charter was granted, February 11, 1829, Rev. Jacob Lindley, a member of the Board, began a thirty-four-day agency for the Seminary. Beginning in Walnut Hills, Lindley visited twelve villages in southern Ohio, and traveled as far north as Dayton. The churches of other members of the Board which he visited were the least inclined to subscribe, and on March 23, Lindley reported that, although he had obtained subscriptions for over $550, he had been able to collect only $22.[93] Two weeks later, the Pandect, a local Presbyterian paper under Wilson's control, printed an appeal "To the Friends of a Literary and Religious Education" asking for "assistance" because "Nothing now prevents the opening of the school but the want of funds;... "[94] In June, the Board obtained the services of "Rev. Mr. Cox from New York," an agent of the American Home Missionary Society, to solicit funds in the Cincinnati vicinity for a "short time. "[95]

In order to offset some of the excuses given for not subscribing, the Pandect, in September, answered the "QUERY. Where is the Lane Seminary," with an address "To the Benevolent." After giving the origin and plan of the Seminary, the writer of the article exclaimed "shall it still remain only in prospect and exist in name!" The sectarian nature of the Seminary, an excuse all non-Presbyterians could use not to contribute, was minimized. The supposed difficulty of forcing students to perform manual labor, another excuse, was proved to be absent on the basis of the success of other manual labor institutions. The major reason for not giving to the Seminary, the "inexpediency" of presenting yet another worthwhile cause to the public "at the present time," was refuted by referring, not to what had been accomplished, but to what still needed to be done to fulfill God's will.[96]

With all of these efforts, only about $5,000 was subscribed in the local area.[97] In spite of this, the Seminary opened on November 18, 1829.[98] Rev. George C. Beckwith, of Lowell, Massachusetts, had been appointed Professor of Sacred Literature and Ecclesiastical History in April, and had arrived in Cincinnati shortly before November 1.[99] Within three weeks, he had planned a course of instruction in theology and had begun teaching several students.[100] The Walnut Hill School, preparatory department of the Seminary, was to open "as soon as the necessary arrangements can be made" by the trustees.[101] This department, which would provide education to prepare students for college, was highly favored in letters to the Pandect (it was the one department of the school which would appeal to all citizens because it was nonsectarian), and apparently opened in November.[102]

Beckwith, at the request of the trustees, presented "an Address in reference to the objects of" Lane Seminary on the first Sunday in January, 1830.[103] On February 24, he was appointed agent to raise funds for the Seminary in the East, a task for which he had neither ability nor interest. [104] Although he sent a description to Wilson of the manual labor system in use at the Oneida Institute, Beckwith did little to gain subscriptions. [105] After submitting traveling expenses of almost two hundred dollars, he resigned as agent and teacher on August 24. [106]

Beckwith's letters to the trustees written at this time and later indicate the lack of support which the institution had received. Beckwith had accepted the position of professor at Lane on the assurances "that provision had already been made for my support." His own discouragement reflected that of the trustees in their failure to secure more than $5 thousand in subscriptions locally. His only suggestion was that the Board should appoint a prominent clergyman to head the Seminary and then approach prospective financial backers in the East. [107]

When the Board met on September 29, they represented a Seminary that had no teachers, no students, little endowment, and the foundation of one building. [108] At that "solemn meeting," each member of the Board presented his views regarding the "raising of funds." Wilson, displaying his bias, stated that he had never had confidence in receiving aid from the East, and asserted that the Seminary should concentrate its fund-raising efforts solely in the West. Other members of the Board had as little confidence in obtaining support in the West as Wilson had in the East. A "dark cloud seemed to hang over the prospects of the Seminary."[109]

After all of the other Board members had spoken, Franklin Y. Vail, secretary of the Western Board of the American Education Society and newest member of the Board, gave his opinion. Picking up on Beckwith's suggestion, Vail insisted that another attempt be made to raise funds in the East. If a prominent churchman, such as Lyman Beecher, could be prevailed upon to join the Seminary, then Eastern funds would flow to support him. The Board responded to Vail's proposal by saying that if he, "the brother who has so much confidence in the East, will go we will send him, & make one more effort. Dr. Wilson," Vail later remembered, "said amen."[110]

Vail described that meeting and his subsequent agency as an opportunity for the New School branch of the Presbyterian Church to gain control of the fledgling Seminary. It had been rumored that the Cincinnati Synod, Old School in sympathy, would endow a professorship, the holder of which would be, naturally, an Old School man.   To counteract that proposed move required haste.   Therefore, Vail resigned his post as secretary of the American Education Society and left for the East three days after the meeting, on September 23.[111]   His agency in the East, although it would insure the Seminary's survival, also would provide material for Lane's future controversies.

Within three weeks of his departure, Vail had visited Philadelphia, New York, and Boston, and had conferred with the "leading men" of these cities regarding possible candidates for the presidency and professorship of theology.   The general consensus of the people Vail consulted was that Lyman Beecher "would be the best man."[112]

Lyman Beecher, "unvanquished Puritan," was one of the best known clergymen of the day.   Born in 1775 in New Haven, Connecticut, he had graduated from Yale in 1797, had studied theology with Timothy Dwight, and had held pastorates on Long Island, New York, in Litchfield, Connecticut, and in Boston.[113]   Through the eyes of his children, the Lyman Beecher of the Autobiography was presented as a rustic, simple, absent-minded, open, naive, and fun-loving country preacher.   He did have a more formidable side and was described as

> below the middle stature, spare and rigid, with bones of brass and nerves of a steel like elasticity. His walk and gesticulation are characteristically rapid and vehement.   His gray eye kindles incessantly with the action of his mind, and the whole contour of his face indicates an energy unsubdued and unsubduable, for the moral fearlessness, before which stern men will involuntarily feel their spirits quailing.[114]

Renowned as a preacher, Beecher was still more famous as a reformer and controversialist, having attacked intemperance, duelling, atheism, Unitarianism, and Roman Catholicism.[115]   He had begun his career as reformer with no long range plans, but with the view that "when I saw a rattlesnake in my path, I would smite it."[116]   Gradually, he developed the idea of a comprehensive and activist united evangelical front to eliminate evil and help bring in God's kingdom. With regard to obvious evils, such as intemperance, Beecher urged all-out warfare to insure their destruction.[117]   In order to complete this task, however, possibly divisive issues, such as doctrine and slavery, had to be resolved. Usually, Beecher tried to do this by minimizing the differences and encouraging the union of opposing parties. [118] In his role as mediator, Beecher would be ineffective at Lane.

Beecher recognized the importance of the West in his desire to reform the nation and the world. In fact, he had considered leaving his home in Boston and going West on his own initiative at least three months before the Lane Board appointed Vail as agent. Calvin Stowe had once heard Beecher state publicly "that he might himself ere long go West," but Stowe had dismissed this "for a mere rhetorical outburst."[119] In July, 1830, Beecher wrote to his daughter, Catherine, that "my interest in the majestic West has been greatly excited and increased. " His desire to go was based on the belief that

> The moral destiny of our nation, and all our insti-
> tutions and hopes, and the world's hopes, turns on
> the character of the West, and the competition now
> is for that of preoccupancy in the education of the
> rising generation, in which Catholics and infidels
> have got the start of us.
> ... If we gain the West, all is safe; if we lose
> it, all is lost. [120]

Because Beecher held this sentiment so strongly, it was no wonder that when Vail approached him on the street in Boston about Lane and the possibility of raising up a generation of ministers in the West, the idea "flashed through my mind like lightning.... It was the greatest thought that ever entered my soul; it filled it, and displaced every thing else. "[121] On October 9, less than three weeks after the meeting of the Board of Trustees, Vail went to Beecher's house with a number of the latter's friends to discuss Lane. After Vail's presentation, each of Beecher's friends expressed his opinion; all agreed that Beecher should go west, notwith-standing the claims upon him by his church and the evangel-ical community in Boston. [122]

Having obtained Beecher's virtual acceptance of Lane's presidency, Vail hurried on to New York and met with Arthur Tappan, a successful businessman and prominent financier of benevolent enterprises. [123] Tappan, who had supported other schools, [124] agreed to give $20,000 to endow a professorship of theology on four conditions: that Beecher should be the first incumbent; that two other professorships be endowed for $15,000 each within a year; that $10,000 to $20,000 be raised in the West for buildings; and that further conditions would be prescribed to insure "a succession of orthodox Professors and to give security to the investment of the funds." The principal would be paid to the Seminary at Tappan's death; until then he would pay an amount equal to the interest of the sum to pay Beecher's salary. [125]

When the trustees received Vail's letters describing Beecher's willingness and Tappan's donation, they were understandably ecstatic. The usually dour Wilson is said to have "clapped his hands and shouted 'Glory to God in the highest.'"[126] On October 22, he hastily assembled the Board members in his tent at a camp meeting where they unanimously elected Beecher President and "Professor of Didactick & Polemic Theology."[127] "The resolution was passed," wrote James Warren, Secretary of the Board, to Vail, "with reverential silence, not a word was spoken but 'Aye.'"[128]

Meanwhile, Vail was attempting to secure subscriptions for the other two professorships. On November 11, he informed the Board that the subscription for the professorship of ecclesiastical history had been nearly completed in Philadelphia, and that Thomas J. Biggs, pastor of the Presbyterian Church in Frankford, Pennsylvania, had been nominated to fill that chair. In addition, Vail reported that the subscription for the professorship of biblical literature had been half completed in New York. [129] The Board dutifully appointed Biggs on January 17 (he accepted a month later), and looked forward to Beecher's acceptance and the completion of the subscription for the last professorship. At the same time it appointed a superintendent for the manual labor and preparatory departments, and a principal for the Walnut Hill School. [130]

It was difficult, however, to secure the most important cog on which the school depended. Beecher's congregation refused to give its consent for him to leave. His church members wanted to insure that the debt incurred to rebuild their burned-out church, which they had accepted at Beecher's insistence, was paid before he left. [131] In addition, Beecher's colleagues in the evangelical movement, such as his good friend Nathaniel W. Taylor, tried to convince him to remain in the East. Taylor even suggested that they approach Tappan about endowing a professorship for Beecher at Yale instead of Lane. [132]

The Lane trustees could do nothing to influence Taylor, but in early 1831, Wilson, Vail, and James Gallaher wrote a letter to Beecher's church expressing their reasons for needing Beecher. After presenting their "general view of the character, claims, and prospects of our seminary," the three stated the consensus that Beecher was the most qualified person for the presidency of Lane, and that the general approbation towards his appointment as President and Professor of Theology indicated "the will of Providence in this matter." The final and major reason that Beecher was required at Lane was that a total of $60 to $70 thousand had been subscribed to the Seminary on the condition that Beecher be connected with it. Without Beecher and the funds that would come because of him, "we see not how our Institution can be sustained, as extensive funds are indispensable, and cannot possibly be obtained here among our infant churches."133

On March 9, Beecher answered the Board's letter, which he seems not to have shown to his congregation. He presented six reasons in favor of his moving to the West. First, he emphasized the importance of a seminary which would spread evangelicalism throughout the West and then the world. Second, he believed that "from the beginning God has been preparing me in some respect to teach theology." His espousal of the Gospel against infidelity, hyper-Calvinism, Arminianism, and Unitarianism had trained him "in explaining and vindicating the doctrines of the Reformation and in adapting them to popular apprehension and in commending them for purposes of conviction and conversion to the conscience and hearts of men...." Third, he believed he should go because the training of the ministry for the West should be accomplished at the West. Fourth, the task of opening the Seminary had to be done immediately. He believed that his work in Boston was near an end and he had already made up his mind to go to Cincinnati, with or without a call. Finally, Beecher was certain that the influences keeping him in Boston, such as the rebuilding of his church, were temporary and should not force him to lose the opportunity of doing greater good.134

Beecher then enumerated the arguments of his "most judicious friends" for his remaining in Boston. Five of these arguments dealt specifically with the rebuilding of Beecher's church and the impossibility of his leaving until that project was completed. Sixth, Beecher's church was considered representative of the evangelical movement in Boston, and Beecher's absence would harm that movement. Seventh, the Unitarian conflict was not ending, as Beecher supposed, and his efforts were needed more than ever. [135]

Having presented the reasons for and against his removal, Beecher stated his major reason for not being able to give his consent. Because the rebuilding of his church had been undertaken by a group of stockholders which included members of the society as well as of the church, and because Beecher had pledged to these stockholders that he would remain, he doubted that he could gain their consent to go. He simply did not have the influence over the society that he had over his own church members. [136]

Finally, Beecher wanted to make clear that his refusal had to be taken as final and not temporary. His declining of the call to Lane had to be "considered as without any secret or confidential understanding that I may be called again after the exigency here is passed, and that if called then I will come." He emphasized this point because rumors were already spreading that he would decline "with a secret understanding that if called again a short time hence, I will come. "[137]

Beecher's premature rejection of any "understanding" may have put the idea into the Board members' heads. In the spring, Vail was dispatched to the East to confer with Beecher and some of his advisers, and to collect more subscriptions. [138] After several days discussion, Vail left with the idea, which Beecher evidently intimated, that while Beecher could not then leave, he might be able to in one or two years. On May 14, Vail wrote to the Board with two pieces of good news. First, "The important object of securing our funds may be regarded as obtained; ... " Second, Vail believed that Beecher would come to Lane sometime in the future. [139] Indeed, it is difficult to believe that Vail could have obtained funds without some assurances that Beecher would come to Lane. For the time being, however, the Board and Seminary could only wait.

Religious Conflict and Beecher's Acceptance

While waiting for something to happen in the East, the Board announced the reopening, on April 12, 1831, of the Walnut Hill School. Operating out of James Kemper's old school house, the school had Rev. Lewis D. Howell as Principal and William Boal as Superintendent of the boarding house and

manual labor department. To gain admittance, students had
to demonstrate "a good acquaintance with the common branches
of an English education, [and] testimonials of a good moral
character and industrious habits. " Preference was to be
given to those preparing for the ministry and those who planned
to complete their education at Lane.   Every student was
required to perform three hours of manual labor per day and
to "submit to the continual supervision of the professors and
teachers. "[140]

   Although the school at last seemed to be prospering--
at least it was in operation--by 1831 disputes about theology,
polity, and missions were taking place in the Presbyterian
Church, and these would have an impact on the theological
and institutional orientation of Lane. [141] In fact, Lane was
one of the prizes over which the Old School and New School
fought in Cincinnati. In the beginning, it looked as if Lane
would be an Old School institution. Wilson was the most
prominent churchman in Cincinnati in the 1830's, and James
Kemper was viewed as the city's Presbyterian patriarch.
Both had had roles in the founding of Lane Seminary and both
were Old School men. Wilson, especially, had great influence on the Board of Trustees and was its President from
the beginning. However, the addition of more Presbyterian
churches in Cincinnati, due at first to the revival which began in 1828 and then to the influx of New School advocates
from the East into the area, changed the character of the
Board of Trustees and the extent of Wilson's power. Of the
eight men elected to the Board between 1829 and 1831, one
was an Old School man while four were definitely New School,
two were probably New School, and the last became affiliated
with the New School later. [142] In addition, the increased acceptance of New School doctrines, the result of revival suc-
cesses, and possible objections to Wilson's domination of the
Board by discontented trustees contributed to a decline of Old
School influence.

   The matter was brought to a head at the annual meeting of the Board when Asa Mahan, New School pastor of the
Sixth Church and theological opponent of Wilson, was elected
to the Board. Wilson had acquiesced a year before when
Amos Blanchard was elected to the Board. As noted, Wilson
opposed Blanchard because of the latter's views on "the doctrines of Original Sin and the Atonement. "[143] Mahan's election was too much for Wilson; he sensed a conspiracy.

   On November 17, Wilson resigned from the Board.

After noting his objection to the Board's admittance of older students to the Preparatory Department, he presented his major reasons for resigning. In excluding Wilson's candidate from the Board, another from the Executive Committee, and still another from the office of Corresponding Secretary, there was "left, on my mind, no doubt, that the full determination of the Majority is to render the Lane Seminary entirely subservient to the New School Theology." This determination was demonstrated clearly by the "suspicious" reason given for the election of Mahan: that it would give the Sixth Church (of which Mahan was pastor) representation on the Board. However, Wilson stated, three members of the Sixth Church were already on the Board, while no one represented the Fifth Church, which favored the Old School. Finally, the Board's move towards the New School was most obvious in its appointment of Lyman Beecher as President and Professor of Theology. Wilson no longer felt he could support Beecher as the head of the Seminary, and he had said so back in July. "Dr. B. is not a Presbyterian--nor can he honestly become so without a great change in his theological opinions."[144] No longer a supporter of the Seminary, Wilson in the future did all he could to oppose it.

Wilson's opposition and his encouragement of Old School churches to do the same forced the Board to take action to raise the funds which might otherwise have been subscribed by Wilson and his supporters. Besides, almost a year had passed since Lyman Beecher had refused the Seminary's call, and if the call were renewed, Tappan's condition of $20,000 raised in the West had to be complied with. On December 29, in the sessions room of the Second Presbyterian Church, a meeting of "a number of the friends of Lane Seminary" was held for the purpose of raising funds to meet the school's "present exigencies." Vail was the main speaker and presented Lane's special role in the West, its manual labor system, and its need of support. He described the subscription of $50,000 in the East, given on the condition that the West raise money for buildings. The purpose of the meeting, he said, was to raise the funds to meet that condition. Vail and another Board member each offered $1,000. A total of $8,200 was subscribed at the meeting, and by January 6 this had increased to $12,000.[145] The money subscribed in the Cincinnati area secured the Eastern pledges and also demonstrated the Seminary's ability to operate successfully without Wilson and the Old School.

Also in January, the Board published an article in the

Cincinnati Journal describing the "Character, advantages and present prospects" of Lane Seminary. It presented the two divisions of the Seminary, literary (or preparatory) and theological and stated that $63,000 had been subscribed. The theological department, under Thomas J. Biggs, would open in the spring and a "grammar school" for boys ten to fifteen years old would open by summer. One building was already completed, which housed the steward and his family, and another was being planned. The manual labor system was in successful operation and students highly favored it. [146] This article, as well as a front-page article in the Cincinnati Journal by the Seminary's agent in England, Calvin Colton, was written to demonstrate the Seminary's prosperity in spite of Wilson and the Old School. [147]

On March 7, the Walnut Hill School opened (again) with Lewis Howell as Principal and Professor of Languages, Rev. Thomas Cole of New Richmond, Indiana, as Professor of Mathematics, and Horace Bushnell, teacher in the "grammar school."[148] By the middle of April, Biggs was expected "in a few days" to begin teaching all branches of theology. [149]

In spite of these indications that Lane was progressing and growing, problems still remained with the Old School faction in Cincinnati and its opposition to the school. Amos Blanchard, Corresponding Secretary of the Board, and Professor Biggs wanted to hire a former teacher of Biggs as a professor of mathematics of the Walnut Hill School to replace Cole (who had resigned in April). Biggs's teacher, an Old School man who supported the Seminary and had sided with the New School during the missions controversy, would ease some of the Old School opposition. "But if he is refused," Blanchard warned Vail, "and an eastern man and a New School man appointed I should not be surprised if it should cool many of our friends."[150]

By July, 1832, Blanchard was frantic. He wrote to Vail in New York that,

> Such is the pressure here that money cannot be obtained on the subscriptions.... There is a general coldness manifested against the institution. Owing to the unfounded calumnies constantly found out against it. Nearly 20 students have left here for Hanover. Still we are full.

Wilson and the Old School faction, said Blanchard, were going

into the churches to "preach against New School men," and
they were determined to "revolutionize this Presbytery," and
bring it totally within the Old School sphere. With the prospects of the Seminary bound up with the extent of New School
influence in Cincinnati, Blanchard was understandably disturbed about the welfare of the New School faction of the
Presbyterian Church against the inroads of "Dr. Wilson and
his men." After noting the recent and expected departures
of several New School clergymen from the Presbytery, Blanchard warned, "If you and D[r]. B[eecher] & some others do
not come on soon the New School will be left in a bare minority. You will say I am low spirited. This is not so. I
am only looking at stubborn facts." For himself, he had received another call and was leaving. [151]

Throughout most of 1832, the Seminary, though established, was still struggling. Wilson's opposition had made
it clear that someone of his own stature was needed to offset
his negative influence. The most obvious choice was still
Lyman Beecher, on whose acceptance of Lane's presidency
rested the Eastern donation. If he came, in addition to working to save the West from infidelity and Roman Catholicism,
he would also have to represent the Seminary in an intrade-
nominational conflict. In fact, the more important work could
not really begin until the opposition in the Presbyterian Church
was either won over or overcome. In the beginning of 1832,
another effort was made by the newly reconstituted Board to
secure Beecher for the Seminary.

Beecher had not been idle for the past year. In January, 1831, he had begun a series of lectures to awaken his
countrymen to the threat of Catholicism. Besides this, he
had been witness to the Taylor-Tyler controversy and had
been involved in theological discussions with Leonard Woods
of Andover Seminary. [152] Uneasy at the idea of open theological bickering within evangelicalism, Beecher had tried to
play a conciliatory role and had kept the more aggressive
Taylor from pressing the issues. [153]

On January 23, 1832, the Board of Trustees of Lane
again encouraged Beecher to accept the presidency and professorship of theology. No longer was the cause simply one
to raise up an evangelical ministry to convert the West. Now
there was an additional reason for Beecher to go to Cincinnati. Controversies within the churches were threatening
God's cause, and ministers, instead of preaching the Gospel
and saving souls, were "engaged in hunting heresy, in defaming

the character of their brethren [including Beecher's], and in
blowing the coals of strife and division. " Only Beecher could
save the situation. Using familiar imagery, the Board pleaded:

> The armies of Israel need a leader. The land is
> before us in the length and the breadth of it, but
> the Amalekite and the Canaanite dwell there, to-
> gether with the sons of Anak, and the people's
> heart is discouraged because we have no Joshua to
> say, "Go up, for the Lord will deliver it into our
> hand. "[154]

Thomas H. Skinner, pastor of the Arch Street Church
in Philadelphia, encouraged Beecher to go, and was specific
regarding the latter's role in the West:

> Arm the spirit which now reigns in the evangelical
> churches with just views of moral government and
> agency, and you bring the Millennium to the very
> doors. Now where in all the world can you do half
> as much to impart and disseminate such views as
> in the great Western Valley--the Valley of Decision
> in respect to this, and probably all other nations?[155]

In other words, Skinner encouraged Beecher to win the battle
in the West against the Old School and its doctrines, which
hindered the spread of the Gospel, so that the West could
then rightly serve its purpose as the religious and national
center from which to convert the world.

In March, Beecher answered another plea from Mahan,
Vail, and Blanchard with the statement that, even though he
was still needed in Boston, he would come to Cincinnati to
look over the situation and to assure himself that if he came
he would receive "cordial co-operation" from his associates
and within the community. If there appeared to be "a rational
prospect of success" for the Seminary, he would accept the
call in the fall. [156]

Arriving in Cincinnati about the middle of April,
Beecher spent his time looking over the Seminary grounds,
lecturing and preaching in the Presbyterian churches open to
him and visiting relatives. [157] The Second Presbyterian
Church, vacant since David Root had left in 1830, was so
impressed with his preaching (and probably his reputation),
that it unanimously called him as pastor. He declined to
answer the call until he had made up his mind about Lane.[158]

Beecher's daughter, Catherine, who had accompanied him to
Ohio, wrote to her sister that their father's reception had
been friendly everywhere, almost.

> I see no difficulties or objections [she wrote]; every
> thing is ready, and every body gives a welcome ex-
> cept Dr. Wilson's folks, and they are finding that
> it is wisest and best to be still, and we hope that
> before a great while they will be friendly. Father
> is determined to get acquainted with Dr. Wilson,
> and to be friendly with him, and I think he will
> succeed. 159

Beecher's strategy was to be conciliatory, and to minimize the differences between him and Wilson. He either
underestimated Wilson, completely misunderstood the local
situation, or both. Perhaps he believed, somewhat naively,
that Wilson and his colleagues held the same vision that
Beecher did. If so, he was as badly mistaken as Catherine's
prophecy.

Beecher's trip to Cincinnati made him feel "much more
settled in his own mind" about moving west. 160 Upon his return to Boston, he held a meeting of a committee of his
church to determine his future. After seven hours, Beecher
convinced the majority that the necessity of his going west
far outweighed any reasons for staying in Boston. On June
21, Vail, who may have been at that meeting, wrote jubilantly
to Blanchard and Mahan. "You will be happy to learn," he
wrote, "after waiting with much anxiety, that the great question of Dr. B's removal to the west is at length decided in
the affirmative."161 On August 10, Mahan publicly announced
"Dr. Beecher's Acceptance" in the Cincinnati Journal. The
Seminary's first president had become a Presbyterian and
would officially enter upon his duties after he arrived about
November 1. 162

In early July, Beecher informed his church and society
of his decision to accept Lane's call and resigned as pastor.
In what was probably a veiled reference to the Old School's
growing antipathy towards revivals, he stated that too often
the doctrines of evangelicalism were "inculcated in such a
manner as to be attended by no revivals and few conversions. "
"And the question whether the first and leading seminary of
the West shall be one which shall inculcate orthodoxy with or
without revivals" was of the utmost importance. As far as
he was concerned, Lane would be "a revival seminary. "

Beecher then, in language almost identical to his letter to
the Board of March 9, 1831, listed the "leadings of Providence" which he perceived had prepared him for his new task.
He was glad that he was leaving because in doing so he would
not be forced to take part in theological controversies in New
England. "Against the enemies of the Lord I can lift up the
spear with good will, but with the friends of Jesus Christ I
can not find it in my heart to enter into controversy. No,
I can not, I can not do it."[163] Moving west, however, would
not allow Beecher to avoid controversy.

In October, Beecher preached a farewell sermon to
his Bowdoin Street Church[164] and then he and his family began the long peregrination to Cincinnati. On the way, Beecher
preached many times, begged money for the endowment of a
chair of Biblical Literature (to which Calvin E. Stowe had
been appointed in August), conducted prayer meetings, and
taught an Andover Seminary graduate the proper way of
preaching. After a wait at Wheeling, Virginia, and Granville,
Ohio, to avoid the cholera in Cincinnati, the family arrived
on November 14, thirteen days after the Seminary term had
begun.[165] Within two weeks, Beecher was received unanimously into the Presbytery of Cincinnati, began his duties as
preacher at the Second Presbyterian Church (he was inducted
the following spring), quieted the apprehensions and animosity
of some of the church members who had been made suspicious
of him by Wilson, and rode out twice a week to the Seminary
to conduct classes in theology.[166]

On December 26, 1832, at 10:00 A.M., Beecher and
Biggs were inducted officially into their respective offices of
Lane Seminary by Vail, Mahan, and Gallaher.[167] None of
the three inducting ministers had been members of the original Board of Trustees. Franklin Y. Vail, who had done so
much to secure Beecher, was an Eastern man and an advocate of voluntary benevolent societies under minimum denominational control. Asa Mahan had been a colleague of Finney
in New York and represented the growing New School doctrinal
influence in the West. James Gallaher, once a close associate of Wilson, had begun to practice the new measures of
revivalism. These participants in the inauguration of Beecher
and Biggs symbolized the Seminary's position in the break that
had occurred in the Presbyterian Church in the West, a break--
in everything but name--occasioned by differences over church
polity and missions, theology, and practice.

The induction service, in the Second Presbyterian

Church, lasted almost three hours. Vail began it by leading
the congregation in a hymn. Mahan followed with a prayer.
Gallaher then performed the actual induction service. First
Beecher and then Biggs assented to a "formula of Christian
doctrine and duty" which the Board had prescribed. This
formula included a statement of belief in the Old and New
Testaments as the word of God and in the Confession of Faith
of the Presbyterian Church as containing the doctrines of
Scripture, the acceptance of the Presbyterian form of government and discipline, and the pledge "to be zealous & faithful
in my endeavours, to maintain the purity, & peace of the
church, & to qualify those young men who may be under my
care, to explain[,] defend, & apply the truths of the Gospel. "
Following the adoption of the formula, Gallaher presented each
man with a copy of the laws of the Seminary, symbolic of
"the authority with which you are now intrusted" and "the office you have now received. " Gallaher then made brief remarks expressing the satisfaction of the Board, congratulated
Beecher and Biggs on the privileges "of presiding over an
important school of the prophets, " and reminded them of the
responsibility of training many of "the future ministers of the
West. "168

      Biggs's address was a voluble, pedantic one, filled
with historical examples and "copious references to the Bible. "
He closed it by giving Biblical injunction to Lane with a reference to what he considered "the original model manual labor
school of the prophets, " established by the prophet Elisha on
the banks of the Jordan. 169

      Following the singing of Psalm 67, Beecher rose to
deliver his inaugural address, the central purpose of which
was to show his conception of the role of the ministry and
the purposes for which the ministry was to be trained. The
central trait of a minister's character had to be piety, without which the ministry was merely another profession. Manual labor (which Beecher had always practiced himself) would
provide the foundation for hard work and ministerial action,
and would counter the deleterious effects that continuous study
had on the constitution. With manual labor providing the basis for ministerial labor, intellectual discipline would be developed which would lead, not to the unreflecting acceptance
of other men's ideas, which had been the cause of the destruction of the Church's peace and purity, but to "original investi-
gations. " The minister should communicate evangelical doctrine (which Beecher assumed would result from "original in-
vestigations" and would be consonant with the Bible) in the

"explanatory mode" to insure he was understood by the people. Any mistakes in delivery or fact would be excused if the overriding "holy love" of the minister shone through. [170]

Beecher's reason for coming west to Lane had been the raising up of such a ministry. He believed the West contained "the great causes which are to decide the destinies of this nation." Religious and educational institutions, with God's blessing, were the only hope for harnessing the great energy and resources of the West for the good. [171]

Gallaher's benediction closed the service to induct Beecher and Biggs into their offices. The service symbolized the completion of the establishment of Lane Seminary. In spite of a number of conflicts and the continued opposition of a significant portion of the Church, the Seminary had been raised in the West for the purpose of saving the West, the nation, and the world. It had received a charter, secured an endowment, constructed buildings, and acquired a faculty. It would train a group of ministers who would be

> inspired with zeal, enlarged by comprehensive views, blessed with a discriminating intellect, and an acute but animated and popular argumentation, untrammeled by reading written polished sermons, and able, with a clear mind and full heart, to look saint and sinner in the face with an eye that speaks, and a hand that energizes, and a heart that overflows, and words that burn; competent and disposed, under the guidance of the wisdom which is from above, to convince gainsayers, allay fears, soothe prejudice, inspire confidence and cooperation in revivals and public charities, and all good things on the part of all, of every name, who substantially hold fast the truth, and love our Lord Jesus Christ in sincerity. [172]

Beecher wanted a ministry which would be zealous in building up the Kingdom of God, one more interested in cooperation than conflict, one more capable of raising up than tearing down. His theological views were attuned with his temperament and were turned toward the vision of uniting all evangelical Christians in the building and expanding of the domain of God. He would be opposed by men holding a vision of another kind.

Notes

1. U. S. , Department of Commerce, Bureau of the Census,
    Tenth Census of the United States, 1880, vol. 19, Re-
    port on the Social Statistics of Cities, pt. 2, p. 344;
    and Maurice F. Neufield, "Three Aspects of the Eco-
    nomic Life of Cincinnati from 1815-1840," Ohio State
    Archaeological and Historical Quarterly 44 (January
    1935): 69-70.

2. Ibid. , p. 358.

3. Richard C. Wade, "The Negro in Cincinnati, 1800-1830,"
    Journal of Negro History 39 (January 1954): 48-49,
    50-57; T. G. Steward, "The Banishment of the People
    of Colour from Cincinnati," Journal of Negro History
    8 (July 1923): 331-32; Frank Quillin, The Color Line
    in Ohio: A History of Race Prejudice in a Typical
    Northern State (Ann Arbor, Mich. : George Wahr,
    1913), pp. 21-23; and Charles Theodore Greve, Cen-
    tennial History of Cincinnati and Representative Citi-
    zens, 2 vols. (Chicago: Biographical Publishing Co. ,
    1904), 1:547.

4. [Benjamin Drake], "Cincinnati at the Close of 1835,"
    Western Monthly Magazine 5 (January 1836): 26-31.

5. Cincinnati Journal, 6 January 1832; Warren Jenkins, The
    Ohio Gazetteer, and Travelers Guide, rev. ed. (Co-
    lumbus: Isaac N. Whiting, 1837), p. 524; and Charles
    Frederick Goss, Cincinnati: The Queen City: 1788,
    1912, 4 vols. (Cincinnati: S. J. Clarke Pub. Co. ,
    1912), 2:180.

6. Harry N. Scheiber, Ohio Canal Era: A Case Study of
    Government and the Economy, 1830-1861 (Athens:
    Ohio University Press, 1969), pp. 225, 222; and William
    Alexander Mabry, "Ante-Bellum Cincinnati and Its
    Southern Trade," in American Studies in Honor of
    William Kenneth Boyd by Members of the Americana
    Club of Duke University, ed. David Kelly Jackson
    (Durham, N. C. : Duke University Press, 1940), pp.
    60-85.

7. Frederick Marryat, A Diary in America with Remarks on
    Its Institutions, ed. with Notes and Introduction by Syd-
    ney Jackman (New York: Alfred A. Knopf, 1962),
    p. 222.

8. Ibid., pp. 223-24; Jenkins, Ohio Gazetteer, p. 112; History of Cincinnati and Hamilton County, Ohio (Cincinnati: S. B. Nelson & Co., 1894), pp. 104, 127; and William H. Hildreth, "Mrs. Trollope in Porkopolis," Ohio Archaeological and Historical Quarterly 58 (January 1949): 36.

9. Cincinnati Journal, 6 January 1832; and David Donald, ed., "The Autobiography of James Hall, Western Literary Pioneer," Ohio State Archaeological and Historical Quarterly 56 (July 1947): 295-304.

10. Cincinnati Journal, 6 January 1832.

11. The Cincinnati Directory for the Year 1834 (Cincinnati: E. Deming, 1834), pp. 240-45.

12. Cincinnati Journal, 6 January 1832; and Amos Blanchard to Charles G. Finney, 1 January 1831, Charles Grandison Finney Papers, Oberlin College Archives, Oberlin, Ohio (Cleveland: Recordak Corporation for Oberlin College, 1958), Roll 2.

13. Greve, History of Cincinnati, 1:508, 527, 516-17; 2:211.

14. Cincinnati Directory for the Year 1834, pp. 240-45.

15. Cincinnati Journal, 21 November 1834; and Thomas Brainerd to C. E. Babb, 24 December 1860, in M. Brainerd, Life of Rev. Thomas Brainerd, D.D., for Thirty Years Pastor of Old Pine Street Church, Philadelphia (Philadelphia: J. B. Lippincott & Co., 1870), p. 80.

16. Sydney E. Ahlstrom, "Theology in America: A Historical Survey," in Religion in American Life, 3 vols., ed. James Ward Smith and A. Leland Jamison, Princeton Studies in American Civilization, no. 5, vol. 1: The Shaping of American Religion (Princeton: Princeton University Press, 1961), p. 265; and Ahlstrom, Religious History, pp. 464-65.

17. Ahlstrom, Religious History, pp. 465-68; and William Warren Sweet, ed., Religion on the American Frontier, 4 vols., vol. 2: The Presbyterians, 1783-1840: A Collection of Source Materials (New York: Harper & Bros., 1936), pp. 99-125.

18. Raymond Lee Hightower, "Joshua L. Wilson: Frontier Controversialist" (Ph. D. dissertation, University of Chicago, 1933); and an article of the same title in Church History 3 (December 1934): 300-16. Further references are to the dissertation only.

19. E. H. Gillett, History of the Presbyterian Church in the United States of America, 2 vols., rev. ed. (Philadelphia: Presbyterian Board of Publication and Sabbath-School Work, 1864), 2:329-32, 358-59.

20. Joshua L. Wilson to A. Cameron, 12 September 1828, in Sweet, ed., The Presbyterians, p. 734.

21. Greve, History of Cincinnati, 1:620-21.

22. Gillett, History of the Presbyterian Church, 2:358-59.

23. Ibid.; Cincinnati Christian Journal and Religious Intelligencer, 9 March 1830; and Hightower, "Joshua L. Wilson," pp. 153-54.

24. Quoted in Gillett, History of the Presbyterian Church, 2:258; and Joshua L. Wilson to R. J. Breckinridge, 12 February 1834, in Sweet, ed., The Presbyterians, p. 740.

25. Gillett, History of the Presbyterian Church, 2:331.

26. Cincinnati Journal, 5 August 1831. Blanchard was supported by the Synod, which still stated that his exposition of original sin and the atonement merited the Presbytery's displeasure. Cincinnati Journal, 4 November 1831. Wilson's dislike of Blanchard may have been increased by the latter's refusal to publish a tract by Wilson attacking the American Home Missionary Society, in March, 1831. See Hightower, "Joshua L. Wilson," pp. 172-75.

27. M. E. Thalheimer, "History of the Vine Street Congregational Church of Cincinnati," Papers of the Ohio Church History Society 9 (1898): 41-56.

28. A recent biography of Mahan is Barbara Brown Zikmund, "Asa Mahan and Oberlin Perfectionism" (Ph. D. dissertation, Duke University, 1969).

29. Hightower, "Joshua L. Wilson," pp. 176-81.

30. Clifford Merrill Drury, Presbyterian Panorama: One Hundred Years of National Missions History (Philadelphia: Board of Christian Education, 1952), p. 81; and Frederick Irving Kuhns, "Operations of the American Home Missionary Society in the Old Northwest: 1826-1861" (Ph. D. dissertation, University of Chicago, 1947). A brief history is in David G. Horvath, ed. , A Guide to the Microfilm Edition of the Papers of the American Home Missionary Society, 1816 (1826-1894) 1936 (Glen Rock, N. J. : Microfilming Corporation of America, 1975), pp. 1-7.

31. Kuhns, "American Home Missionary Society," p. 32; H. Shelton Smith, Robert T. Handy, and Lefferts A. Loetscher, American Christianity: An Historical Interpretation with Representative Documents, 2 vols. (New York: Charles Scribner's Sons, 1960-1963), 2:89; and Thomas Barr to Clement Vallandingham, 22 September 1830, in E. B. Welch, "The Presbyterian Church in the U. S. A. : Their [sic] Old Synod of Ohio, 1814-1837," in Buckeye Presbyterianism: An Account of the Seven Presbyterian Denominations with Their Twenty-One Synods and More than Sixty Presbyteries which at One Time or Another Have Functioned Wholly or in Large Part within the State of Ohio, by United Presbyterian Synod of Ohio. n. p. : United Presbyterian Synod of Ohio, 1968), pp. 66-69.

32. "Central Committee for Home Missions in the Western States," in Sweet, ed. , The Presbyterians, pp. 670-73.

33. Cincinnati Journal, 31 December 1830; Presbyterian Church in the United States of America, Minutes of the General Assembly of the Presbyterian Church in the United States of America from A. D. 1821 to A. D. 1837 Inclusive (Philadelphia: Presbyterian Board of Publication and Sabbath School Work, n. d.), pp. 298-300, 301, 333; and Gillett, History of the Presbyterian Church, 2:451.

34. Gillett, History of the Presbyterian Church, 2:451.

35. 9 September 1831.

36. <u>Cincinnati Journal</u>, 21 October 1831.

37. <u>Ibid.</u> Kemper donated part of the land for Lane Seminary; see pp. 31-35 above. All of the others were
members of Lane's Board of Trustees at one time
or another; <u>Lane Theological Seminary General Cata-
logue</u>, p. 7.

38. J. C. White, "Reminiscences of Lane Seminary, " in
<u>Pamphlet Souvenir of the Sixtieth Anniversary in the
History of Lane Theological Seminary, Containing
Papers Read before the Lane Club</u>, ed. Howard A.
Johnston, John H. Walter, and Nelson A. Shedd
(Cincinnati: Elm Street Printing Co. , 1890), pp. 5-
7; and Horace Bushnell to A. Barnes, 31 May 1867,
in Brainerd, <u>Life of Brainerd</u>, pp. 48, 44. One
participant at the meeting noted that the discussion
about Bushnell's licensure "was not conducted with
all that christian candor and meekness which ought
to characterize a judicatory of Jesus Christ. " <u>Cin-
cinnati Journal</u>, 14 October 1831.

39. <u>Cincinnati Journal</u>, 21 October 1831. Of the Old School
members of the "Low Church" faction, F. Slack was
a former teacher and friend of Thomas J. Biggs
(Professor of Church History at Lane from 1832 to
1839), and was without charge; J. Thomson had a
church in Springfield; T. Cole of New Richmond,
Indiana, and A. T. Rankin of Felicity, Ohio, were
both missionaries for the A. H. M. S. <u>Ibid.</u>; and <u>Lane
Theological Seminary General Catalogue</u>, p. 11.

40. Greve, <u>History of Cincinnati</u>, 1:621-22; Thomas Brainerd
to Wait Talcott, 8 January 1832, and Thomas Brain-
erd to C. E. Babb, 24 December 1860, in Brainerd,
<u>Life of Brainerd</u>, pp. 72-73, 82, 44.

41. For accounts of the many reform societies of the nineteenth century, see Clifford S. Griffin, <u>Their Brothers' Keepers: Moral Stewardship in the United States,
1800-1865</u> (New Brunswick, N. J. : Rutgers University
Press, 1960); Charles I. Foster, <u>An Errand of Mercy:
The Evangelical United Front, 1790-1837</u> (Chapel Hill:
University of North Carolina Press, 1960); and Robert
T. Handy, <u>A Christian America: Protestant Hopes
and Historical Realities</u> (New York: Oxford University Press, 1971).

42. Approximately 90 percent of all college presidents before the Civil War were clergymen. Ahlstrom, <u>Religious History</u>, p. 641, n. 3. Of the forty-five institutions of higher learning incorporated in Ohio before 1850, at least twenty-one were under specific "denominational influence." Edward A. Miller, "The History of Educational Legislation in Ohio from 1803 to 1850," <u>Ohio State Archaeological and Historical Quarterly</u> 27 (1919): 106, 112-13. Works dealing with church-related colleges in this period are Donald G. Tewksbury, <u>The Founding of American Colleges and Universities before the Civil War; with Particular Reference to the Religious Influences Bearing upon the College Movement</u> (New York: Bureau of Publications, Teachers College, Columbia University, 1932); and Vernon Franklin Schwalm, "The Historical Development of the Denominational Colleges in the Old Northwest to 1870" (Ph.D. dissertation, University of Chicago, 1926).

43. Winthrop S. Hudson, <u>Religion in America</u> (New York: Charles Scribner's Sons, 1965), p. 156.

44. Samuel J. Baird, <u>A History of the Early Policy of the Presbyterian Church in the Training of Her Ministry; and of the First Years of the Board of Education</u> (Philadelphia: Presbyterian Board of Education, 1865), p. 3.

45. Sweet, ed., <u>The Presbyterians</u>, pp. 78-80; and William Warren Sweet, "The Rise of Theological Schools in America," <u>Church History</u> 6 (September 1937): 267.

46. The support given to these two organizations is detailed in Drury, <u>Presbyterian Panorama</u>, pp. 21-41, 52-90; and Kuhns, "American Home Missionary Society in the Old Northwest."

47. "Copy of a Letter on the Subject of a Theological Seminary in the West," September 1822, in Sweet, ed., <u>The Presbyterians</u>, pp. 590-91.

48. Presbyterian Church, <u>Minutes of the General Assembly</u>, p. 144.

49. <u>Cincinnati Christian Journal</u>, 8 December 1829.

50. James Blythe to Joshua L. Wilson, 2 September 1825, in Sweet, ed., The Presbyterians, p. 593.

51. Presbyterian Church, Minutes of the General Assembly, pp. 169-71, 177; and Gillett, History of the Presbyterian Church, 2:349.

52. Ibid., p. 209; and Jesse Johnson, "Early Theological Education West of the Alleghanies," Papers of the American Society of Church History, 2d series, 5 (1917): 128.

53. Jesse Johnson, "Early Theological Education," pp. 128-29.

54. Lane Seminary, Formal Minutes of Meetings of the Board of Trustees, 1828-1838, Meetings of 27 September and 1 October 1828, Office of the Treasurer, Lane Theological Seminary, Cincinnati (hereafter cited as Lane Seminary, Trustees Formal Minutes, LTS); Edward D. Morris, "Leaves from the Early History of Lane," in Thirty Years in Lane and Other Lane Papers (n.p., 1896), p. 54; and G. M. Maxwell, "Early History," in Addresses and Proceedings at Lane Theological Seminary, December 18, 1879 (Cincinnati: Elm Street Printing Co., 1879), p. 18.

55. Ebenezer Lane to D. H. Allen, 14 October 1847, Lane Papers, Folder 1, MTS.

56. Reprinted in the Hudson Ohio Observer, 3 April 1834. The Weekly Journal evidently did not consider Isaac G. Burnet to have been a Baptist; although baptized by Rev. John Boyd, pastor of the Enon Baptist Church about 1826, he joined the Second Presbyterian Church in 1831 or 1832. Memorial Association, In Memoriam. Cincinnati, 1881. Containing Proceedings of the Memorial Association, Eulogies at Music Hall, and Biographical Sketches of Many Distinguished Citizens of Cincinnati (Cincinnati: A. E. Jones, 1881), p. 111.

57. Cincinnati Pandect, 7 April, 8 September 1829. Information on the members of the Board of Trustees is contained in Gillett, History of the Presbyterian Church, 2:292; Lane Theological Seminary General Catalogue, p. 7; Greve, History of Cincinnati, passim; Goss, Cincinnati, passim; and History of Cincinnati and Hamilton County, Ohio, passim.

58. "To the [Members of?] the Senate & House of Represent-
    atives of the State of Ohio in General Assembly,"
    Lane Papers, Folder 1, MTS; "Lane Seminary.
    Charter & Amendments," Lane Papers, Folder 1,
    MTS; and History of the Foundation and Endowment,
    Catalogue, and Trustees, Alumni, and Students of
    the Lane Theological Seminary (Cincinnati: Ben
    Franklin Printing Press, 1838), pp. 4-5.

59. History of the Foundation and Endowment, pp. 6-7.

60. Ebenezer Lane to Joshua L. Wilson, 7 December 1828,
    in John Vant Stephens, The Story of the Founding of
    Lane: Address Delivered at the Centennial of Lane
    Theological Seminary, June 25, 1929 (Cincinnati,
    n.p., 1929), p. 5.

61. History of the Foundation and Endowment, p. 3; Lane
    Seminary, Trustees Formal Minutes, Meeting of
    1 June 1829, LTS.

62. Andrew Lane to Franklin Y. Vail, February and 28
    November 1834, Lane Papers, Folder 1, MTS.

63. Cincinnati Pandect, 7 April 1829.

64. "To the [Members of?] the Senate & House of Represent-
    atives," Lane Papers, Folder 1, MTS.

65. "Lane Seminary. Charter & Amendments," Lane Papers,
    Folder 1, MTS; and Miller, "History of Educational
    Legislation," p. 117.

66. Ibid.

67. "An act to incorporate the 'Lane Seminary,' " Lane
    Papers, Folder 1, MTS.

68. Ibid.

69. "Lane Seminary. Charter & Amendments," Lane Papers,
    Folder 1, MTS.

70. Lane Seminary, Trustees Formal Midutes, Meetings of
    28 October, 15 November, and 15 December 1828,
    LTS; and Greve, History of Cincinnati, 1:619-20.

71. Biographical materials on Elnathan Kemper are in Marie

Dickore, ed., "The Elnathan Kemper Account Book, 1829-1843," Bulletin of the Historical and Philosophical Society of Ohio 17 (January 1959): 69-73; Cincinnati Daily Gazette, 19 August 1834; and Cincinnati Journal, 5 September 1834.

72. History of Cincinnati, pp. 548-49; Greve, History of Cincinnati, 1:359, 2:192; and [Earl R. North, ed.], One Hundred and Fifty Years of Presbyterianism in the Ohio Valley, 1790-1940 (Cincinnati: Presbytery of Cincinnati, 1941), pp. 8-18, 24-31.

73. Greve, History of Cincinnati, 1:619; Morris, "Leaves," p. 56, n.; and James Kemper, description of Walnut Hills Academy, donated by Elnathan and Peter Kemper and run by Rev. James Kemper (copy), Lane Seminary Papers, Folder 2, Cincinnati Historical Society, Cincinnati (hereafter cited as Lane Papers, CHS).

74. James Kemper to Ezra Stiles Ely, 27 April 1827 (copy), Lane Papers, Folder 1, CHS.

75. "To the Commissioners for locating a Western Theological Seminary for the Presbyterian Church," Lane Papers, Folder 6, CHS.

76. Elnathan Kemper, answer to complaint of David Kemper and others in respect to lands [1834], Lane Papers, Folder 2, CHS.

77. Lane Seminary, Trustees Formal Minutes, Meetings of 1 and 12 January 1829, LTS; and A. A. Halsey to Elnathan Kemper, 13 January 1829, Lane Papers, Folder 1, CHS.

78. Elnathan Kemper to Joshua L. Wilson, 14 January 1829, Kemper Family, Collection of Letters, Documents and Miscellanea of Many Members of the Kemper Family, Box 1, Cincinnati Historical Society, Cincinnati (hereafter cited as Kemper Family Collection, CHS). A portion of this letter is quoted in History of the Foundation and Endowment, p. 8.

79. Elnathan Kemper, answer to complaint of David Kemper and others in respect to lands [1834], Lane Papers, Folder 2, CHS.

80. Charles A. Kemper, answers to questions regarding disputes in the Kemper family, 28 September 1832, Lane Papers, Folder 3, CHS.

81. Questions and answers of a Kemper family member (probably Charles A.) regarding the family dispute, 28 July 1830, Lane Papers, Folder 3, CHS.

82. Elnathan Kemper, answer to complaint of David Kemper and others in respect to lands [1834], Lane Papers, Folder 2, CHS. The deed provided that, in case the Seminary failed, the donation would be divided between the American Bible Society, the American Tract Society, the American Colonization Society, and the American Education Society, instead of reverting back to the original donors or their heirs. Elnathan's brothers may also have been distrubed at this provision. The writer of the History of the Foundation and Endowment, p. 9, stated that this provision "was not acceded to by the rest of the family, till a few days before the deed was made out,... "

83. Elnathan Kemper, answer to complaint of David Kemper and others in respect to lands [1834], Lane Papers, Folder 2, CHS; "David R. Kemper vs James Kemper Senior, James Birdsell, Elnathan Kemper," Lane Papers, Folder 6, CHS; and questions and answers of a Kemper family member (probably Charles A.) regarding the family dispute, 28 July 1830, Lane Papers, Folder 3, CHS.

84. Elnathan wrote to Peter complaining of the latter's "deranged state of your mind & the strength of your prejudice" and that he should "keep your Diabolical stuff to yourself. " Elnathan Kemper to Peter Kemper 27 April 1832, Kemper Family Collection, Box 1, CHS.

85. Daniel Gano, abstract of David R. Kemper vs James Kemper Senior, James Birdsell, and Elnathan Kemper, 12 April 1834, Lane Papers, Folder 3, CHS.

86. History of the Foundation and Endowment, p. 9.

87. James Kemper to Thomas J. Biggs and Lyman Beecher, 13 June 1833, Lane Papers, Folder 8, MTS. Elnathan wrote that his father "denounces the Seminary & has not to my knowledge ever gone to see for himself. "

Elnathan Kemper to Benjamin Chambers, 31 October
1833, Kemper Family Collection, Box 1, CHS.

88. Willis N. Kemper, "History of certain lots in Lane
Seminary Subdivision, deeded back to the heirs of
Elnathan Kemper by the Seminary Trustees," 17
September 1908, Lane Papers, Folder 2, CHS.

89. Cincinnati Journal, 5 September 1834; and Boston Recorder, 18 January 1834.

90. Dickore, ed., "Elnathan Kemper Account Book," p. 71.

91. Peter H. Kemper to Mr. and Mrs. Archibald Peterson,
25 August 1834, Kemper Family Collection, Box 1,
CHS; and Cincinnati Journal, 5 September 1834.
Theodore D. Weld offered the prayer at Elnathan's
funeral. Sereno W. Streeter to Theodore D. Weld,
18 August 1875, Theodore Dwight Weld, Angelina
Grimké Weld, and Sarah Grimké Papers, Box 15,
William L. Clements Library, University of Michigan,
Ann Arbor (hereafter cited as Weld-Grimké Papers,
WLCL). Elnathan's father, James, died of cholera
two days after his son's funeral. Cincinnati Daily
Gazette, 21 and 23 August 1834.

92. Lane Seminary, Trustees Formal Minutes, Meetings of
26 January and 23 March 1829, LTS; and History of
the Foundation and Endowment, pp. 9-10.

93. Jacob Lindley to the Board of Trustees, 23 March 1829,
Lane Papers, Folder 5, MTS.

94. 7 April 1829.

95. Lane Seminary, Trustees Formal Minutes, Meetings of
1 June and 18 August 1829, LTS; and Absalom Peters
to Joshua L. Wilson, 22 July 1829, in Sweet, ed.,
The Presbyterians, pp. 597-98.

96. 8 September 1829.

97. History of the Foundation and Endowment, p. 10.

98. The trustees announced, in a statement dated November
18, that Lane "is now open, at Walnut Hills, for the
reception of students in theology." Cincinnati Christian Journal, 24 November 1829.

99. Maxwell, "Early History," p. 21; George Beckwith to James Warren, 11 August 1829, Lane Papers, Folder 18, MTS; Cincinnati Pandect, 1 September 1829; and Cincinnati Christian Journal, 3 November 1829.

100. Cincinnati Christian Journal, 10 and 17 November 1829.

101. Ibid. , 24 November 1829.

102. Ibid. , 1, 8, and 29 December 1829.

103. Ibid. , 29 December 1829.

104. Lane Seminary, Trustees Formal Minutes, Meeting of 24 February 1830, LTS.

105. George Beckwith to Joshua L. Wilson, 21 July 1830, Lane Papers, Folder 18, MTS.

106. George Beckwith to James Warren, 24 August 1830, Lane Papers, Folder 18, MTS; and George Beckwith to Franklin Y. Vail or David Root, 25 August 1830, Lane Papers, Folder 18, MTS.

107. Ibid; George Beckwith to David Root, 19 July 1830, Lane Papers, Folder 18, MTS; and George Beckwith to Franklin Y. Vail, 15 June 1835, Lane Papers, Folder 18, MTS.

108. History of the Foundation and Endowment, p. 10.

109. Lane Seminary, Trustees Formal Minutes, Meeting of 20 September 1830, LTS; and Franklin Y. Vail to the Executive Committee of the Board of Trustees, 20 April 1836, Lane Papers, Folder 3, MTS.

110. Franklin Y. Vail to the Executive Committee of the Board of Trustees, 20 April 1836, Lane Papers, Folder 3, MTS.

111. Ibid. The Old School character of much of the Cincinnati Presbytery is noted in Welsh, "The Presbyterian Church in the U. S. A. ," p. 76.

112. Franklin Y. Vail to the Board of Trustees, 14 October 1830, in Cross, ed. , Autobiography of Beecher, 2:181.

113. Biographical information on Beecher is from Henry, Unvanquished Puritan; Harding, "Lyman Beecher"; and Cross, ed., Autobiography of Beecher.

114. Cincinnati Chronicle and Literary Gazette, 14 December 1833.

115. Henry, Unvanquished Puritan, pp. 92-95, 57-58, 51-52, 136-39, 156-57.

116. Quoted in Calvin E. Stowe, "Sketches and Recollections of Dr. Lyman Beecher," Congregational Quarterly 6 (July 1864): 225.

117. Henry, Unvanquished Puritan, pp. 92-95.

118. When arguments within Congregationalism arose over doctrine and threatened to divide potential allies, Beecher "hesitated, temporized, compromised." Stowe, "Sketches," p. 228. Beecher's plan of uniting abolitionists and colonizationists is well-known. Henry, Unvanquished Puritan, p. 198.

119. Stowe, "Sketches," p. 232.

120. In Cross, ed., Autobiography of Beecher, 2:167.

121. Ibid., 2:184.

122. Franklin Y. Vail to the Board of Trustees, 14 October 1830, in Cross, ed., Autobiography of Beecher, 2:181; and Franklin Y. Vail to James Warren, 15 October 1830, Lane Papers, Folder 19, MTS.

123. Lewis Tappan wrote a biography of his brother, The Life of Arthur Tappan (New York: Hurd & Houghton, 1871). A modern biography of both Lewis and Arthur is Bertram Wyatt-Brown, "Partners in Piety: Lewis and Arthur Tappan, Evangelical Abolitionists, 1828-1841" (Ph.D. dissertation, The Johns Hopkins University, 1963), which was reworked and published as Lewis Tappan and the Evangelical War against Slavery.

124. Arthur Tappan gave money to Auburn Theological Seminary, Western Reserve College, Kenyon College, Yale College, and Amherst College, as well as to

numerous benevolent enterprises. [Tappan], Life of Arthur Tappan, pp. 407-10; Frederick Clayton Waite, Western Reserve University: The Hudson Era. A History of Western Reserve College and Academy at Hudson, Ohio, from 1826 to 1882 (Cleveland: Western Reserve University Press, 1943), p. 120; and George Frederick Wright, Charles Grandison Finney, American Religious Leaders (Boston: Houghton Mifflin & Co., 1891), pp. 122-23.

125. Arthur Tappan to Franklin Y. Vail, 14 October 1830, Lane Papers, Folder 5, MTS.

126. Cross, ed., Autobiography of Beecher, 2:211.

127. Lane Seminary, Trustees Formal Minutes, Meeting of the Executive Committee, 22 October 1830, LTS; Gillett, History of the Presbyterian Church, 2:462-63, n. 2; and James Warren to Franklin Y. Vail, 23 October 1830, Lane Papers, Folder 19, MTS.

128. James Warren to Franklin Y. Vail, 23 October 1830, Lane Papers, Folder 19, MTS; portions of this letter were quoted in History of the Foundation and Endowment, p. 12.

129. Franklin Y. Vail to James Warren, 11 November 1830, Lane Papers, Folder 19, MTS.

130. Lane Seminary, Trustees Formal Minutes, Meetings of 17 January and 10 March 1831, LTS; Thomas J. Biggs to James Warren, 15 February 1831, Lane Papers, Folder 6, MTS; and Cincinnati Journal, 21 January, 25 February, and 1 April 1831.

131. Lyman Beecher to "Dear Brother" (probably Vail), 9 March 1831, in "Appendix," in The Life and Services of Rev. Lyman Beecher, D.D. as President and Professor of Theology in Lane Seminary. A Commemorative Discourse, Delivered at the Anniversary, May 7th, 1863, by D. Howe Allen (Cincinnati: Johnson, Stephens & Co., 1863), p. 4.

132. Nathaniel W. Taylor to Lyman Beecher, 8 November 1830, in Cross, ed., Autobiography of Beecher, 2:185-86.

133. Joshua L. Wilson, Franklin Y. Vail, and James Galla-
     her to the Hanover Church and Congregation of
     Boston, [February] 1831, in Cross, ed. , Autobiog-
     raphy of Beecher, 2:182-83.

134. Lyman Beecher to "Dear Brother" (probably Vail), 9
     March 1831, in "Appendix, " pp. 1-2.

135. Ibid. , pp. 2-3.

136. Ibid. , p. 4.

137. Ibid. , pp. 4-5.

138. Lane Seminary, Trustees Formal Minutes, Meeting of
     28 March 1831, LTS.

139. Franklin Y. Vail to James Warren, 14 May 1831, Lane
     Papers, Folder 19, MTS.

140. Cincinnati Journal, 1 April 1831; and Lane Seminary,
     Trustees Formal Minutes, Meetings of 10 and 24
     March, and 18 April 1831, LTS.

141. See above, pp. 22-26.

142. Lane Theological Seminary General Catalogue, p. 7;
     Joshua L. Wilson to E. D. Mansfield, May 1839,
     in Sweet, ed. , The Presbyterians, pp. 600-603;
     Cincinnati Journal, 21 October 1831; Joshua L.
     Wilson to the Trustees of Lane Seminary, 17 No-
     vember 1831, Lane Papers, Folder 16, MTS; and
     Amos Blanchard to Franklin Y. Vail, 13 July 1832,
     Lane Papers, Folder 16, MTS. Between 1831 and
     1836, at least ten of fifteen new Board members
     were New School.

143. Lane Seminary, Trustees Formal Minutes, Meeting of
     26 October 1831, LTS; and Cincinnati Journal, 5
     August 1831.

144. Joshua L. Wilson to the Trustees of Lane Seminary,
     17 November 1831, Lane Papers, Folder 16, MTS.

145. Lane Seminary, Trustees Formal Minutes, Meeting of
     Executive Committee, 5 January 1832, LTS; and
     Cincinnati Journal, 6 January 1832.

146. Cincinnati Journal, 27 January 1832.

147. Ibid., 2 March 1832. Colton was in Europe to purchase books for the Seminary. He was competing
   against the agent for the General Assembly's Seminary at Alleghanytown for donations for books and
   did not think very highly of the quality of the latter's
   selections. Calvin Colton to James Warren, 26
   March 1832, Lane Papers, Folder 13, MTS.

148. Lane Seminary, Trustees Formal Minutes, Meeting of
   10 March 1831, LTS; and Cincinnati Journal, 27
   January, 23 and 30 March 1832.

149. Cincinnati Journal, 13 April 1832.

150. Ibid., 21 October 1831; and Amos Blanchard to Franklin Y. Vail, 28 May 1832, Lane Papers, Folder
   14, MTS. Biggs's former teacher was offered the
   position in July, but, having been offended by some
   Board members, he turned it down in December.
   Lane Seminary, Trustees Formal Minutes, Meetings
   of Executive Committee, 12 July and 23 December
   1832, LTS.

151. Amos Blanchard to Franklin Y. Vail, 13 July 1832,
   Lane Papers, Folder 16, MTS. In fact, Blanchard
   had already resigned from the Board. Lane Seminary, Trustees Formal Minutes, Meeting of Executive Committee, 12 July 1832, LTS.

152. Cross, ed., Autobiography of Beecher, 2:187, 194-98.

153. Stowe, "Sketches," p. 228.

154. Lane Seminary, Trustees Formal Minutes, Meetings of
   Executive Committee, 5 and 23 January 1832, LTS;
   a portion of this letter is in Cross, ed., Autobiography of Beecher, 2:188-89.

155. Thomas H. Skinner to Lyman Beecher, 16 February
   1832, in Cross, ed., Autobiography of Beecher,
   2:189-90.

156. Lyman Beecher to Asa Mahan, Franklin Y. Vail, and
   Amos Blanchard, 17 March 1832, in Cross, ed.,
   Autobiography of Beecher, 2:190-92.

157. Catherine Beecher to Harriet Beecher, 17 April 1832, in Cross, ed. , Autobiography of Beecher, 2:199-201; Cincinnati Journal, 20 April 1832.

158. Cincinnati Journal, 15 June 1832.

159. Catherine Beecher to Harriet Beecher, 17 April 1832, in Cross, ed. , Autobiography of Beecher, 2:201.

160. Ibid. , p. 200.

161. Franklin Y. Vail to Amos Blanchard and Asa Mahan, 21 June 1832, Lane Papers, Folder 19, MTS.

162. Cincinnati Journal, 10 August 1832. Beecher joined the Third Presbytery of New York City, to which Finney belonged, and then transferred his membership to the Cincinnati Presbytery. Fletcher, History of Oberlin, 1:53.

163. An extract of Beecher's address is in Cross, ed. , Autobiography of Beecher, 2:204-206.

164. Cincinnati Journal, 12 October 1832.

165. Extracts of letters in Cross, ed. , Autobiography of Beecher, 2:207-10; and Cincinnati Journal, 24 August 1832. Stowe was appointed Professor of Biblical Literature at the Executive Committee's meeting on August 9. Lane Seminary, Trustees Formal Minutes, LTS.

166. Cincinnati Journal, 14 December 1832; and Cross, ed. , Autobiography of Beecher, 2:212, 221, 214.

167. Accounts of the inauguration were printed in the Cincinnati Journal, 28 December 1832, and 4 and 11 January 1833. The "Order of Exercises" and "Formula" are in the Lane Papers, Folders 27 and 6, MTS.

168. Cincinnati Journal, 4 January 1833; and "Formula, " Lane Papers, Folder 6, MTS.

169. Ibid.

170. Ibid.

171. Ibid. Edward Weed, a student at the Seminary, attended the inauguration and was "highly delighted with" the addresses of Biggs and Beecher. Weed thought Beecher "treated the whole subject of education with a masterly hand." Diary entry, 26 December 1832, in [James Lillie], Faith and Works: or the Life of Edward Weed, Minister of the Gospel (New York: C. W. Benedict, 1853), p. 27.

172. Extract of Beecher's address, in Cross, ed., Autobiography of Beecher, 2:205-206.

CHAPTER III

THE LANE DEBATE

Lane Seminary: 1832-1833

After the inauguration of Lyman Beecher as President and Professor of Theology, the faculty and students of Lane experienced a period of calm. Although he was still opposed by Joshua Wilson, Beecher concentrated on his Seminary duties of teaching twice a week, raising funds to complete the endowment, and supervising the day to day activities of the school. [1]*

Thomas J. Biggs taught church history, participated in meetings of the Presbytery, and occasionally supplied the pulpit of the Third Presbyterian Church. [2] Some of the students considered him to be an incompetent teacher, and even threatened to boycott his classes. [3] A colleague thought Biggs was "a good natured nothing."[4]

Calvin E. Stowe, a graduate of Andover Theological Seminary and former editor of the Boston Recorder, was the third member of the theological faculty. He arrived in Cincinnati in June, 1833, to begin his work as Professor of Biblical Literature. Easily the best scholar in the Seminary, Stowe was charged with planning the course of study. He was well-liked by the students because of his teaching ability, and because of his ironic, sarcastic brand of humor and his talents as a mimic. He and Beecher became friends and their friendship increased when Stowe married Beecher's daughter, Harriet, in 1836. [5]

A number of people taught in the Preparatory Department. Lewis Howell, who had been named the Principal of the Department in March, 1831, left, with some bitterness, in November, 1832. [6] Thomas Cole, who taught mathematics,

---

*Notes to Chapter III begin on page 96.

stayed at Lane only a month. [7] Nathaniel S. Folsom was
Professor of Languages until leaving for Western Reserve
College in Hudson, Ohio, in February, 1834. [8] Thomas D.
Mitchell, a local physician, taught chemistry. [9] John Morgan,
graduate of Williams College, was Professor of Mathematics
and Natural Philosophy. [10] More intimate with the students
than any of his colleagues, Morgan often visited them in their
rooms in the dormitory. [11] He wrote to a friend, "I have
thrown myself among among [sic] their familiarity & they
seem both to love & respect me. "[12] In addition to all these
men, former students, such as Horace Bushnell, and advanced
students, such as Enoch N. Bartlett, taught in the Preparatory Department. [13]

Between 1831 and 1833, Lane had between fifty and
one hundred students in attendance. Most of the earlier students had been from Ohio, but, beginning in the summer after
Beecher's induction, students began arriving from more dis-
tant places. [14] By January, 1834, a plurality of students,
thirty-eight, listed their home residences as New York.
Eighteen were from Ohio. In regional terms, forty-four came
from the Mid-Atlantic states, twenty-three from the Midwest,
seventeen from New England, and only eight from the South.[15]
This predominantly Northern and Eastern student body found
itself within a community with Southern economic ties, Southern sentiments, and a large Southern-born segment of the
population.

The students had other distinctive traits besides their
origins. While the theological students were as old as those
in other seminaries in the country, most of the students in
the Preparatory Department, which was supposed to prepare
students for college, were nearly as old as their classmates
in the Theological Department. [16] Within Lane's student body
were men of considerable talents. Theodore Weld already
had a national reputation as a reformer, and had been offered
a professorship at Lane. [17] Huntington Lyman had been active
in the state militia and politics in New York. [18] Thomas
Williamson had been a practicing physician in Ripley, Ohio,
before deciding to come to Lane to prepare himself as a missionary to the Indians. [19] Many students had been agents or
colporteurs for different benevolent societies. [20] In addition,
a number of students were from prominent families. For
example, John T. Pierce was the nephew of Arthur and Lewis
Tappan. [21]

The most significant characteristics of the student body

were its acceptance of the manual labor system and its evangelicalism. The manual labor system had originated at Phillipp von Fellenberg's academy in Switzerland, and was promoted in the United States by William Channing Woodbridge.[22] It became popular for several reasons. First, by combining labor with study, students were able to pay for their own education. Second, the healthful benefits of physical exercise were stressed.[23] Third, manual labor was presented as a means of eliminating class distinctions and "acquiring a knowledge of mankind."[24] Fourth, manual labor was shown to be a way of inspiring students "with the independence of character, and the originality of investigation, which belongs peculiarly to self-made and self-educated men."[25]

The manual labor system at Lane was not significant because it was unique; in 1830, Lane was only one among twenty schools in ten states which had manual labor programs.[26] The significance of Lane's program was the prominence given to it as a "fundamental principle" by which the West itself would train ministers to spread the gospel.[27]

At Lane, the manual labor department was directed by Samuel F. Dickinson, Superintendent and Steward.[28] Each student worked in either the printing, farming, or mechanical departments under the immediate supervision of student "work monitors," who reported the amount of work performed, compensation for each worker, and damage to tools. The most popular department, by far, was the printing department, which used six presses and produced, among other works, 150,000 copies of Webster's spelling book in 1833.[29] Manual labor was the means for producing independent, healthy, and knowledgeable ministers.

The force which led the students to enter a manual labor seminary in the West was evangelicalism. Some, like Charles P. Bush, Marius Racine Robinson, Henry B. and Robert L. Stanton, and Weld, had been converted in the revivals of Charles G. Finney, the new measures revivalist who preached man's ability and responsibility.[30] As a result of this evangelical emphasis, men came to Lane to become "God's stewards [who] act for him, live for him, transact business for him, eat and drink for his glory, live and die to please him."[31] Like Edward Weed, students asked "in what business or occupation can I be most useful, in promoting the cause of Christ, and the welfare of my fellow-men?" Coming to Lane was the means to prepare oneself for God's "business."[32]

Coming to Lane was also the means to continue God's work, because there was to be no separation between preparation for the ministry and immediate involvement in saving the world. [33] In this, the students were encouraged by the faculty and trustees, who believed

> that the exigencies of the church and the world demand that our prospective ministry, instead of confining their attention exclusively to study, and thus losing the holy ardor and zeal of their first love, should be trained to habits of christian activity, self-denial, and usefulness during their whole preparatory course. [34]

Within the Seminary, students formed societies concerned with inquiry about missions, mutual improvement, foreign missions, colonization, and miscellaneous discussion. [35] In the community, students assisted in forming temperance societies, conducted prayer meetings, distributed tracts, and established twenty-one Sabbath schools with 1,172 students, many of whom were from "the most destitute neighborhoods."[36]

Lane's students were encouraged and were eager to engage in the promotion of "all the great enterprises of christian benevolence."[37] Their maturity, abilities, self-reliance, and evangelical fervor marked them as an exceptional student body, "a set of glorious good fellows."[38] The first test of their character came when the cholera struck.

On October 25, 1832, a legal clerk in Cincinnati wrote:

> Cincinnati is filled with gloom. The demon has reached us, and has let slip the dogs of death. Cholera, Cholera. The word is upon every tongue, its poison is in every constitution. [39]

The first deaths in the city had been reported on September 20. For thirteen months, the disease remained in Cincinnati; it killed over eight hundred people and forced an estimated five thousand to flee. [40]

Students and faculty at Lane experienced no sickness for almost ten months. Their isolation on Walnut Hills, a reputedly healthy area, as well as the coming of winter accounted for this. [41] On July 17, a month after the term began, a student experienced "premonitory symptoms" of cholera; in response, the faculty appointed a student Board of Health to obtain the services of a physician, issue health regulations, determine the health of each student, and distribute disinfectant. On Friday the nineteenth, the first student died. In less than a week there were four deaths, nine cases of cholera, and twenty-six cases of premonitory symptoms. [42]

While the epidemic lasted, there were "a few instances of alarm; but they were so surrounded by such a power of steadfast christian self-possession, as effectually repressed the contagion of panic fear;... " Only one student left the Seminary, at the insistence of his parents. The rest, when not ill, provided food and medicine, and nursed their friends and fellow students. [43] Theodore Weld's experience of going without sleep for forty-eight hours at a time was inspiring but typical. [44] When the cholera had departed, by July 30, the students were not only mature, able, self-reliant, and evangelical, but united as well.

Prelude to the Lane Debate

By early 1834, events had occurred which moved the antislavery movement into national prominence. Prudence Crandall, operator of an illegal school for black girls in Canterbury, Connecticut, had been imprisoned in late June, 1833. The American Anti-Slavery Society had been formed in December, 1833, and had announced its commitment to immediate emancipation. William Lloyd Garrison's Liberator had become more offensive to Southerners and their supporters. [45]

In southern Ohio, the slavery issue became important not only because of the national attention the antislavery movement had received. Situated on the border of a slave state, Cincinnati's contacts with slavery were numerous. Groups of slaves being shipped South stopped occasionally at the Cincinnati wharf, to be viewed with pity and outrage by those not used to such spectacles. Attempts of slaves to gain freedom were not uncommon; in 1832, a captured fugitive jumped to his death rather than be returned to slavery. [46]

In Cincinnati some efforts were made to alleviate the sufferings of the city's blacks. In January, 1817, a "Female association for the benefit of Africans" was formed to organize Sabbath schools for black children. However, by 1825 the secretary of the society noted its "negligence in the performance of known duty. "[47] Joshua L. Wilson's First Presbyterian Church maintained "a large and increasing African School" in 1829. [48] For the most part, however, Cincinnatians preferred the emigration rather than assimilation of blacks, and supported the forced removal of more than 1,100 blacks in 1829. [49]

In southern Ohio, few people would have heartily approved of the continuation of slavery. Most would have agreed with the resolution of the Cincinnati Synod of 1830 which labelled the slave trade "a heinous sin."[50] The issue in Cincinnati, as elsewhere, centered around the best means of eliminating slavery. On the one hand, some believed that the ending of slavery implied, even necessitated, the removal of blacks. On the other hand, others asserted that the ending of slavery carried with it the belief in the equality of blacks and whites. Cincinnati's proximity to a slave state and strong anti-black bias made the former alternative more favorable.

The American Colonization Society, founded in late 1816, favored the removal of free blacks from the United States to settlements in Africa. [51] In southern Ohio, any program which advocated the removal of blacks was popular, because blacks were not welcome in white society. In the fall of 1832, an article in the Cincinnati Journal expressed this common conviction:

> Independent of the evils arising from the existence, in the midst of our population, of a foreign and discontented people, it will be at once foreseen that the association of these two classes must exert a most pernicious influence upon the morals of both. It is unnecessary to refer to facts in support of this position, for they are within the observation of every body. [52]

The Cincinnati Colonization Society had been organized in 1826, and had contributed money to the national organization until 1829. After a short period of decline, it was revitalized by the national society's agent, Robert S. Finley, and almost five hundred dollars was raised to send a shipload of blacks from New Orleans to Liberia in 1831. [53] By 1833, prominent Presbyterian clergymen, such as Joshua L. Wilson, Lyman Beecher, James Gallaher, and Asa Mahan, supported the local society. [54]

The Chillicothe Presbytery of the Cincinnati Synod

contained many former Southerners who had moved to the Old Northwest to avoid slavery[55] and who rejected the assumption of colonizationists that the removal of free blacks would end slavery gradually. In 1831, Rev. Samuel Crothers, pastor of the Presbyterian church at Greenfield, Ohio, wrote fifteen letters to the Cincinnati Journal under the title "An Appeal to Patriots and Christians in Behalf of the Enslaved Africans." These letters asserted the sin of slavery, refuted pro-slavery arguments, and stated that the solution to the problem of slavery was to "obey God. Lose [sic] the bands of wickedness, break every yoke and let the oppressed go free."[56]

In August, 1831, Crothers headed a committee appointed by the Cincinnati Synod, which wrote "An Address to the Churches on the Subject of Slavery." "The way of truth and duty," Crothers wrote, "is clear and plain; the way of error and sin is dark and perplexed. The direction is not resolve to do it; but, do it.... The command of heaven is imperative [regarding slavery]. The direction is: 'BREAK OFF.'"[57]

With a slave state just across the river, the extensive newspaper discussions of slavery in the Cincinnati Journal, the existence of the Cincinnati Colonization Society, the religious context in which slavery was discussed, and the demand by men such as Crothers for the immediate release of the slaves, it was no wonder that there was discussion of slavery at Lane Seminary. In the summer of 1832, one of the student societies debated the question, "If the slaves of the South were to rise in insurrection, would it be the duty of the North to aid in putting it down?" Henry B. Stanton recalled later that, much to his surprise, he was the only student to argue in the negative.[58] The debate elicited no censure from faculty, trustees, or townspeople because the students, with the exception of Stanton, espoused no unfavorable doctrine or program. Their overwhelming approval of Northern assistance to the South to put down slave rebellions signified their acceptance of the anti-black sentiment common in Cincinnati. This may also have indicated something more serious, as reflected in Stanton's charge that "the intellectual and moral condition of the institution is low--very low.... The standard of benevolence--of effort--of piety--all, all are lamentably low--far lower than our reputation."[59]

A year and a half later the situation had changed considerably. By early 1834 Lane was a well-endowed institution with talented students and a notable faculty. The most im-

portant change had occurred in the makeup of the student
body. Twenty of the one hundred students in attendance in
January, 1834, had attended Oneida Institute, where they had
known Theodore Weld. [60] Thirty years old, Weld's peculiar
and unkempt appearance masked an intellectual's brilliance
and a reformer's passion. Converted by Finney, Weld had
accepted the revivalist's conception of stewardship, and had
become a national reform figure by 1833. He was asked to
serve many benevolent organizations, but he gave up most of
his reform activities and, refusing a professorship, entered
Lane as a student in June, 1833. [61] Weld exerted some influence on the Board of Trustees through Asa Mahan and
Franklin Y. Vail, and his relations with Beecher were cordial. [62] Many of the students considered him the real leader
of Lane. [63]

Weld had spent a year as agent for the Society for the
Promoting of Manual Labor in Literary Institutions and in
January, 1833, he recommended Lane Seminary for the location of a projected manual labor seminary. [64] However, his
reasons for coming to Lane went beyond an interest in manual labor. Weld informed the Tappan brothers that he knew
of "a number" of men from the South who were going to attend Lane. In addition, many of Weld's friends from the
Oneida Institute were also expected to enroll. A student body
representing the two major regions of the nation in a Seminary headed by a nationally known figure such as Lyman
Beecher provided the perfect setting for the promulgation of
the doctrine of immediate emancipation. Weld told the Tap-
pans of his "intentions to improve the excellent opportunity
to introduce antislavery sentiments, and have the whole subject thoroughly discussed. "[65]

Weld had no intention of holding an open debate on the
pros and cons of antislavery. His idea was like that of Elizur Wright, soon to be Corresponding Secretary of the American Anti-Slavery Society, who wrote to Weld in November,
1833, "I rejoice that you have prepared the line of attack for
a general pitched battle with the colonizationists. "[66]

Weld began the groundwork for the discussion of slavery early. Most likely he had already spoken to the Allan
brothers, two of those coming to Lane from the South, about
the sin of slavery. [67] During his trip down the Ohio River
with other prospective students, the major subject of conversation was slavery. [68] Even after this work, Weld said that
he found "not a single immediate abolitionist in this seminary"

in July, 1833, shortly after the term had begun. Abolitionism "was regarded as the climax of absurdity, fanaticism and blood. "[69] Weld wrote one correspondent that "This Institution stands fiercely committed for Colonization <u>against</u> Abolition. " However, he predicted that "in due time you may expect to hear from this Institution--a more favorable Report. "[70]

Weld began to inculcate his immediatist views among his fellow students, one at a time. William Allan, heir to a slave estate, was the first whose "noble soul broke loose from its shackles" and embraced immediate emancipation. [71] Weld, Allan and several others "selected each his man to instruct, convince, and enlist in the cause. Thus we carried one after another, and, before ever we came to public debate, knew pretty well where we stood. "[71] Although "a majority were still opposed" to immediatism before the debate commenced, those favoring colonization were also unsure of their support and asked for a postponement until they were better prepared. [73]

The faculty members were approached regarding the discussion on February 4, 1834. Beecher's immediate response was favorable and he is reported to have said, "Go ahead, boys--that's right; I'll go in and discuss with you. "[74] Later, at a faculty meeting called to examine the students' invitation, Beecher realized (or was made aware of) the difficulties in debating such controversial issues as immediatism and colonization in a region with strong Southern ties and anti-black prejudice. "After mature deliberation, the faculty agreed that such a discussion was, at the present time, inexpedient, and ought to be postponed.... "[75]

That evening Beecher presented the faculty's reasons to the students assembled in the Prayer Hall. Such a discussion, he said, would "create and perpetuate a disproportioned interest, unfriendly to the best prosecution of literary and theological studies. " It would cause "unpleasant and permanent divisions" within the student body. It would commit the school to a subject on which the community was divided; and because Lane was just forming its character, was surrounded by theological opposition, and needed additional funds, the school could not afford to offend a significant portion of the community. Although the "subject is one of the very first importance, " a public discussion "is not the best way to secure accurate, well-balanced, and judicious views. " The positive results of a public discussion could be secured, and evils avoided, by "conference, and temperate explanation and definition, " which would lead to "unanimity. " There were no reasons urging that the discussion take place immediately, and no evils that would occur if it were postponed. Finally, the faculty believed that the time was approaching when the subject could be examined freely and openly. [76]

On the fifth, Weld and George Whipple, another student, informed the faculty of the students' desire to commence the discussion. To this the faculty replied that it did not approve.

> Still the Faculty never have intended, and do not now intend, to interpose by authority to prevent the discussion. They have given their advice, with the reasons for it; and do not feel called upon to do any thing more. [77]

Thus, in the winter of 1834, the pro-South, pro-colonization and anti-black sentiments of most Cincinnatians; the recognition among Presbyterians of the sin of slavery; the status of Lane Seminary; and the evangelically based abolitionism of Weld and many other students combined to produce a discussion which would be noticed nationwide.

The Lane Debate and a Theology for Antislavery

The students of Lane announced their intention of going forward with the debate against the advice of the faculty on February 5, 1834. [78] Shortly thereafter, perhaps that same evening, the discussion began. Two questions were discussed: first, "Ought the people of the Slave holding States to abolish Slavery immediately?" and second, "Are the doctrines, tendencies, and measures of the American Colonization Society, and the influence of its principal supporters, such as render it worthy of the patronage of the Christian public?" Each question was examined for nine evenings, two and one half hours per night. [79]

The majority of the students attended some or all of the sessions. John Morgan, supporter of the students, attended every meeting, while Beecher and Stowe were present at some. It appears that Biggs was the only faculty member who refused to attend any of the meetings. [80] A Dr. Shane, a Cincinnati physician who had accompanied a group of emigrants to Liberia in 1831, sent the students a statement concerning that colony. [81] Catherine Beecher, daughter of the President, was present at one meeting and prepared a state-

ment in response to the ideas expressed there. [82]   Finally,
members of the antislavery Presbytery of Chillicothe, such
as John Rankin, William and James H. Dickey, James Gilli-
land, Jesse Lockhart, and Samuel Crothers may have attended,
as well as interested citizens of Cincinnati. [83]

A total of eighteen students participated in the debate
during the first nine evenings.   All of them had either been
born and raised in the South or had lived there for at least
six months. [84]   Apparently, none of them spoke in the negative.   William T. Allan, the heir to a slave inheritance who
had been convinced by Weld of the sin of slavery, began the
debate and continued for "nearly three nights. "   Augustus
Wattles reported that Allan "commenced by asking this ques-
tion--'What is slavery?'   'Before we can prescribe a remedy,'
said he, 'we must understand the disease.   We must know
what we are attempting to cure, before we give the medicine. ' "[85]   He presented facts illustrating slavery and its effects on politics, on social relations, and on the slaves themselves. [86]

"Conclusions and inferences were then drawn from
these facts, and arguments founded upon them favourable to
immediate abolition,... "[87]   Allan ridiculed the belief that
immediate emancipation was dangerous, and emphasized the
definition of immediatism. [88]   As a plan, in distinction from
a doctrine, immediate emancipation stressed that the slaves
would not be turned loose, nor would they be given political
rights immediately.   They would be placed under the protection of the law, rather than the oppression of bondage; they
would work as free laborers, rather than as slaves; they
would be placed under the guidance of disinterested super-
visors, rather than overseers; and they would receive religious and secular education. [89]

Having presented the plan of immediate emancipation,
Allan began a litany of eyewitness accounts to demonstrate,
through sheer volume, that, in the treatment of slaves,
"Cruelty is the rule, and kindness the exception. "   Henry P.
Thompson of Kentucky, Coleman S. Hodges of Virginia, Andrew Benton of Missouri, among others, presented gruesome
tales of debasement, torture, and murder. [90]

The most moving account of the evils of slavery and
of the ability of blacks to overcome those obstacles was that
recounted by James Bradley, a former slave and the only
black in the Seminary.   Kidnapped as a child from Africa,

Bradley had become manager of his owner's plantation and,
by working for five years during his free time, had earned
enough to purchase his freedom. He spoke for nearly two
hours. "This shrewd and intelligent black, cut up these
white objections" that immediatism was unsafe for the community and would leave the blacks helpless, "and withered
and scorched them under the sun of sarcastic argumentation,
for nearly an hour, to which the assembly responded in repeated and spontaneous roars of laughter...." Then for an
hour Bradley described the earnest desires of all slaves for
" 'liberty and education.' "[91] In recounting Bradley's comments fifty years later, George Clark wrote, "I doubt if there
was a dry eye in the chapel."[92]

The debate on the first question was one-sided: no
one spoke against immediatism. At the end of the ninth
evening, a vote was taken. Four or five students refused
to vote "on the ground that they had not made up their opinion." The rest of the students signified their acceptance of
immediate emancipation.[93]

At the next session, the discussion began on the second
question: was colonization "worthy of the patronage of the
Christian public?" The students examined the annual reports
of the American Colonization Society, numbers of that society's
organ, the African Repository, and the "Declaration of Sentiments" of the recently organized American Antislavery Society,[94] which had just been published in Cincinnati.[95] During the second nine evenings, only two people spoke, one for
each side. A third "read some testimony in favour of the
Colony" of Liberia, the statement furnished by Dr. Shane.[96]

Originally, a number of students had intended to speak
in favor of colonization. Augustus Wattles, for example, had
been president of the colonization society at Oneida Institute.
"But before he had an opportunity to take the floor [in the
debate], facts pressed upon him, (he was always open to conviction,) he changed his views, [and] became the decided opponent of the Society...."[97] Wattles wrote, "I disclaim all
connection" with the Colonization Society.

> ... I believe its doctrines, tendencies and measures
> are calculated to subvert the best interests of the
> colored people, to strengthen prejudice, to quiet the
> conscience of the slave-holder, and put far off the
> day of emancipation.[98]

The "facts" which convinced Wattles and other colonizationists to end their support for the American Colonization
Society was the program of colonization, which emphasized
the removal of free blacks. Not only did free blacks dislike
the idea of emigration, but the colonization program strength-
ened rather than weakened slavery by removing possible
sources of slave rebellion. [99]

When the vote on the second question was taken, only
one student, probably John E. Finley, a son of the agent for
the Colonization Society, defended colonization. At the beginning of the debate, he had "defied the Abolitionists to
wring out of him a vote against the Colonization Society. "[100]
Except for this one show of defiance, the debate was characterized by "great earnestness, but no unworthy heat, and no
impeachment of the motives of the disputants on either
side. "[101] No "unpleasant excitement" occurred; instead, "the
kindest feelings prevailed. There was no crimination, no de-
nunciation, no impeachment of motives. "[102]

The Lane debate has been characterized as a "revival
in benevolence; ... a debate only in name. "[103] Certainly its
similarity to the revivals of Charles G. Finney was no coin-
cidence; Weld had participated as a member of Finney's "holy
band" and had eagerly "advocated brother Finneys [sic] cause,
and those called 'new measures,' with much of the unhallowed
feeling of a political partizan. "[104] The debate owed a great
deal to Finney, and through Weld's agency, the revivalist's
influence was present in the debate's leadership, techniques,
and message.

The organizer, leader, and guiding spirit of the antislavery discussion was, of course, Weld, "a man of great
originality and force of character, and highly esteemed for
his piety and self-consecration. "[105] He did not speak until
the end of the discussion against the doctrines of colonization.
His role as an antislavery "revivalist" who brought "sinners"
to a conviction of sin, repentance, and conversion is illustrated in the comments of John Tappan Pierce, nephew of
Lewis and Arthur Tappan. Years later Pierce wrote:

> I was a strong Colonizationist at the time, full of
> prejudice, & would not attend the lectures & debates
> till my conscience compelled me to go & listen to
> one or two of the last, & was genuinely converted
> & have been a strong abolitionist ever since. This
> is the reason why I have no precise recollection of

the debates, saving br. Weld, who was the means of opening my blind eyes, under God, in the closing of the debate, when I confessed myself a full convert to Abolition, immediate & unconditional. [106]

Weld and his "holy band" used several techniques to influence the neutral students or those who favored colonization to recognize their sin in supporting slavery, to repent of that sin, and to be converted to immediatism. They had spent months preparing fallow ground by talking individually with fellow students about slavery. [107] Most likely they followed Finney's detailed advice, later published in 1835 in his Lectures on Revivals of Religion, which was addressed to Christians on "the private efforts of individuals for the conversion and salvation of men. "[108] A second measure, the most obvious, was the protracted character of the debate: forty-five hours on the subject of slavery.

The progress of the debate itself was similar to that of a revival (and even to the form of one of Finney's sermons). First, definitions were presented and the reason appealed to on the basis of "facts, FACTS, FACTS. "[109] Repeated accounts of atrocities committed against slaves focussed the listeners' attention on the subject through emotional identification with the slaves. [110] Most of the students would have been aware of the truth of the sin of slavery. Weld and his associates followed Finney's lead in that "It is indeed the pressing of truth upon the sinner's consideration that induces him to turn. "[111]

Having appealed to reason and pressed the truth of the sin of slavery, Weld and his associates attempted to secure a decision from the "convicted" sinners and "enlist" them in the cause of antislavery. [112] The public testimony of other converted sinners, particularly Southerners, provided more than information about the cruelties of slavery. It was also a means of public confession, advocated by Finney, which aided in pressing the truth on those still unconverted. [113] By the end of the debate, the majority of students were "converted," like James A. Thome, who wrote that "the great principles of duty stood forth, sin revived, and I died" to sin. [114] Like Pierce, each of those students who was converted came "over to Anti-Slavery ground with his whole soul" and was "a full convert to Abolition, immediate & unconditional. "[115]

Statements regarding conversion to immediatism were

not simply exercises in rhetoric or habit. This antislavery evangelicalism extended beyond a use of evangelical ideas and doctrines which supplied the doctrine of immediatism with its justification, vocabulary, and method. [116] Being evangelicals preparing for the ministry, the Lane students, as well as most seminary students and religious men and women of the time, were theologians. The basis of their antislavery was evangelicalism, a basis most fully explicated in the evangelical theology of Finney.

Finney's role in the antislavery movement has been minimized because of his personal unwillingness to make abolition his predominant concern. [117] This unwillingness was the result of his refusal to let any cause dissuade him from what he conceived to be his major task: the saving of souls. [118] For his timidity in regard to abolitionism he was severely castigated by Lewis Tappan. [119] Finney's personal reticence, however, should not lead one to think his influence on Weld, who addressed him as "My dear father in Christ," was minimal. [120] The similarities between Finney's revivals and the Lane debate indicate a larger influence, especially if the theological basis of his revivals is understood. Finney's theology of revivalism was transposed to an antislavery setting; the only difference was the strident emphasis on the sin of slavery. In terms of the sovereignty of God, the nature of sin, the moral agent, and benevolence, Finney's revivalistic theology lent itself to Weld's (and consequently the Lane rebels') antislavery evangelicalism. In this way Finney's influence was considerable. More important, he is representative of the way evangelicalism undergirded the antislavery movement.

Finney's theology at the time of the Lane debate was best expressed in his sermon "Sinners Bound to Change Their Own Hearts," which he preached in 1831 and published thereafter. [121] A brief examination of his ideas of God's sovereignty, sin, the moral agent, and benevolence in this sermon reveals the appropriateness of Finney's theology as a basis for the antislavery evangelicalism of the Lane rebels.

Finney's moral theology was based on the concept of the moral government of God, an idea implicit in this sermon. God is the moral governor, or sovereign, of the universe and rules through the influence of His laws on His subjects, who are free moral agents capable of conforming to or rejecting those laws. Because God is sovereign, the breaking of His laws is a sin not only against any victim, but also against God Himself, the architect of those laws. [122]

Sin for Finney was "self-gratification" or "selfishness. "
The person "who actually prefers his own selfish interest to
the glory of God, is an impenitent sinner. " Finney believed
that sin is not constitutional or a principle or substance within the nature of man which must be changed; it is the voluntary "preference of self-interest to the glory of God and the
interests of his kingdom. " By preference, Finney meant an
act of the will; sin itself is in the act, not in the nature of
man. [123]

Finney's notion of sin as selfishness coincided per-
fectly with the idea of the sin of slavery. Slavery was man-
stealing, the theft of another's life, labor, and soul for one's
own self-gratification. "Licentiousness" was an obvious expression of the sin of slavery which degraded both the slave
and master. [124] Although the idea of slavery as sin had been
expressed often before 1834, [125] Finney's concept of sin provided the Lane students with a theological framework in which
the sin of slavery could be placed.

More important for Lane's abolitionism was Finney's
concept of the moral agent. Man is a free moral agent and
bound to sin by nothing except his voluntary preference. The
change of heart, from the "preference for one's self-gratification to that for God's glory and the interests of his immense
kingdom" involves a moral, or voluntary, change. This moral
change must be voluntary, because man is responsible or ob-
ligated for his sin. One's obligation is "commensurate with
his ability. "[126]

The idea of the free moral agent who is responsible
for his actions was significant for antislavery evangelicalism
at Lane in two respects. First, it cast the sin of slavery
into a much stronger light. If man were created by God as
a free moral agent, to keep him in bondage was to deny him
this God-given freedom and to defy God's demand for personal
responsibility. It was therefore a sin against God's laws and
even Himself. [127] As Weld wrote, "God has committed to
every moral agent the privilege, the right and responsibility
of personal ownership. This is God's plan. Slavery annihi-
lates it, and surrenders to avarice, passion and lust, all that
makes life a blessing. "[128] Second, because man is responsible and therefore able to stop sinning, the demand that he
quit sinning immediately could not be refuted. Pressed home
by the spirit, through the agency of the antislavery revivalist,
the truth of the enormity of the sin of slavery demanded of
the sinner an immediate action to repudiate his sin; that is,
the severing of any connection with slavery whatsoever. [129]

Immediate emancipation was the positive statement of the logical consequence of the idea of the free, responsible individual required to quit sinning immediately.

Just as sin is the voluntary act or preference of the individual for selfish reasons, so a change of heart is the act of placing God and his kingdom as one's "governing preference of the mind." The converted sinner is never passive, and benevolence is "a preference of the glory of God and the interests of his kingdom to one's own happiness." It is "good will." As Finney wrote:

> Benevolence to God, is preferring his happiness and glory to all created good. Benevolence to men is the exercise of the same regard to, and desire for their happiness, as we have for our own. [130]

The key to Finney's notion of benevolence is "exercise." Benevolence, or good will, is an active preference of the will for one's ultimate object, God and His creation; it is "willing good to the object of it." Benevolence is a duty of the Christian, who should will it because it is right, not just because God demands it of him. It is "disinterested," although it does promote the happiness of the moral agent, because it advances happiness in general. One who is benevolent will also be happy. [131]

Finney's idea of benevolence as action meant that the natural condition of the convert would be one of useful conduct. He was quoted as saying that converts "should set out with a determination to aim at being useful in the highest degree possible."[132] This was not to be interpreted as a conscious attempt to prove one's conversion by good works (although this probably happened at times in practice). Rather, if the convert were truly imbued with "the principles of the gospel at the outset," he would "take right ground, on any subject that may be proposed" such as for "the education of ministers, for missions, for moral reform, for slaves."[133]

The notion of benevolence as action for the glory of God and the happiness of mankind and as the natural condition of the Christian convert was expressed in antislavery terms in Weld's statement to Elizur Wright, Jr. "Abolition immediate universal is my desire and prayer to God; and as long as I am a moral agent I am fully prepared to act out my belief in that thus saith the Lord--'Faith without WORKS is dead.' "[134]

Regarding Finney's contribution to antislavery at Lane, it must be asked if there were something unique in his evangelical theology which lent itself to antislavery. An examination of the works of Nathaniel W. Taylor, the foremost exponent of New England theology, brings forth many of the same ideas which Finney expressed.[135] But Taylor cannot be said to have influenced Finney.[136] Taylor's sermon based on Ezekiel 18:31, "The Sinner's Duty to Make Himself a New Heart," is similar in theology to that of Finney.[137] However, the sermons differ in emphasis. Taylor's stresses the truth of the doctrine of the sinner's duty from the nature of the new heart, from the nature of man, from the commands of God, from "facts," from the law of God, from the nature of the gospel, and from the character of God.[138] Finney's sermon shows what a change of heart is not (he states in three different ways that it is not a constitutional change) and what it is. Finney's sermon is not so much concerned with proving the truth of the doctrine as it is with bringing sinners to a conviction of and acceptance of that truth.[139]

Finney's theology was practically oriented. It had an activist bent which appealed to and "energized" would-be reformers.[140] This "energizing" influence was, in part, an emotional appeal to perform good works. However, Finney was aware of the volatile nature of human emotion and preferred those converted under his preaching to act on the basis of reason rather than feeling.[141] The moral stridency of the evangelical reformers converted by Finney issued from his idea of the character of benevolence. As has been noted, Finney believed that benevolence is active. Further, and unlike Taylor, Finney asserted that the willing of good is good in itself, regardless of its tendency actually to promote its goal. The "governing preference of the mind" for God's glory and His kingdom is good in itself whether or not one actually promotes those ends.[142] Of course Finney assumed that if one's "preference" were for God's glory and kingdom, then the promotion of those ends would naturally follow.[143] The point is that such an emphasis on ends could be seen as an outrageous demand for moral purity, such as total abstinence from alcohol or immediate emancipation. Thus, the Lane students' emphasis on immediatism without equal emphasis on plans for emancipation, and an appearance of self-righteousness are understandable. It did not matter whether or not immediatism was practicable, because willing immediatism was good in itself.

This "energizing" influence of Finney was probably

more evident because of Finney's lack of connections with institutions through which the reform impulse could be channeled (and restrained). Unlike Lyman Beecher, Finney had few denominational, theological, or institutional traditions to bind him. This "democratic" (versus Beecher's more "theocratic") bias led to greater freedom of expression and a willingness to bypass, condemn, or leave institutions which were not perceived to be morally stringent. [144]

In the hands of a person such as Weld, who rivalled Finney in ability, such a theology could provide a powerful incentive, as well as a framework for antislavery evangelicalism. Also, in such a context as that provided by Lane Seminary, with its highly talented student body and its proximity to locales of strong pro-Southern and anti-black sentiment, such a theology could become combustive.

Effects of the Lane Debate: March-July, 1834

The students' belief in the responsibility of the converted sinner to work in God's cause led them to engage in pro-black and antislavery activities. These in turn aroused opposition in both the community and faculty. The conflict which resulted brought to light two major and interrelated issues: the function of theological education in American society; and the proper roles of individuals in regard to slavery.

The majority of the students responded to the debate by answering the call to action explicit in antislavery evangelicalism. On March 10, a week after the debate ended, they formed an antislavery society, the object of which was the

> immediate emancipation of the whole colored race, within the United States; the emancipation of the slave from the oppression of the master, the emancipation of the free colored man from the oppression of public sentiment, and the elevation of both to an intellectual, moral, and political equality with the whites.

The method of operation was to be moral suasion. They would abolish slavery "By approaching the minds of slaveholders with truth, in the spirit of the gospel," by appeals to economic interests, and by the dissemination of information. [145]

In addition to forming an antislavery society, students became involved with the blacks in Cincinnati. "But I must tell you something more," wrote Weld to Lewis Tappan. "We believe that faith without works is dead." As a logical result of their antislavery evangelicalism, the students "formed a large and efficient organization for elevating the colored people in Cincinnati."[146] They lectured to crowds of 250 to 300 at the black-supported, biweekly lyceum, and helped secure a circulating library and reading room. Working in rotation, students taught reading three nights a week to blacks who ranged in age from fifteen to sixty. They also organized three Sabbath schools and Bible classes.[147]

The work of Augustus Wattles with the blacks of Cincinnati indicates the impact of the antislavery evangelicalism which resulted from the Lane debate. Formerly president of the colonization society at Oneida Institute, Wattles had become convinced of the sin of slavery during the debate.[148] In late February, he went to President Beecher and expressed his feelings of guilt for having supported colonization and his desire to aid the blacks of Cincinnati. Beecher was moved to tears and gave Wattles an honorable dismission and his blessing.[149]

On March 1, Wattles opened a day school in a black church in a black section of Cincinnati. So many people tried to attend the first day that he was forced to stagger the classes.[150] To meet this need, Marius R. Robinson, a theological student, took a leave of absence from Lane in May and opened another school.[151] Sometime that spring, Wattles travelled to New York where he recruited several women to come to Cincinnati to work in the black schools.[152] Arthur Tappan, at the request of Weld, sent funds to aid Wattles, and also paid the expenses of the women to Cincinnati.[153] By the beginning of July, Wattles was superintending four schools with five teachers and a total of two hundred students.[154] He was supported by funds provided by Arthur Tappan, the black community, the students of Lane, and Elnathan Kemper.[155]

Besides working in the local black community, the members of the Lane Anti-Slavery Society worked to propagate and disseminate pro-abolitionist information. In May, Henry B. Stanton and James A. Thome attended and addressed the anniversary meeting of the American Anti-Slavery Society in New York. Stanton's remarks centered on the abolitionist doctrine that "prejudice was vincible; that being a sin it could

be repented of, being a folly it could be cured. " Abolitionists, as opposed to colonizationists, "do not slander human
nature and blaspheme Christianity by saying that neither religion nor reason can overcome or eradicate" prejudice. [156]
Thome, by his very presence as well as his speech, demonstrated the power of antislavery over slaveholders if it were
presented properly. After stating such items as the duties
of slaveholders, the sufferings of slaves, and the licentiousness of both classes, he pleaded for more efforts by the
American Anti-Slavery Society to convince Southerners of the
necessity of abolishing slavery. [157] In June, James Bradley,
the only black at Lane, wrote a brief autobiography which
was published in Maria Lydia Child's Oasis and was widely
reprinted. [158] On July 15, Elizur Wright, Jr. , sent Weld a
box containing 400 copies of the Annual Report of the American Anti-Slavery Society, 150 copies of the Antislavery Re-
porter, and 73 handbills, and asked that Weld and his fellow
students "set them all at work without delay. "[159]

In addition to these overt efforts, students assisted in
the preparation of James G. Birney's Letter on Colonization,
Addressed to the Rev. Thornton J. Mills, Corresponding
Secretary of the Kentucky Colonization Society. Weld, John
Morgan, and two other students critiqued an early version of
the Letter. Students contributed $108 to pay for extra copies,
Henry B. Stanton travelled to Lexington, Kentucky, to pick
them up from the printer, and students distributed eight thousand of them throughout the Ohio Valley. [160]

Weld, Stanton, and Edward Weed apparently did more
than teach in the schools or disseminate information. Huntington Lyman was "willingly ignorant" of the use made of his
horse by some of his classmates. 'It was understood that
that horse might be taken without question by any brother who
had on hand 'Business of Egypt. ' " In other words, Weld,
Stanton and Weed might have been conductors on the Underground Railroad. Lyman himself was quite familiar with one
of the local stations of the Railroad. He had very strong
suspicions about his classmates, but all he would admit to
knowing was "My horse was hard used. "[161]

Not all of the activities in which the students engaged
should have been objectionable in themselves to the responsible
citizens of Cincinnati. The operation of black schools in the
city had several precedents, the most recent being one operated by a black Presbyterian licentiate, John Jones. [162] The
speeches of Stanton and Thome may have offended some, but

those speeches had been given in far off New York and were matter-of-factly reported by the editor of the <u>Cincinnati Journal</u>, Thomas Brainerd, who had attended the anniversary of the American Anti-Slavery Society as an observer. [163] The students' work distributing antislavery materials, their aid to Birney and their possible assistance to runaways were not generally known to the public.

A major objection was raised against the formation of an antislavery society within an educational institution. In the May issue of his <u>Western Monthly Magazine</u>, James Hall published an article entitled "Education and Slavery." Because of the "violent conflicts of opinion" common in a free republic, he wrote,

> There certainly ought to be some spot hallowed from the contests of party, sacredly protected from the contamination of the malignant passions, where the mind might be imbued with the lessons of truth, and peace, and honor, unalloyed with prejudice.

Hall questioned the propriety of a seminary which would allow its students to discuss questions such as slavery, "which might be calculated to disturb its harmony, to prevent the most amicable intercourse among its members, or to distract the attention of the pupil from his main purpose, which is the acquisition of knowledge." Slavery was too difficult and perplexing an issue "to be made the theme of sophomoric declamation" by "young gentlemen at school, dreaming themselves into full-grown patriots...."[164]

After the appearance of Hall's article, Weld went to see him and asked "if he would correct any of the misrepresentations of his article." Hall strongly refused, and when Weld reminded him that such virulence was unbecoming a Christian, Hall told him to leave. [165]

Weld then wrote a public letter to Hall, which was published in the <u>Cincinnati Journal</u>. He showed that the students were responsible and mature adults and severely criticized Hall for the latter's misrepresentations. The main thrust of Weld's reply to Hall concerned the role of theological education. Why, Weld asked,

> should not theological students investigate and discuss the sin of slavery? Shall those who are soon to be ambassadors for Christ--commissioned to cry

> aloud--to show the people their transgressions--
> shall they refuse to think, and feel, and speak,
> when that accursed thing 'exalts itself above all
> that is called God'--and wags its impious head,
> and shakes its blood-red hands at heaven? Why,
> I ask, should not students examine into the subject
> of slavery? Is it not the business of theological
> seminaries to educate the heart, as well as the
> head? to mellow the sympathies, and deepen the
> emotions, as well as to provide the means of
> knowledge? If not, then give Lucifer a professor-
> ship. He is a prodigy of intellect, and an encyclo-
> pedia of learning.

No public pressure should inhibit the free discussion of important issues in educational institutions, particularly those
which would train ministers. "He who would preach in the
nineteenth century, must know the nineteenth century. "[166]

Weld's article itself caused a sensation. Thomas
Brainerd, who had been in New York at the time of its publication, criticized his publisher for presenting Weld's article. [167] In response to angry complaints from people who
had received unsolicited copies of the article, the Cincinnati
Journal announced that "These were sent out, not by us, but
by the individuals who purchased them. "[168]

The second major objection of local people to the activities of the Lane students concerned the manner in which
they involved themselves with the black community. To teach
black children was one thing, a Christian duty to be perse-
vered in. To treat blacks as equals seemed to go beyond the
dictates of Christian charity. As a matter of principle, the
students believed it right to "treat men according to their
character without respect to condition or complexion. "[169]
Weld wrote that "while I was at Lane Seminary my intercourse
was with the Colored people of Cincinnati I think I may say
exclusively. "[170] Wattles lodged and boarded with black families and twice was seen escorting a black woman. Groups of
blacks were entertained by the students at the Seminary. [171]
On one occasion, "to break down what they called a wicked
caste in society, they brought a colored woman into church,
and seated her beside one of the most prominent white ladies
in the city;... "[172]

The social contacts of the students with blacks exacerbated an already tense racial situation. Students at the Semi-

nary received numerous threatening letters. Wattles, though
no longer a student, and the teachers in the black day schools
were the major targets of abuse. They were "daily hissed
and cursed, loaded with vulgar and brutal epithets, oaths and
threats; filth and offal were often thrown at them as they came
and went;..."[173] Rumors of mob violence circulated, especially in mid-June when Wattles was observed escorting a
black woman to a religious meeting.[174]

Articles in the Cincinnati Journal criticized the students (never by name) for self-righteousness in all of their
activities. One article, entitled "Theological Students," complained of the Seminarians' "high-handed spirit of overbearing
censoriousness."

> Do these persons think, that because they choose
> to arrogate to themselves a standard of moral ex-
> cellence, and to lay down rules for the exercise of
> the social and civil relations, when they have noth-
> ing but unfledged inexperience for the basis, that
> others, who have grown grey in the work of disci-
> pline, and in the salutary exercise of the reforming
> virtues, will bend to these dogmas?

Theological students should attend to "their business," which
is study, and leave reform to those more qualified.[175]

The issue which led to complaints against the students
for self-righteousness was not antislavery but "Amalgamation."
"Benezet," in the Cincinnati Journal, stated his belief that
God had ordained the separation of the races. Although he
supported the antislavery movement, he abhorred "the indis-
cretion of some of its headlong friends" who were attempting
to force the "commixture" of blacks and whites, even in the
churches. These attempts had produced "a repellency of feeling in truly christian minds, that might be avoided and should
never be provoked."[176] In late June, "A Ruling Elder" went
so far as to recommend that the trustees of the Seminary pass
regulations to proscribe the students' antislavery activities.[177]

The two criticisms raised in the community against the
students concerned the place of theological education in society
and the role of individuals regarding slavery. The responses
of members of the faculty indicated their concern with these
same issues. Their activities in relation to colonization were
indirect attempts to counteract the discussions, publications
and actions of the students which had given Lane a reputation

for abolitionism. At the annual meeting of the Cincinnati Colonization Society, on June 4, Lyman Beecher defended colonization and expressed his belief that colonization and abolitionism had their proper spheres of action, the former in the conversion of Africa and the latter in the abolition of American slavery. Members of both societies should work harmoniously. Beecher emphasized that "great care is needed that in this division of labor, the children of benevolence should not fall out by the way. How mournful would be the sight, should the Christians of the United States array themselves in antagonist societies." Controversy over slavery should be avoided because it might enter the churches and "separate very friends, now harmonious in the great enterprises of the day, and send discord and dismay through the sacramental host. The unhallowed controversy might break out in colleges, and theological seminaries...."[178]

Beecher was trying to hold together all evangelical Christians in his grand scheme to Christianize and civilize the world. To do so he had to try to please everyone, and in this speech he apparently succeeded. The African Repository called it an "eloquent speech" and it was reprinted in at least eight other papers.[179] On the other side, John Morgan said Beecher's speech "was quite abolitionist."[180]

Five days after Beecher spoke, on June 9, Calvin Stowe spoke to the local colonization society. He added his endorsement of the national society's activities and defended the society against what he considered to be unjust criticisms.[181] Thomas Biggs, the third member of the theological faculty, was scheduled to speak at yet another colonization meeting on the eleventh. Instead, he began a series of articles for the Cincinnati Journal espousing African colonization.[182]

Throughout this period, from March to the end of the term in July, Beecher tried to resolve the second issue, the role of the individual regarding slavery. First, he attempted to convince the students of the need for discretion in their relations with blacks. He advised them to follow his example "never to take a public stand in favour of any new subject that is likely to excite controversy, until I was fully assured that public sentiment was so far advanced in its favour as to sustain me in its advocacy."[183] Beecher told Weld, "If you want to teach colored schools, I can fill your pockets with money, but if you will visit in colored families, and walk with them in the streets, you will be overwhelmed."[184]

When the majority of students rejected his advice, Beecher encouraged those students who had not endorsed anti-slavery evangelicalism to form a colonization society. [185] At least this would help to offset the negative public sentiment towards the students of the Seminary. On July 7, this society issued a Constitution, a statement of reasons for its formation, and four resolutions. These students made it clear that they had no objections to the activities of abolitionists, "so far as they are judiciously directed to that object only." They would not, however, endorse

> that mistaken philanthropy which would introduce a promiscuous association of all classes, without regard to the principles of equality based upon intellectual and moral culture, and thereby increase the very difficulty sought to be removed. [186]

As the summer vacation approached, Beecher felt pleased with the success of the Seminary and the quality and conduct of students. He himself had no objection to the "commixture" of the races: after a social gathering for the students at his home he expressed his regret that James Bradley had felt it best not to attend. [187] Beecher believed that the Seminary's affairs were well in hand, except for the "inconvenience" encountered when the students had failed to heed the faculty's advice about their discussion of slavery and their insistence on treating blacks as equals. [188] On the whole, he would have agreed with Morgan, who wrote, "Things, I think, will be judiciously managed by the 'powers that be' here."[189] The faculty members were apparently united in the belief, wrote Beecher, "that, if we and our friends do not amplify the evil by too much alarm, impatience, and attempt at regulation, the evil will subside and pass away."[190]

Beecher did not realize that the only one who could keep the Seminary's friends from amplifying the evil was himself, and he left on a fund-raising trip to the East after the term ended on July 19. [191] Nor was he aware of the extent of the students' continued activities. Many intended to stay at Lane during the summer in order to aid Wattles in the black schools and to disseminate Birney's next publication. [192] Because he was new to the West, was relatively isolated at Walnut Hills from the Cincinnati community, and had "not a little of the old Connecticut prejudice about the blacks"[193] Beecher did not realize the extent of the anti-black and anti-abolitionist sentiment in the city. He did not understand the fears of the trustees, who had worked so hard to maintain the school and now found it being transformed from a New School Seminary to an abolitionist training ground. Finally, Beecher did not perceive the resentment and dislike Biggs had for the students. The issues that had been raised between the time of the debate and the end of the term, concerning theological education and the individual's response to slavery, would be argued and resolved, for the most part, without him.

Notes

1. Lyman Beecher to Benjamin Wisner, 8 January 1833, in Cross, ed., Autobiography of Beecher, 2:214; and Lyman Beecher, "To the Friends of the Lane Seminary and the West," 24 April 1833, Lane Papers, Folder 19, MTS.

2. Cincinnati Journal, 14 December 1832; and Sweet, ed., The Presbyterians, p. 741, n. 19.

3. Cross, ed., Autobiography of Beecher, 2:241.

4. John Morgan to Mark Hopkins, 17 September 1833, Morgan-Hopkins Correspondence, Box 4, Oberlin College Archives, Oberlin, Ohio (hereafter cited as Morgan-Hopkins Correspondence, OCA).

5. R. W. Patterson, "Reminiscences of Professor Calvin E. Stowe, D.D. Read before the Lane Club," Lane Papers, Folder 24, MTS; and L. J. Evans, "In Memoriam--Calvin Ellis Stowe, D.D., Professor of Biblical Theology in Lane Seminary, 1833-1850," in Pamphlet Souvenir, eds. Johnston, Walter, and Shedd, pp. 56-82.

6. Cincinnati Journal, 1 April 1831; Lane Seminary, Trustees Formal Minutes, Meeting of Executive Committee, 20 November 1832, LTS; and Order of the Executive Committee regarding Lewis Howell, Lane Papers, Folder 6, MTS.

7. Thomas Cole to the Executive Committee of Lane Seminary, 7 March 1832, and to Amos Blanchard, 24 April 1832, Lane Papers, Folder 14, MTS.

8. W. S. Kennedy, The Plan of Union: or a History of the Presbyterian and Congregational Churches of the Western Reserve; with Biographical Sketches of the Early Mis-

sionaries (Hudson, Ohio: Pentagon Steam Press,
1856), pp. 90, 120-21; and Waite, Western Reserve
University, p. 114.

9.   Lane Seminary, Fourth Annual Report of the Trustees
of the Cincinnati Lane Seminary: Together with a
Catalogue of the Officers and Students, January, 1834
(Lane Seminary: Students' Typographical Association,
1834), p. 24.

10. Ibid.; Fletcher, History of Oberlin, 1:29.

11. Theodore D. Weld to James G. Birney, 17 June 1834,
in Dwight L. Dumond, ed. , Letters of James Gillespie Birney, 1831-1857, 2 vols. (New York: D.
Appleton-Century Co. , 1938), 1:115.   Morgan knew
some of the students from New York because he had
taught them at the Rochester Manual Labor Institute.
Henry B. Stanton to Theodore D. Weld, 7 May 1832,
in Barnes and Dumond, eds. , Letters of Weld, 1:71.

12. John Morgan to Mark Hopkins, 17 September 1833,
Morgan-Hopkins Correspondence, Box 4, OCA.

13. L. J. Evans, "The Faculty," in Addresses and Proceedings, p. 25; Thomas J. Biggs to Franklin Y. Vail,
2 July 1833, Lane Papers, Folder 26, MTS; and Cincinnati Journal, 30 March 1832.

14. "Catalogue of Students in Lane Seminary, 1831," Lane
Papers, Folder 8, MTS; and Thomas J. Biggs to
Franklin Y. Vail, 2 July 1833, Lane Papers, Folder
26, MTS.

15. Lane Seminary, Fourth Annual Report, pp. 25-28; and
Fletcher, History of Oberlin, 1:54-56.

16. Banner, "Religion and Reform," p. 688; and Theodore
D. Weld to James Hall, May 1834, in Barnes and
Dumond, eds. , Letters of Weld, 1:138.

17. Abzug, "Theodore Dwight Weld"; and Franklin Y. Vail
to Theodore D. Weld, August 1832, in Cross, ed. ,
Autobiography of Beecher, 2:240-41.

18. Barnes and Dumond, eds. , Letters of Weld, 1:179,
n. 5.

19. Lane Theological Seminary General Catalogue, p. 21; and R. C. Galbraith, The History of the Chillicothe Presbytery, from Its Organization in 1799 to 1889. Prepared in Accordance with the Order of the Presbytery (Chillicothe, Ohio: H. W. Guthrie, Hugh Bell, & Peter Platter, 1889), p. 122.

20. Cincinnati Journal, 30 May 1834.

21. Portrait and Biographical Album of Henry County, Illinois, Containing Full-page Portraits and Biographical Sketches of Prominent and Representative Citizens of the County. Together with Portraits and Biographies of All the Governors of Illinois, and of the Presidents of the United States. Also Containing a History of the County, from Its Earliest Settlement to the Present Time (Chicago: Biographical Publishing Co., 1885), pp. 331-332.

22. Cincinnati Journal, 15 December 1829; and Fletcher, History of Oberlin, 1:117.

23. Ibid., 15 December 1829, 4 January 1833.

24. Theodore Weld, agent for the Society for Promoting Manual Labor in Literary Institutions, lectured in Cincinnati in March, 1832, on the benefits of manual labor, and stressed this democratic aspect. Ibid., 23 March 1832.

25. Lane Seminary, Fourth Annual Report, p. 8.

26. Report on manual labor system, 1830, Lane Papers, Folder 11, MTS. The extent of the popularity of manual labor is discussed in the Cincinnati Journal, 15 December 1829; Waite, Western Reserve University, p. 75; and Leonard, Story of Oberlin, pp. 229-30.

27. "Lane Seminary, Charter & Amendments," Lane Papers, Folder 1, MTS.

28. Lane Seminary, Fourth Annual Report, p. 24; and Samuel F. Dickinson to Franklin Y. Vail, 3 December 1833, Lane Papers, Folder 21, MTS.

29. Lane Seminary, Fourth Annual Report, pp. 8-9.

30. Charles P. Bush to Charles G. Finney, 27 January
1873, Finney Papers, Roll 6; Nye, "Marius Robinson," pp. 138-39; Henry B. Stanton, Random Recollections, 2d ed. (New York: MacGowan & Slipper,
1886), pp. 25-26; Robert L. Stanton, "Remarks of
Rev. R. L. Stanton, D. D. , of Cincinnati, " in Reminiscences of Rev. Charles G. Finney, Speeches and
Sketches at the Gathering of His Friends and Pupils,
in Oberlin, July 28th, 1876. Together with President Fairchild's Memorial Sermon, Delivered before
the Graduating Classes, July 30, 1876 (Oberlin: E.
J. Goodrich, 1876), p. 26; and Cross, ed. , Autobiography of Beecher, 2:233-34. Two of the better
studies on Finney are William G. McLoughlin, Introduction to Lectures on Revivals of Religion, by
Charles Grandison Finney (Cambridge: Harvard University Press, Belknap Press, 1960); and Melvin L.
Vulgamore, "Social Reform in the Theology of Charles
Grandison Finney" (Ph. D. dissertation, Boston University, 1963). Finney's emphasis on man's ability and
responsibility is apparent in his sermons, "Sinners
Bound to Change Their Own Hearts," and "Stewardship, " in his Sermons on Important Subjects, 3d ed.
(New York: John S. Taylor, 1836), pp. 3-42, 197-
207.

31. Finney, "Stewardship," p. 207.

32. Diary entry, 27 April 1827, in [Lillie], Faith and Works,
p. 14.

33. Donald M. Scott explores this point in terms of "ministerial styles," in Pastors and Providence: Changing
Ministerial Styles in Nineteenth-century America, The
1975 M. Dwight Johnson Lecture in Church History
(Evanston, Ill. : Seabury-Western Theological Seminary, [1975]), pp. 18-24.

34. Lane Seminary, Fourth Annual Report, p. 14, under the
title of "Active Usefulness Combined with Theological
Training. "

35. See letters to the Society of Inquiry on Missions at Lane
Seminary in the Cincinnati Journal, 4 July and 29
August 1834; and in the Lane Papers, Folder 10, MTS;
see also Cincinnati Journal, 3 June 1831, 22 February
1833, and 14 March 1834; Eliza and Henry H. Spalding

to Lorena Hart, 31 March 1834, Presbyterian Historical Society, Philadelphia; African Repository, 7 (September 1831): 208; and [Tappan], Life of Arthur Tappan, pp. 225-26.

36. Cincinnati Journal, 7 February 1834; Cincinnati Temperance Society to Theodore D. Weld, 1 July 1833, Weld-Grimké Papers, Box 2, WLCL; Lane Seminary, Fourth Annual Report, p. 14.

37. Lane Seminary, Fourth Annual Report, p. 14.

38. Lyman Beecher to Theodore D. Weld, 8 October 1834, in Barnes and Dumond, eds., Letters of Weld, 1:172.

39. Isaac Appleton Jewett to Joseph Willard, 25 October 1832, in Jewett, " 'Cincinnati is a Delightful Place': Letters of a Law Clerk, 1831-34," ed. James T. Dunn, Bulletin of the Historical and Philosophical Society of Ohio 10 (October 1951): 270.

40. Greve, History of Cincinnati, 1:588; and Isaac Appleton Jewett to Joseph Willard, 25 October 1832, in Jewett, " 'Cincinnati is a Delightful Place,' " p. 271.

41. Cincinnati Pandect, 1 April 1829.

42. Cincinnati Journal, 17 May, 26 July 1833.

43. Ibid., 2 August 1833; and Obadiah Davisson to the Faculty and Trustees of Lane Seminary, 7 August 1833, Lane Papers, Folder 8, MTS.

44. Cross, ed., Autobiography of Beecher, 2:237.

45. Louis Filler, The Crusade Against Slavery, 1830-1860, New American Nation Series (New York: Harper Torchbooks, 1963), pp. 60-67.

46. Cincinnati Journal, 22 March 1833, 10 February 1832; and Wendell Phillips Dabney, Cincinnati's Colored Citizens: Historical, Sociological, and Biographical (Cincinnati: Dabney Publishing Co., 1926; reprint ed., New York: Negro Universities Press, 1970), pp. 63-64.

47. Female Association for the Benefit of Africans, Consti-

tution, Members, Proceedings, Reports, etc., Minutes of Meetings of 19 January 1817 and 1825, Cincinnati Historical Society, Cincinnati.

48. Cincinnati Christian Journal, 29 September 1829.

49. Wade, "Negro in Cincinnati," p. 56.

50. Quoted in Samuel Crothers, James H. Dickey and William Graham, An Address to the Churches on the Subject of Slavery (Georgetown, Ohio: D. Ammen & Co., 1831), p. 2.

51. Staudenraus, African Colonization Movement, pp. 29-30.

52. Cincinnati Journal, 7 September 1832.

53. Richard Frederick O'Dell, "The Early Antislavery Movement in Ohio" (Ph. D. dissertation, University of Michigan, 1948), pp. 347-48, 351-53.

54. "Intelligence," African Repository 9 (May 1833): 88-89.

55. For an account of the exodus of Southern antislavery advocates to the Old Northwest, see Gordon Esley Finnie, "The Antislavery Movement in the South, 1787-1836: Its Rise and Decline and Its Contribution to Abolitionism in the West" (Ph. D. dissertation, Duke University, 1962), pp. 343-546.

56. Cincinnati Journal, 4 February through 13 May 1831; quotation from 13 May 1831. Crothers was identified as the author in William Birney, James G. Birney and His Times: The Genesis of the Republican Party with Some Account of the Abolition Movements in the South before 1828 (New York: D. Appleton & Co., 1890), p. 168 Crothers had come North to get away from slavery. Galbraith, History of the Chillicothe Presbytery, pp. 93, 210-12. From 1832 to 1839 he was a member of Lane's Board of Trustees. Lane Theological Seminary General Catalogue, p. 7.

57. Crothers, Dickey, and Graham, Address to the Churches, pp. 21-22.

58. H. Stanton, Random Recollections, pp. 27-28.

59. Henry B. Stanton to Theodore Weld, 2 August 1832, in Barnes and Dumond, eds., Letters of Weld, 1:84.

60. Lane Seminary, Fourth Annual Report, pp. 25-28; and Fletcher, History of Oberlin, 1:55, n. 43. Abzug, "Theodore Dwight Weld" is the most recent biography of Weld. Benjamin P. Thomas, Theodore Weld: Crusader for Freedom (New Brunswick, N.J.: Rutgers University Press, 1950), is still useful.

61. Franklin Y. Vail to Theodore D. Weld, August 1832, in Cross, ed., Autobiography of Beecher, 2:240-41; and Nathaniel S. Folsom to "Mr. Bingham," 12 June 1833, Lane Papers, Folder 8, MTS.

62. Theodore D. Weld to James G. Birney, 27 September 1832, in Dumond, ed., Letters of Birney, 1:27; Henry B. Stanton, Edward Weed, Sereno W. Streeter, and Calvin Waterbury to Theodore D. Weld, 2 and 4 August 1832, in Barnes and Dumond, eds., Letters of Weld, 1:78-87; and Cross, ed., Autobiography of Beecher, 2:241.

63. Beecher commented that the other students thought Weld "was a god." Cross, ed., Autobiography of Beecher, 2:241. Weld was not oblivious to this adulation. See Theodore D. Weld to Angelina Grimké, 12 March 1838, in Barnes and Dumond, eds., Letters of Weld, 2:593.

64. Cross, ed., Autobiography of Beecher, 2:235. This version was recorded by Charles Beecher shortly after he heard it from Weld.

65. Ibid.

66. Elizur Wright, Jr. to Theodore D. Weld, 2 November 1833, in Barnes and Dumond, eds., Letters of Weld, 1:119.

67. In June, 1832, Weld had stayed at the home of Dr. Allan, where he discussed slavery with Allan, James G. Birney, and, presumably, Allan's two sons. Birney, Birney and His Times, pp. 105-108.

68. Cross, ed., Autobiography of Beecher, 2:235.

69. Theodore D. Weld to Lewis Tappan, 18 March 1834, in Barnes and Dumond, eds., Letters of Weld, 1:132. This letter was published originally in the New York Evangelist, 5 April 1834.

70. Theodore D. Weld to Amos A. Phelps, 17 September 1833, Amos A. Phelps Papers, Ms. A. 21. 4, p. 62, Boston Public Library, Boston (hereafter cited as Phelps Papers, BPL); and Abzug, "Theodore Dwight Weld," pp. 101-102.

71. Theodore D. Weld to Lewis Tappan, 18 March 1834, in Barnes and Dumond, eds., Letters of Weld, 1:132.

72. Quoted in Cross, ed., Autobiography of Beecher, 2:235. Eighteen years later James Steele wrote to George Whipple, "In 1834, at the Lane Seminary, I had some of the common prejudice against colored people, but as the discussion was about to commence there, I had frequent conversation with individuals on the subject. One day S. F. Porter said to me, Do you not expect to go to heaven with colored people, or words to that effect. The appeal was successful, and from that day to this there has been nothing either in my views or feelings, relating to the colored race, for which the most sound Abolitionist could reproach me." James Steele to George Whipple, 31 January 1852, American Missionary Association Archives, Amistad Research Center, Dillard University, New Orleans (microfilm), Illinois-Roll 1 (hereafter cited as AMA Archives).

73. Theodore D. Weld to Lewis Tappan, 18 March 1834, in Barnes and Dumond, eds., Letters of Weld, 1:132; O. Johnson, Garrison and His Times, p. 167; and Theodore D. Weld to Amos A. Phelps, 17 September 1834, Phelps Papers, Ms. A. 21. 3, p. 40, BPL.

74. O. Johnson, Garrison and His Times, p. 167.

75. Lane Seminary, Minutes of Meetings of the Faculty, 1833-1879, Meeting of 4 February 1834, Office of the Treasurer, Lane Theological Seminary, Cincinnati (hereafter cited as Lane Seminary, Faculty Minutes, LTS).

76. Ibid. Another slightly different version was printed in

Lyman Beecher, Thomas J. Biggs, and Calvin E.
Stowe, "Statement of the Faculty concerning the
Late Difficulties in the Lane Seminary," in Fifth
Annual Report of the Trustees of the Cincinnati Lane
Seminary; Together with the Laws of the Institution,
and a Catalogue of the Officers and Students. November 1834 (Cincinnati: Corey & Fairbank, 1834),
p. 35. The only substantial difference between these
two versions was the inclusion in the latter of a reference to the "example of a kindred institution in this
state, being greatly depressed by the introduction of
this subject,... " This institution was Western Reserve College, which had endured conflicts over slavery in 1832 and 1833. The faculty and many students
had favored immediatism, while the trustees had favored colonization. See Carroll Cutler, A History of
Western Reserve College, during Its First Half Century, 1826-1876 (Cleveland: Crocker's Publishing
House, 1876), pp. 24-31. Weld learned of the controversy at Western Reserve from Elizur Wright,
Jr. , one of the professors there. See letters from
Wright to Weld, 1 February and 5 September 1833,
in Barnes and Dumond, eds. , Letters of Weld, 1:101-
104, 114-117.

77. Lane Seminary, Faculty Minutes, Meeting of 5 February
1834, LTS.

78. Ibid.

79. Contemporary accounts of the debate include letters from
Henry B. Stanton, Theodore D. Weld, Huntington Lyman, and Augustus Wattles published in the following
papers: New York Evangelist, 22 March and 5 April
1834; the Emancipator, 25 March and 22 April 1834;
and an anonymous letter from a Lane student in the
Emancipator, 8 April 1834.

80. O. Johnson, Garrison and His Times, p. 168; and New
York Evangelist, 22 March 1834.

81. Emancipator, 25 March 1834.

82. Ibid. ; and O. Johnson, Garrison and His Times, pp.
167-68.

83. Dumond, Antislavery, p. 161. I have found nothing to

confirm or deny Dumond's assertion that members of the Chillicothe Presbytery attended. One of those citizens of Cincinnati who was greatly influenced by the Lane debate was Gamaliel Bailey, a physician who later became a prominent abolitionist editor. Stanley C. Harrold, Jr. , "The Perspective of a Cincinnati Abolitionist: Gamaliel Bailey on Social Reform in America, " Cincinnati Historical Society Bulletin 35 (Fall 1975): 175.

84. New York Evangelist, 22 March 1834; and Cincinnati Journal, 30 May 1834.

85. Emancipator, 22 April 1834. Historians have usually asserted that Weld was the first speaker in the debate, and have based this on Stanton's account in the New York Evangelist, which did not identify the first speaker as a Southerner. The account of Wattles, however, identified the first speaker as being from Alabama. Moreover, Marius R. Robinson, another student, wrote in the names of the speakers in his copy of Wattles's account. Newspaper clipping in volume of clippings and notes, Marius R. Robinson Papers, Folder 3, Western Reserve Historical Society, Cleveland (hereafter cited as Robinson Papers, WRHS).

86. New York Evangelist, 22 March 1834.

87. Ibid.

88. Emancipator, 5 April 1834.

89. Ibid. The plan was that adhered to by the Emancipator.

90. Ibid. Some of these accounts were later incorporated into Weld's American Slavery as It is: Testimony of a Thousand Witnesses (New York: American Anti-Slavery Society, 1839; reprint ed. , New York: Arno Press & The New York Times, 1968), pp. 46, 87-88.

91. New York Evangelist, 22 March 1834.

92. George Clark to Theodore D. Weld, 10 October 1884, Weld-Grimké Papers, Box 16, WLCL.

93. New York Evangelist, 22 March 1834.

94. Ibid. The writings of Garrison were not used by the students because they wanted to examine the stated policies of the American Colonization Society, and because they mistrusted him because he was not an evangelical. Emancipator, 25 March 1834; and George Clark to William Smith, 4 August 1884, James Gillespie Birney Papers, Box 17, William L. Clements Library, University of Michigan, Ann Arbor (hereafter cited as Birney Papers, WLCL).

95. Cincinnati Chronicle and Literary Gazette, 8 February 1834.

96. New York Evangelist, 22 March 1834.

97. Ibid.

98. Emancipator, 22 April 1834.

99. New York Evangelist, 22 March 1834.

100. Quoted in O. Johnson, Garrison and His Times, p. 169.

101. Ibid. , p. 168.

102. New York Evangelist, 22 March 1834.

103. Barnes, Antislavery Impulse, p. 66.

104. Thomas, Theodore Weld, p. 16; and Theodore D. Weld to Charles G. Finney, 22 April 1828, in Barnes and Dumond, eds. , Letters of Weld, 1:16-17.

105. O. Johnson, Garrison and His Times, p. 168.

106. John T. Pierce to Theodore D. Weld, 12 September 1884, Weld-Grimké Papers, Box 16, WLCL. Finney gave his view on the role of the revivalist in his sermon, "Sinners Bound to Change Their Own Hearts, " p. 39. The goal of the revivalist, he said, "is so thoroughly to convince, so completely to imbue their minds with the subject, as to get their intellect, and conscience, and heart to embrace his views of the subject. "

107. New York Evangelist, 5 April 1834. Huntington Lyman wrote that some students had "been prayerfully in-

vestigating the subject" since the previous June, the
same month that Weld entered the Seminary. Emancipator, 25 March 1834.

108. Finney, Lectures on Revivals, p. 156.

109. New York Evangelist, 22 March 1834. Finney's appeal
to the reason is intimated in Weld's criticism of
revival preachers in the West. Theodore D. Weld
to Charles G. Finney, 28 February 1832, in Barnes
and Dumond, eds. , Letters of Weld, 1:67. Finney's
statement that he "talked to the people as I would
have talked to a jury" is instructive. See Charles
G. Finney: An Autobiography. Specially Prepared
for English Readers (London: Hodder & Stoughton,
1882), p. 70; and "Sinners Bound to Change Their
Own Hearts, " pp. 31-32.

110. Finney, "How to Change Your Heart, " in Sermons,
p. 52; and Scott, "Watchmen on the Walls of Zion, "
pp. 359-61.

111. Finney, "Sinners Bound to Change Their Hearts, "
p. 34.

112. New York Evangelist, 5 April 1834; Finney, "How to
Change Your Heart, " p. 55; and Scott, "Watchmen
on the Walls of Zion, " pp. 359-61.

113. Scott, "Watchmen on the Walls of Zion, " pp. 359-61.
See Finney's description of Theodore Weld's public
confession, made after the latter's conversion.
Charles G. Finney, Memoirs of Charles G. Finney.
Written by Himself (New York: A. S. Barnes &
Co. , 1876), pp. 187-88.

114. James A. Thome, "Speech of James A. Thome, of
Kentucky, Delivered at the Annual Meeting of the
American Anti-Slavery Society, May 6, 1834, " in
Debate at the Lane Seminary, Cincinnati. Speech
of James A. Thome, of Kentucky, Delivered at the
Annual Meeting of the American Anti-Slavery Society,
May 6, 1834. Letter of the Rev. Dr. Samuel H.
Cox, against the American Colonization Society
(Boston: Garrison & Knapp, 1834), p. 7.

115. New York Evangelist, 5 April 1834; and John T. Pierce

to Theodore D. Weld, 12 September 1884, Weld-
Grimké Papers, Box 16, WLCL.

116. Loveland, "Evangelicalism and 'Immediate Emancipation,' " p. 174.

117. McLoughlin, Modern Revivalism, pp. 108-111.

118. Theodore D. Weld to Lewis Tappan, 17 November 1835,
in Barnes and Dumond, eds., Letters of Weld,
1:243.

119. Noted in McLoughlin, Modern Revivalism, p. 110.
A recent study about Finney asserts that he maintained "a firm commitment to abolitionism" which
previous studies have ignored or underestimated.
For Finney, "Far from being mutually exclusive
enterprises, the progress of revivals and the abolition of slavery formed part of a single process by
which men hastened the onset of the millennium."
James David Essig, "The Lord's Free Man: Charles
G. Finney and His Abolitionism," Civil War History 24 (March 1978): 25. There can be no question that Finney was more of an abolitionist than he
has sometimes been given credit for. Nonetheless,
he was less an abolitionist than reformers such as
Tappan and Weld would have liked.

120. Theodore D. Weld to Charles G. Finney, 20 March
1832, in Barnes and Dumond, eds., Letters of
Weld, 1:71. Weld called Finney "that blessed
man," a "modern Paul," and considered him to be
the best preacher he had ever heard. Theodore D.
Weld to Zephaniah Platt, 16 November 1829, Finney
Papers, Roll 2. The character of Finney's influence
on Weld was not in urging him to adopt immediatism
or supplying him with antislavery tracts. These
were actions taken by Charles Stuart, an eccentric,
retired British army officer who paid for Weld's
education, and after whom Weld named his first-
born son. Abzug, "Theodore Dwight Weld," p. 97.
Finney's influence was more subtle and, in the long
run, of more significance. From Finney, Weld received a theological framework and moral impulse
by which he could formulate and express his antislavery.

121. George Frederick Wright, <u>Charles Grandison Finney</u>,
      American Religious Leaders (New York: Houghton
      Mifflin & Co. , 1891), p. 179.   McLoughlin has
      called this sermon a "key" to Finney's theology.
      <u>Modern Revivalism</u>, p. 66.   It is examined here
      because it epitomizes Finney's theology at the time
      of the Lane debate.   Finney's theology did not change
      materially over the succeeding years, although there
      is a continuing discussion concerning his notion of
      "perfectionism, " and the ideas he expressed in this
      sermon appear in different and later works.   For
      example, on Finney's ideas on the doctrine of hu-
      man ability in regeneration, see his "Sinners Bound
      to Change Their Own Hearts, " pp. 20-23; <u>Lectures
      on Revivals</u>, pp. 195-97; and <u>Lectures on Systema-
      tic Theology, Embracing Moral Government, the
      Atonement, Moral and Physical Depravity, Natural,
      Moral, and Gracious Ability, Repentance, Faith,
      Justification, Sanctification, &c. </u>, ed. , rev. and
      intro. by George Redford (London: William Tegg
      & Co. , 1851), pp. 408-14.   Finney's theology is
      discussed in Vulgamore, "Social Reform in Finney";
      McLoughlin, Introduction to <u>Lectures on Revivals</u>,
      by Finney; James E. Johnson, "The Life of Charles
      Grandison Finney" (Ph. D. dissertation, Syracuse
      University, 1959), pp. 272-313; and James E. John-
      son, "Charles G. Finney and a Theology of Revi-
      valism, " <u>Church History</u> 38 (September 1959): 338-
      58.

122. Finney briefly discussed moral government in "Sinners
      Bound to Change Their Own Hearts, " pp. 14-15.
      The relevance of Finney's idea of the sovereignty of
      God for his own antislavery is discussed in Vulga-
      more, "Social Reform in Finney, " p. 149.   The idea
      of God's sovereignty eventually led Finney to develop
      the doctrine of the "higher law, " which provided a
      basis for civil disobedience for antislavery advocates.
      See Cole, <u>Northern Evangelists</u>, pp. 208-10; and
      Vulgamore, "Social Reform in Finney, " p. 149.

123. Finney, "Sinners Bound to Change Their Own Hearts, "
      pp. 15, 10; and Vulgamore, "Social Reform in
      Finney, " pp. 79-84.

124. Thome, "Speech, " pp. 8-9; and <u>New York Evangelist</u>,

3 May 1834. See also Ronald G. Walters, "The Erotic South: Civilization and Sexuality in American Abolitionism," American Quarterly 25 (May 1973): 177-201.

125. For example, see Elizur Wright, Jr. , The Sin of Slavery, and Its Remedy; Containing Some Reflections on the Moral Influence of African Colonization (New York: Printed for the Author, 1833).

126. Finney, "Sinners Bound to Change Their Own Hearts," pp. 19, 24.

127. See J. L. Hammond, "Revival Religion and Antislavery Politics," American Sociological Review 39 (April 1974): 177, 184; Vulgamore, "Social Reform in Finney," p. 149.

128. Theodore D. Weld to Arthur Tappan, Joshua Leavitt, and Elizur Wright, Jr. , 22 November 1833, in Barnes and Dumond, eds. , Letters of Weld, 1:120.

129. Finney, "Sinners Bound to Change Their Own Hearts," pp. 20-23. Finney's preaching of immediate repentance from sin in his revivals of 1826 was described by him in his Autobiography, pp. 158-59.

130. Ibid. , pp. 16-17, 10, 41.

131. Finney, "How to Change Your Heart," pp. 43-44. For a discussion of the relationship between Finney's theology and that of Samuel Hopkins, see McLoughlin, Introduction to Lectures on Revivals, by Finney, pp. xlii-xliii.

132. Finney, Lectures on Revivals, p. 404.

133. Ibid. , p. 426; and Richard C. Wolf, "Charles Grandison Finney: Mr. Oberlin, 1835-1875," Oberlin Alumni Magazine 71 (September-October 1975): 12. "Finney was a Christian evangelist who expected reform as a consequence of conversion. "

134. Theodore D. Weld to Elizur Wright, Jr. , 10 January 1833, in Barnes and Dumond, eds. , Letters of Weld, 1:99.

135. The standard biography of Taylor is Sidney Earl Mead, Nathaniel William Taylor, 1786-1858: A Connecticut Liberal (Chicago: University of Chicago Press, 1942).

136. The first theological discussion between Finney and Taylor appears to have occurred around 1836. George Clark, "Remarks of Rev. George Clark of Oberlin," in Reminiscences of Finney, p. 49.

137. In Practical Sermons (New York: Clark, Austin & Smith, 1858), pp. 397-412.

138. Ibid.

139. A typical statement from Finney's sermon is "And now, sinner, while the subject is before you, will you yield? To keep yourself away from under the motives of the Gospel, by neglecting church, and neglecting your Bible, will prove fatal to your soul." Finney, "Sinners Bound to Change Their Own Hearts," p. 41.

140. The term is from Vulgamore, "Social Reform in Finney," p. 253.

141. See Finney, "How to Change Your Heart," pp. 30-39, 53.

142. Finney's doctrine of the "foundation of moral obligation" is fully explained in his Lectures on Systematic Theology, pp. 42, 54; and Wright, Charles Grandison Finney, pp. 212-19. This is implicit throughout Finney, "Sinners Bound to Change Their Own Hearts."

143. Finney, Lectures on Revivals, p. 415.

144. Finney's "democratic" aspect is discussed in McLoughlin's Introduction to Lectures on Revivals, pp. viii-x; Vulgamore compares Finney and Beecher, "Social Reform in Finney," pp. 202-4; see also Banner, "Religion and Reform." However, Leonard I. Sweet asserts that Finney was basically a conservative. "The View of Man Inherent in New Measures Revivalism," Church History 45 (June 1976): 206-21.

145. Cincinnati Standard, 28 March 1834. Weld wrote the "Preamble and Constitution of the Anti-Slavery Society of Lane Seminary. " Liberator, 26 April 1834.

146. In the New York Evangelist, 5 April 1834.

147. Ibid. ; Augustus Wattles, "Statement in Regard to Cincinnati, " in Proceedings of the Ohio Anti-Slavery Convention. Held at Putnam, on the Twenty-second, Twenty-third, and Twenty-fourth of April, 1835 (n. p. : Beaumont & Wallace, [1835]), p. 21; and O. Johnson, Garrison and His Times, p. 169.

148. New York Evangelist, 22 March 1834. On Wattles, see O. E. Morse, "Sketch of the Life and Works of Augustus Wattles, " Collections of the Kansas Historical Society 17 (1928): 290-99.

149. O. Johnson, Garrison and His Times, pp. 169-70.

150. Wattles, "Statement in Regard to Cincinnati, " p. 21.

151. Ibid. ; Lane Seminary, Faculty Minutes, Meeting of 6 May 1834, LTS; and Nye, "Marius Robinson, " p. 143.

152. Morse, "Sketch of Wattles, " p. 291. The women who worked in the black schools in Cincinnati included Susan E. Lowe, who later married Wattles; Lucy Wright, sister of Elizur Wright, Jr. ; Phebe Mathews, who later married Edward Weed, another student; Emeline Bishop, from Ohio, who married Robinson; and Maria Ann Fletcher, from Oberlin. Barnes and Dumond, eds. , Letters of Weld, 1:178, n. 2.

153. Theodore D. Weld to Lewis Tappan, 1 January 1870, in [Tappan], Life of Arthur Tappan, p. 236.

154. Wattles, "Statement in Regard to Cincinnati, " p. 21; and Emancipator, 3 July 1834.

155. Theodore D. Weld to Lewis Tappan, 1 January 1870, in [Tappan], Life of Arthur Tappan, p. 236; Wattles, "Statement in Regard to Cincinnati, " p. 27; New York Evangelist, 5 April 1834; Dickore, "Kemper Account Book, " p. 71.

156. *Liberator*, 24 May 1834.

157. Thome, "Speech"; also published in the *Liberator*, 17 May 1834.

158. *New York Evangelist*, 1 November 1834.

159. Elizur Wright, Jr. to Theodore D. Weld, 15 July 1834, Weld-Grimké Papers, Box 2, WLCL.

160. Theodore D. Weld to James G. Birney, 17 June and 14 July 1834, in Dumond, ed. , *Letters of Birney*, 1:115, 127; Huntington Lyman to William Smith, April 1884, Weld-Grimké Papers, Box 16, WLCL; and Lyman, "Lane Seminary Rebels," p. 63.

161. Huntington Lyman to Theodore D. Weld, 16 November 1891, Weld-Grimké Papers, Box 17, WLCL; and Huntington Lyman to Wilbur H. Sieburt, 1 April 1898 (copy), Wilbur H. Sieburt Papers, Box 106, Ohio Historical Society, Columbus (hereafter cited as Sieburt Papers, OHS).

162. *Cincinnati Baptist Weekly Journal*, 17 January 1834; and [North, ed.], *Presbyterianism in the Ohio Valley*, p. 59. Other precedents for black schools are noted above, pp. 74-75.

163. *Cincinnati Journal*, 23 May 1834.

164. [James Hall], "Education and Slavery," *Western Monthly Magazine* 2 (May 1834): 267, 271, 268.

165. Theodore D. Weld to James G. Birney, 28 May 1834, in Dumond, ed. , *Letters of Birney*, 1:114.

166. *Cincinnati Journal*, 30 May 1834.

167. *Ibid.* , 27 June 1834.

168. *Ibid.* , 20 June 1834.

169. Quoted in Beecher, Biggs, and Stowe, "Statement of the Faculty," p. 40.

170. Theodore D. Weld to Lewis Tappan, 9 March 1836, in Barnes and Dumond, eds. , *Letters of Weld*, 1:273.

171. O. Johnson, Garrison and His Times, p. 170; A Statement of the Reasons which Induced the Students of Lane Seminary, to Dissolve Their Connection with that Institution (Cincinnati: n. p. , 1834), pp. 24-25; and Beecher, Biggs, and Stowe, "Statement of the Faculty," p. 37.

172. Quoted in Brainerd, Life of Brainerd, p. 108.

173. Quoted in O. Johnson, Garrison and His Times, p. 171; and John B. Shotwell, A History of the Schools of Cincinnati (Cincinnati: School Life Co. , 1902), pp. 449-50.

174. Asa Mahan stated that "The most influential citizens openly talked of sending up an organized mob to demolish the buildings, and drive the Faculty and students from the ground. " Mahan, Autobiography, pp. 36-37.

175. Cincinnati Journal, 16 May 1834; see also "Hints to Reformers," Cincinnati Journal, 11 July 1834.

176. Reprinted in the Liberator, 21 June 1834.

177. Cincinnati Journal, 27 June 1834.

178. Ibid.

179. "Dr. Beecher's Address," African Repository 10 (November 1834): 279; and Cincinnati Journal, 22 August 1834.

180. John Morgan to Franklin Y. Vail, 9 June 1834, Lane Papers, Folder 26, MTS. Beecher's desire for union between abolitionists and colonizationists is indicated in his article, "Union of Colonizationists and Abolitionists," Spirit of the Pilgrims 6 (July 1833): 396-402. See also the reply to this article by Lewis Tappan in Spirit of the Pilgrims 6 (October 1833): 569-78.

181. Cincinnati Journal, 4 July 1834.

182. Ibid. , 20 June 1834. James Hall spoke at this meeting and "advocated the cause of colonization with great energy. " In a rare editorial comment, the Journal

stated, "We are glad, that this movement has taken place, and just at this time. To counteract the bane, the antidote should speedily follow." Cincinnati Journal, 13 June 1834. Biggs's first article was published in the Cincinnati Journal, 8 August 1834.

183. Quoted in Mahan, Autobiography, p. 175.

184. Cross, ed., Autobiography of Beecher, 2:244.

185. Statement of Reasons, p. 22.

186. Cincinnati Journal, 11 July 1834.

187. Statement of Reasons, p. 26.

188. Cross, ed., Autobiography of Beecher, 2:244.

189. John Morgan to Franklin Y. Vail, 9 June 1834, Lane Papers, Folder 26, MTS.

190. Cross, ed., Autobiography of Beecher, 2:244-45.

191. Cincinnati Journal, 25 July 1834.

192. Huntington Lyman to James A. Thome, 17 August 1834, File 16/5, Box 19, Oberlin College Archives, Oberlin, Ohio (hereafter cited as File 16/5, OCA).

193. Stowe, "Sketches," pp. 232-33.

CHAPTER IV

THE LANE REBELLION

The Trustees: July-October, 1834

To understand the actions of the trustees which preceded the Lane rebellion, it is necessary to examine the backgrounds, attitudes, and concerns of the Board members. Their status as leading citizens, concern for Cincinnati's prosperity, fear of mob violence against the Seminary, disagreement with the abolitionist principles and methods of the Seminary students, and their acceptance of the advice of Professor Biggs all led them to impose the drastic regulations which precipitated the students' withdrawal.

In the summer and fall of 1834, there were twenty-five Board members:[1]* six were ministers, two were practicing attorneys, two were lumber merchants, one was a druggist, one a physician, one a book-publisher and merchant, one a pork merchant and banker, one a coach maker, one a banker, one a hardware merchant and financier, one an insurance agent, one a cooper, one a carpenter (or a steamboat captain), and one a general merchant.[2] The occupations of the remaining four have not been identified. Twenty trustees lived and worked in Cincinnati, and most of these were involved in the civic and social life of the city. Isaac G. Burnet had been mayor of Cincinnati for thirteen years and George Neff was a member of the city council. At least sixteen trustees were officers of the local benevolent societies and associations.[3]

The trustees who lived and worked in Cincinnati were concerned with the city's prosperity. As noted, a large portion of Cincinnati's trade was with the South.[4] An indication of the importance of this Southern trade for Cincinnati's prosperity was apparent in 1835, a year after the Lane rebellion,

---

*Notes to Chapter IV begin on page 146.

when a railroad between Cincinnati and Charleston, South
Carolina, was projected to give Cincinnati an additional sea-
board outlet and to open up further the Southern interior to
Midwestern products. [5] One of the main sponsors of the
"Great Rail Road" was George Neff, a Lane trustee. [6] Any
conflicts about slavery could have effectively alienated the
important Southern trade.

Equally important as the trustees' concern for Cincinnati's prosperity was their fear of mob violence. The anti-
abolitionist riots in New York city in July, 1834, were heav-
ily reported in the Cincinnati papers. [7] Rumors had circulated during the summer that mobs might be formed to destroy the Seminary. Wattles's schools and the Lane students'
open and equal treatment of blacks fueled tales of "amalgamation. "[8] At times the trustees' concern about mob violence
spilled over into vituperation against abolitionists. During
the middle of August, one of the trustees castigated Horace
Bushnell, a former student and instructor and an abolitionist,
"as a liar a scoundrel an agitator a traitor to Christ and his
country. An attempt was made to lay upon him the N.Y.
riots and all the blood and violence from that of Cain to that
of Genl. Jackson. "[9]

Besides their concern with Cincinnati's economic prosperity and fear of mob violence, the trustees objected to the
students' anti-slavery beliefs and activities on principle. Only
four of the Board favored abolitionism: Asa Mahan, William
Holyoke and John Melindy (two of the elders of Mahan's
church), and Samuel Crothers, of the Chillicothe Presbytery.[10]
Three Board members had been officers in the local branch
of the American Colonization Society. [11] In addition, the trustees objected to the manner in which students espoused their
beliefs. In their eyes, the students were self-righteous in
their propagation of their belief in the vincibility of race prejudice, and had acted without regard to the consequences of
their actions on the welfare of the Seminary. [12] The speeches
of Stanton and Thome at the May anniversary of the American
Anti-Slavery Society were only the most obvious expressions
of the students' attitude.

Finally, the trustees were encouraged in their fears
by Professor Biggs. Five days after the term ended, Biggs
wrote to Franklin Y. Vail in Boston of his own apprehensions
regarding the position of the Seminary. He believed that Lane
was approaching ruin because of the introduction of antislavery.
The "remedy" to the problem was "within our reach. We are

not yet so far out at sea that we cannot regain the port. It
may take hard pulling--and we may have to lighten the vessel and this surely we shall not hesitate to do, rather than
founder at high sea!" Biggs believed that "prompt and efficient measures ought to be forthwith adopted" by the trustees,
and he requested Vail to return immediately. "That the offensive thing must be expurgated from the institution is my
firm conviction ... and that the seminary must regain its
original ground of non-committal on these subjects." Biggs
intended to see members of the Board but he promised no
action until Vail and Beecher made recommendations. "Something must be done & done speedily or we shall have the
scenes of N.Y. repeated here."[13]

On August 2, students rooming at the Seminary mailed
out sixteen hundred copies of Birney's Letter on Colonization,
a fact reported to the trustees.[14] Four days later, Calvin
Stowe's wife, Eliza, died, and after the funeral he left for
the East, no later than the ninth.[15] August 8 saw the publication of Biggs's first letter to the Cincinnati Journal favoring colonization and opposing the introduction of the slavery
question into the Christian community and theological seminaries.[16] The students' activities, the absence of Stowe,
who seemed on the verge of adopting immediatism,[17] and
Biggs's influence led to a meeting of the Executive Committee of the Board of Trustees on August 9.

Nathaniel Wright, President of the Board, "informed
the Committee that the object of the meeting was to consider
the proceedings of the Students in relation to the subject of
Slavery." After Biggs read the record of the faculty's actions regarding the subject, a special committee was appointed,
headed by Wright, "to consider the subject and report what
steps should be taken...."[18]

On Saturday the sixteenth, the Executive Committee
met again to consider the report of the special committee,
"which was read and considered at some length...." The
report recommended the dissolution of the students' antislavery society and the prohibition of the discussion of slavery
by the students, even in private.[19] Asa Mahan, who had
learned of the meeting upon his return from a trip to the
East, strongly objected to the recommendations, particularly
the one prohibiting discussion of slavery "at table or elsewhere." He reminded the Committee that it was an executive,
not a legislative body, and therefore had no right to pass such
recommendations. The other members of the Executive Com-

mittee agreed, and instructed the special committee to continue the preparation of a report to be presented to the Executive Committee on the twentieth. [20]

Two days before the August twentieth meeting, Biggs
received a letter from Beecher and Vail advising caution.
In reply, Biggs noted the public impression that Lane had
become "the great Laboratory and depot" of antislavery sentiment, and that "The Trustees feel themselves called upon
to furnish something to correct and allay this (not unreason-
ably) excited state of feeling. " In a reference to Weld and
to the perceived fanaticism of the students, Biggs wrote:

> We have among us, as all know, the Master Spirit
> of Abolitionism, we have it here in its publicated
> state. It has already inflated and intoxicated nearly
> all our students. Its exhilirations make them act
> above all our heads, and the principle is now pretty
> well settled that the one whose head has the most
> capacity for this empyrial [sic] gas, why, he's the
> model, and the best theologian and best any thing
> else you please.

For Biggs and the trustees, the issue had become "who shall
govern? Students? or faculty in concurrence with Trustees? ['] The recent history of our seminary has rendered
the question altogether dubious. " The Executive Committee
had "decided that their duty calls them to act & to act with
vigour and promptitude. "[21]

As scheduled, the Executive Committee met on the
twentieth. The report of the special committee "was read
and considered at some length, " and then adopted. Basically
it was the same as that presented at the meeting on the sixteenth. The Executive Committee ordered that the report be
published. [22] Three days later, it ordered "That a sufficient
number of copies of the C. [incinnati] Journal [containing the
report] be obtained to furnish one to each student.... " The
Committee also recommended the firing of John Morgan, the
only faculty member to openly support the students. [23] At
still another meeting, the Executive Committee amended the
recommendation that the entire Board wait for the return of
the faculty before acting to read "unless the Board at large
shall previously act on the subject. "[24] Evidently the Committee was not certain of the position Beecher and Stowe
would take when they returned. In addition, the Committee
may have believed that events would lead to a crisis before
the summer vacation ended.

The report of the special committee was published in the Cincinnati Gazette on August 30, and in the Cincinnati Journal on September 5. The report stated that no theological seminary "should stand before the public as a partizan, on any question, upon which able men and pious christians differ." To do so would alienate the Seminary from the public, and would serve to "preoccupy the minds of the young with bitter party prejudices; to unsettle the judgment, and unfit the mind for genial and useful intercourse with mankind." Therefore, "every thing tending to keep alive a spirit of controversy . . . ought to be excluded from the Seminary." In support of this point of view (which had been advanced by James Hall in April, and later by Biggs), the Executive Committee recommended a resolution which would prohibit the organization of any student societies without faculty permission, prohibit students from speaking in public without faculty permission, abolish the antislavery and colonization societies, prohibit student absences from the Seminary without faculty permission, discourage students from discussing questions not connected with their studies, and provide for the dismission of students who refused to comply with the regulations. [25]

The response to the action of the Executive Committee was mixed. Antislavery papers strongly disapproved. Joshua Leavitt, editor of the New York Evangelist, in a widely republished editorial, asked "In what age do we live? And in what country?" He noted that when students at Yale had asked President Timothy Dwight for permission to discuss the credibility of miracles, Dwight had approved and even had taken part in the discussions. Leavitt could not see how Beecher, Stowe, and Morgan could remain at Lane under such regulations, and he hoped that the entire Board would "pause" before passing the recommendations and realize its folly. [26]

Other papers were not outraged. The Boston Recorder printed the report without comment. [27] The Cross and Baptist Journal of the Mississippi Valley noted only that the activities of the Lane students "have been matters of some notoriety and animadversion for three or four months past" and that the Executive Committee had acted to correct the situation. [28] The Ohio Observer was ambivalent: "Many of their [the trustees'] general remarks meet our full approbation. From some of them however we should demur." [29] On the whole, the public waited to see what actions the trustees, faculty, and students would take in the fall.

Beecher: September, 1834

Since a month would pass before the trustees would
meet to decide whether or not to accept the report and recommendations of the Executive Committee, attention was fixed
on Beecher, who was in the East soliciting funds for a chapel, library, and another professorship.   The Executive Committee's hesitancy in calling for the immediate passage of
the recommendations in its report of August 20 was based,
in part, on uncertainty regarding Beecher's position. [30]   Students were also uncertain.   In September, Henry B. Stanton
wrote, "We hope Beecher will set his face against it [the re-
port], & take the stand which his boasted professions of regard for free inquiry & discussion, would seem to compel
him to assume. "   Stanton added that the students "are a little doubtful as to his course. "[31]

Beecher was kept informed of the actions of the Executive Committee by letters from Biggs, Mahan, and Wright. [32]
Although all three men had assured Beecher that new and
drastic recommendations would be adopted by the Executive
Committee, he evidently had discounted their statements.
Only when Wright informed him that the recommendations had
been adopted by the Executive Committee did Beecher realize
that the situation was approaching a crisis.   Wright's letter,
said Beecher, "has occasioned no small inquietude--. "[33]

Beecher informed Wright, on September 3, that he had
discussed the matter with Stowe and Vail, and that all had
agreed on six points for the Board to consider.   First, there
was no urgent reason requiring action before their return from
the East.   Second, the Executive Committee's recommendations
should be adopted only if absolutely necessary, and then by the
united actions of the trustees and faculty.   Third, if such measures were carried out, they must be done so as to insure
public support, particularly since they involved the issue of
free discussion and inquiry.   Fourth, the publication of such
"projected laws" would limit other future courses of action.
Fifth, rumors of "trouble & confusion in the Seminary" would
repel prospective students and hinder Beecher in the collection
of funds.   Sixth, in a criticism of Biggs, Beecher wrote, "no
one of us in the absence of the other members of the faculty
would have been willing to take the responsibility of advising
to a course of such strong & highly responsible measures. "
In closing, he advised the Executive Committee not to publish
the recommendations until the faculty's return. [34]

Four days later, having learned that the Executive Committee's report had already been published, Beecher wrote again to Wright.

> I have foreseen that what you have done Might be indispensable & had made up my mind to meet the emergency when all hope of averting it had failed, & the necessity was inexorable hoping in the mean time that we might get by the point with out strong measures. But inasmuch as you have taken ground & published [the report], it is to be regarded as the providential will of heaven that this is the best way. 35

Beecher agreed with the Executive Committee that "the Seminary should not be diverted from its main purposes" and promised faculty support "in rooting up & out all ultraism-- which goes to impair the usefullness of the Seminary--. " The problem then confronting the Seminary was how to remove the "ultraism" without public outcry. In an obvious reference to Weld and to rumors that the Executive Committee had talked of expelling him, Beecher presented his own scheme to Wright.

> Our plan of Parental & evangelical government is right & would have carried all before it but for one headlong powerful mind too powerful & too unsafe to be trusted. And which as I believe must be seperated [sic] from the Seminary. But I had rather the committee should not attempt to do it untill [sic] after my return as his friends in New York are eager to take him away as their agent, & I am in hope that I may be able to help them to do it & it will pay off much better in that form than any other. 36

Beecher was adamant that all activities of the faculty and trustees be done cautiously to avoid "throwing the Student[s] by any sudden statement into his [Weld's] power & creating a sort of social mania which would carry them all as a flood away. " Stowe agreed with him that action was necessary "to put down this ultraism & misrule in the Seminary. " Public sentiment would support them if they acted "discreetly. "37

In addition to getting the Eastern abolitionists to remove the instigator of the students' "ultraism, " Beecher was

also working to relieve the tensions at Lane by the formation
of a national antislavery society

> which shall superintend decidedly speedily & effi-
> ciently the whole process of bringing to a close
> Slavery in the shortest time & in the kindest way,
> to conciliate protect & aid the South in doing her
> own work in her own way provided she will do it.

In other words, Beecher wanted a moderate antislavery organization which both abolitionists and colonizationists could
support. Such an organization would temper the radicalism
of the abolitionists while still providing an outlet for the reform impulse. Once this new society was organized, it "will
call for Auxiliaries in Cincinnati & over the land, & will em-
body all our moderate & decent young men."[38]

Beecher's repeated advice to the trustees to be cau-
tious and discreet, and his confidence that he could solve the
problem while in the East demonstrated his ignorance of the
situation in Cincinnati. The fact that Nathaniel Wright, well-
known for his cautiousness, had encouraged such drastic actions as those proposed in the Executive Committee's report
indicated that the trustees believed that the time for caution
was past.[39] On September 13, Wright wrote to Beecher that
the trustees had acted "with great deliberation, and great re-
luctance ... Many of our best citizens were looking upon the
seminary as a nuisance, more to be dreaded than cholera or
plague." In a statement directed at Beecher's ignorance of
local sentiment, Wright said,

> It is impossible for persons not well conversant in
> the slave states, and the part of the country on
> their borders, to realize the state of the public
> mind on these subjects. If once excited, we may
> as well tamper with the whirlwinds and the light-
> ning.[40]

Wright's letter may also have contained accounts of
incidents which indicated the severity of the situation. On
August 30, four blacks had ridden out to Walnut Hills to visit
some of the students at the Seminary. This was promptly
reported to the trustees by an acquaintance of a brother of a
Board member.[41] A total of 3,600 copies of Birney's Letter
on Colonization had been mailed from the Seminary by students
on the ninth, tenth, and eleventh, a fact which probably became
known to the trustees when a committee went out to the Semi-

nary on the tenth. [42] Also, it was no secret that Weld had arranged, by the tenth, to have Birney's more recent Letter to the Ministers and Elders on the Sin of Holding Slaves published in the Cincinnati Journal. [43] In light of these events, the trustees believed that their decision, on September 6, to close the school for the rest of the vacation had been a wise one. [44] On the thirteenth, the same day that Wright wrote to Beecher, the Seminary was closed. [45]

Instead of returning to Cincinnati, Beecher travelled to New York to raise more funds and to put his plan into operation to form a moderate antislavery organization and rid the Seminary of Weld. In New York he met with a number of prominent abolitionists, including Arthur Tappan, John Rankin, S. S. Jocelyn, and Samuel E. Cornish. Beecher stated that he wished to see abolitionists and colonizationists join together. "He said that he did not think the differences were so great that this [conciliation] could not be effected without material sacrifices of opinion and feeling." The abolitionists replied that such a union was impossible because of their objections to colonization. Beecher, said Lewis Tappan, "expressed very great surprise and disappointment." Regarding the actions of the Executive Committee of the Board of Lane, Beecher declared emphatically, when "pressed on the subject," that those actions did not meet with his approval, and that he would not consent to the suppression of the right of the students to discuss slavery. [46]

Beecher had attempted to ease the crisis at Lane by uniting abolitionists and colonizationists, but he had failed to secure the support of the New York abolitionists. On September 29, he and Vail went to see Lewis Tappan at his office, evidently to try to get Tappan to help them get rid of Weld. They related some of the students' indiscretions which had alarmed the trustees, and Beecher expressed his own apprehensions. Beecher was critical of Weld, who "could not be touched with a ten foot pole" and who persisted in going his "own way." "It is evident," Tappan reported to Weld, "that the accounts Dr. B.[eecher] & Mr. Vail have recently received from Cincinnati have alarmed and excited them." "I doubt not," concluded Tappan, "they feel that you must leave or the Institution be sacrificed--unless you will consent to draw in the traces with the President." [47]

Tappan refused to give credence to Beecher's and Vail's tale of student indiscretions. Nor did he offer to encourage Weld to leave Lane to accept a position elsewhere, or agree

to advise him "to draw in the traces with the President."
Instead, Tappan chided Beecher for not becoming an abolitionist, an action he felt would end the strife in the Seminary. Beecher replied that he was an abolitionist, insofar
as he desired an end to slavery. However, he did not accept the abolitionist doctrine that it was possible for blacks
and whites to live together in an open society. [48]

Beecher failed in his plan to combine the actions of
abolitionists and colonizationists, and in his attempt to have
Weld leave the Seminary quietly. In fact, he had compounded
the situation by agreeing to support the trustees' actions and
also by pledging his support of the students' right to free
discussion.

Beecher started west, but at Columbus, Ohio, he
turned north to Granville, and then returned east. [49] In
transit he received a letter from Weld, who had been informed of Beecher's comments about him by Tappan. In
answer to Weld's entreaty that he return immediately to Cincinnati to resolve the problems there, Beecher replied with
a request of his own, "that till I see you, you will not permit the impression that I have spoken improperly concerning
you to Mr. Tappan." Beecher asserted his right to criticize
his students, but insisted that he considered them to be "a
set of glorious good fellows, whom I would not at a venture
exchange for any others." He advised Weld to "pray much,
say little, be humble and wait" for his return. [50]

The Crisis: October, 1834

When Beecher wrote to Weld on October 8, the trustees had already acted. On September 15, two days after
the trustees closed the school, and on the same day that students had begun printing (presumably on Seminary presses)
and mailing out Birney's Letter to the Ministers and Elders,
Robert Boal, Recording Secretary of the Board, informed the
trustees that Wright had called a special meeting of the entire Board to be held on October 6 in the Second Presbyterian
Church. [51] The purpose of the meeting was to discuss the
recommendations of the Executive Committee regarding the
students' activities before the term commenced on October 15.
It was generally assumed that the Executive Committee's recommendations would pass. As early as September 11, Henry
B. Stanton had noted the determination of the trustees to pass
the recommendations "tho it should force every student &

every member of the Faculty from the Seminy [sic]. "[52] Two
days before the meeting, another student, Huntington Lyman,
wrote, "It is about reduced to a certainty that the laws will
pass. "[53]

At 10:00 A. M. on Monday the sixth, seventeen of the
twenty-seven trustees assembled in Beecher's church to decide the Seminary's future course. Refusing to follow the
proposal of one trustee to vote immediately, the Board discussed, "at some length," the report adopted by the Executive
Committee on August 20. [54] A letter was read from Robert
H. Bishop, one of the absent trustees, which favored the
adoption of "all the regulations suggested by the Executive
Committee...."[55] Bishop, who was President of Miami University, had forbidden the discussion of slavery at his school
in June because of threats of possible violence. [56] If any
Lane trustees were still uncertain, Bishop's letter probably
convinced them of the necessity of the proposed recommendations. When the vote was taken, only Mahan and two of his
church elders, William Holyoke and John Melindy, opposed
the acceptance of the Executive Committee's report of August 20. [57]

Having accepted the report, the Board formally promulgated its content and intent in two Standing Rules and two
Orders. The first Standing Rule banned the organization of
any student societies "without the approbation of the Faculty. "
The second forbade students from holding meetings, giving
addresses, or being absent from the Seminary without faculty
permission. Order 1 required the students to disband the
antislavery and colonization societies which had been formed
in the Seminary. Order 2 gave the Executive Committee the
'power to dismiss any student from the seminary, when they
shall think it necessary so to do; & to make any rules &
regulations ... which they may deem expedient. "[58]

After the Executive Committee's report, the Standing
Rules, and the Orders had been passed, it was moved that
they be published. Wright objected to the publishing of Order
2, which he had written, ostensibly because it was not a public matter but belonged solely to the interior operations of the
Seminary. Despite his protest, the Board approved the publishing of all its resolutions. However, as the members were
about to leave, Wright again brought up the matter of Order
2, and moved "to reconsider the order of publication, as to
the last mentioned order.... " This time he received support
from James Gallaher, who was suspicious of Mahan's support

for the publication of Order 2. If Mahan, who supported the students and had voted against all three of the resolutions passed, were in favor of publishing the second Order, then Gallaher was " 'apprehensive that he sees something in this item that we do not.' " Gallaher would therefore vote for Wright's motion not to publish the second Order. Only when Mahan dared the Board members to publish the Order did they defeat the measure. However, to allay any public excitement over this Order, a footnote was added stating that Order 2 referred to a "distribution of duties between the Board & Ex. Com." and could not be properly understood "with out reference to the Charter, bye laws &tc. "[59]

Having passed such stringent measures, the Board wanted to present clearly its intent to the members of the faculty, particularly Beecher, who had not returned from the East. Therefore, it was ordered that the Board members "communicate to the Faculty some explanation of their views in relation to the regulations recently adopted. " This "explanation" stressed the Board's desire not "to impose any undue restraints upon discussion & free enquiry among the students; nor" did the Board wish "to interfere with the Faculty in the details of collegiate government. " The Board's object was "to secure to the Faculty a more direct & certain influence over the conduct of the students without the necessity of adopting for themselves severe or arbitrary regulations. "[60]

The Board noted that the "signs of the times" had demonstrated "a strong & growing propensity to insubordination,--a disposition to set up individual notions or constructions in opposition to lawful authority,--.... " Often this "spirit" manifested itself in rioting or, more recently, in nullification. "Yet it is but the workings of the same spirit, which arrays the students of our colleges in hostility to the regulations established by those constituted rulers. " If theological students, the future regulators of public morality, should partake of this "spirit" of insubordination, "we may well despair of the Republic. "[61]

By adopting such severe measures, the Board intended to strengthen the faculty's ability to eliminate any "propensity to student insubordination. " Students would be required to obtain faculty permission before engaging in almost any activity. The faculty would continue, as it had in the past, to "advise" students concerning possible debates or their relations with people in the city. With the threat of expulsion hanging over them, the students would have to consider the "advice" and "approbation" of the faculty as virtual commands. 62

The Board's "suggestions" to the faculty regarding the new regulations made no mention of Order 2, which empowered the Executive Committee to expel any student at will. This was the ultimate threat, and some of the Board members intended to employ it as soon as possible, either to demonstrate their seriousness by making examples of some students, or to employ their power to correct a troublesome situation. Back in July Biggs had hinted that the faculty should "lighten the vessel ... rather than founder at high sea!"63 In September, Stanton learned that the Executive Committee "have for some time been legislating about expelling Weld!"64 Beecher himself had agreed that it would be best for the school if Weld were gone, but he preferred to remove him quietly and without conflict. 65

After the trustees' meeting adjourned on the sixth, Mahan went to Weld's lodgings and told him and the other students present about what had transpired. Weld wrote to Birney, "Brother Mahan says without doubt I shall be expelled, and perhaps brothers Thome and Stanton." Weld's alienation from the Seminary showed through when he added, "You may rely upon it we shall not die of broken hearts if that takes place. "66

With the passage of the new regulations, the Executive Committee made special arrangements for the commencement of the term. On the tenth, the Committee met and passed three resolutions. First, to limit the students' ability to travel, and perhaps their aiding of fugitive slaves, the Steward was instructed to allow no horses on the grounds except those owned by the Seminary. Second, the Committee informed the Steward that it would "require strict attention to the rules regulating the admission of students. " Third, apprehensive about its new power to dismiss students, the Committee postponed action on the motion to expel Weld and William T. Allan, president of the students' antislavery society. 67 Mahan, Melindy and Holyoke were probably able to convince the Committee to wait for Beecher's return.

When Beecher did return, sometime between the tenth and fourteenth, he "found all in a flurry. If I had arrived a little sooner I should have saved them [students]; but it was too late. "68 Both he and Stowe, however, expressed their acceptance of the new regulations, although they found the "phraseology" of some of the more offensive regulations to be liable to misunderstanding. [69]

Still uncertain was the reaction of the students to the new regulations. Those who had remained in Cincinnati over the summer had made plans in case the trustees passed the regulations. On September 11, Stanton wrote:

> If the law requiring us to disband the Anti-Slavery Society, is passed, we shall take a dismission from the Seminary ... We shall spread the whole matter before the public, & I trust tell a story that will make some ears tingle ... If the laws pass, the theological class will probably all go in a body somewhere, & pursue our studies. We can have money enough to hire good teachers--.... [70]

It is not known whether or not the trustees and faculty knew of the intentions of some of the students. Mahan, in the students' confidence, probably knew. Beecher may have been informed by Lewis Tappan or by Weld. [71] Undoubtedly, the trustees would have preferred the voluntary withdrawal of certain students (such as Weld, Stanton, Thome, and William Allan), which would have alleviated the necessity of expelling them. None of the trustees perceived the extent to which antislavery evangelicalism had influenced the students. Stanton expressed the emotional stridency and dedication of this evangelically grounded abolitionism when he wrote that the majority of the students

> will not only have their names, but their bodies, cast out as evil, before they will hazard for one moment the cause of the oppressed, or yield an inch to the assault of a corrupt & persecuting public sentiment, or swerve one hair from the great principles which have been the basis of all our operations in regard to Slavery & Colonization. No never--never! [72]

When the term commenced on October 15, at least forty-six students from the previous year were present, along with seventeen prospective students. [73] They assembled and sent a delegation to the faculty to request an explanation of the new regulations. The faculty complied. A second delegation of the students asked if they could discuss the new regulations among themselves. To this request the faculty refused permission, saying that each student had to decide for himself whether or not to obey the regulations. A third committee of students requested permission to discuss among themselves whether or not they could remain in the Seminary under the new code. Again, the faculty refused. Asa Mahan later recounted that one of the student leaders then stood up and said that they all should decide whether or not to remain at Lane.

> For himself, he would say, that the most solemn convictions of duty to his God, his conscience, his country, and the race, constrained him to say, that he could not longer continue a student of Lane Seminary. He should, therefore, ask of the Faculty an honourable dismission; and he would request every student present, who was of the same mind and determination with himself, to signify the same by rising and standing upon his feet. [74]

The majority of the students arose. Of the seventeen prospective students, eight refused to enter Lane. [75] Twenty-eight enrolled students requested dismissions from the faculty on the fifteenth, and eleven more did on the sixteenth. [76]

Weld informed the faculty that he would not request a dismission until the trustees had decided whether or not to expel him. The Emancipator wrote that Weld would not avoid "expulsion by skulking out under cover of a regular and honorable dismission while the Board had measures in progress which aimed at thrusting him out branded with disgrace."[77] Weld was reputed to have said that the trustees

> have beaten me openly, uncondemned being an American; and now do they thrust me out privately, bearing the stigma of a culprit? Nay, verily, but let them come themselves and fetch me out. If I have offended, I refuse not to die, but let them show me the wrong I have done. If I am innocent let me stand upon my character. [78]

At a special meeting of the Executive Committee on the sixteenth, Beecher and Stowe were successful in " 'Quashing' " the resolution to expel Weld and Allan. [79] The next day Weld requested "a regular dismission" and left. [80]

On the seventeenth, the faculty members met with the Executive Committee and presented a "declaration of their understanding" of the new regulations "and of the manner in

which they will be administered. " They stated their belief
that the new regulations contained nothing "which is not common law in all well-regulated institutions, since they merely
commit the whole management of the internal concerns of the
seminary to the discretion of the faculty. " They voiced their
approval of the freedom of discussion and association of the
students in the Seminary and in the community. However,
all "benevolent labors" of the students were to be "in subordination to the great ends of the institution" as determined
by the faculty. The faculty would not permit any associations
which would injure students' health and studies, which dealt
with exciting or divisive topics, which offended public sentiment, and which harmed the prospects of the Seminary. The
faculty stated that the trustees' Order to disband the antislavery and colonization societies in the Seminary was "called
for by the necessities of the case. " The power of dismission given to the Executive Committee in Order 2 was viewed
"as simply vesting the executive committee with trustee powers
in certain cases, and not intended to interfere with the appro-
priate duties of the faculty or the rights of the students. "[81]

The majority of students did not agree with the faculty
interpretation. As other students learned of the proceedings
at Lane, they made their own decisions regarding the new
regulations. The Emancipator reported that almost all the
members of the students' antislavery society had resolved independently to leave the Seminary, "however great the amount
of personal sacrifice. "[82] George Clark hurried back from
Kentucky, where he had been working as an agent for the Society for Moral Reform, and requested a dismission.[83] Asa
A. Stone returned "some time after the students had left" to
receive his.[84] Lorenzo D. Butts actually re-entered the
Seminary and stayed until December 9, when he withdrew.[85]

By the end of the year, ninety-five of the one hundred
and three students previously enrolled at Lane had left or had
not returned.[86] Only eight entered at the beginning of the
term, six of whom were avowed colonizationists.[87] Of the
ninety-five who did not enter, nineteen had left before the
trustees took action and one had died.[88] Therefore, a total
of seventy-five students withdrew from Lane in the fall and
winter of 1834. Fifty-one of these went on record as having
withdrawn because of the trustees' and faculty's actions.[89]
In addition, at least three more were later considered to be
members of this group.[90] The remaining twenty-one left no
record of their reasons for not re-entering the Seminary.
However, Weld wrote:

> We are not apprized of the reasons which have de-
> terred the remainder from joining the Seminary,
> but can only say, that their minds have been changed
> <u>since</u> the proceedings of the executive committee,
> and of the trustees, were published. [91]

A total of seventy-five students, then, could lay claim to
being "Lane rebels. "[92]

Cumminsville and the "Statement of Reasons"

Most of the seceding students returned to their homes
or went to other schools. [93]   Four recanted and requested
permission to re-enter the Seminary. [94]   "About a dozen" of
those who had been most active moved as a group to Cumminsville, a village about four and one-half miles northwest
of the Seminary. [95]   James C. Ludlow gave the students the
use of a building in which to live and study.   This building
may have been the "Hall of Free Discussion" which Ludlow
had built in 1832, and had dedicated to " 'the interest of education, literature, and religion. ' "[96]   From Arthur Tappan
in New York came $1,000 for the support of the "Cummins-
ville band. "[97]

At Cumminsville, the students continued their work in
the black community.   William T. Allan, Andrew Benton,
Marius R. Robinson, Henry B. Stanton, and George Whipple
taught in the Sabbath schools.   John W. Alvord, Huntington
Lyman, Henry B. Stanton, James A. Thome, and Samuel
Wells gave lectures twice a week in the black community.
The students also alternated in preaching at eight different
churches, including two black churches.   They helped support
Augustus Wattles's teachers and schools, enlisted the cooperation of local black ministers, and kept Weld, now an anti-
slavery agent, and Joshua Leavitt informed of local events. [98]

In addition to their benevolent activities, the students
continued their studies.   Gamaliel Bailey, a local physician
influenced by the Lane debate and who would later gain prominence as an abolitionist editor, came out to Cumminsville
and gave lectures on physiology. [99]   George Whipple taught
Hebrew, Greek, and theology. [100]   John W. Alvord, Huntington Lyman, John T. Pierce, Marius R. Robinson, Sereno W.
Streeter, Edward Weed, and Samuel Wells lectured on topics
such as revelation, the trinity, and Christology. [101]   Thome
wrote, "This is a new point in my life at least.   I never

studied so successfully. "[102] Whipple added that the Cumminsville students "are doing well. It is a pleasure to teach such young men, and I believe they will make a noise in the world. "[103]

A profound sense of fate and feelings of piety pervaded the students' activities. Thome believed

> that the Lord has been gracious to me in throwing me into such circumstances. Indeed, He has led me by strange paths ever since I first entered Lane Seminary. From a previous life of reveri[e]s and sunshine, I was at once thrust amid the conflict of high solemn principles, calculated to draw out my soul. Sin[ce] then my feelings and associations have been entirely changed; and I seem all swallowed up in the causes which never troubled my thoughts before. Bless God! Though I have lost the favor of the gay and the smile of folly, I have secured friendship with Heaven and peace of soul.[104]

Benjamin Foltz, a prospective student who had refused to enter Lane and had joined the group at Cumminsville, recorded in his diary numerous instances of private prayer and soul searching. [105]

The benevolent and devotional activities of the students were expressions of the evangelicalism which formed the basis of their abolitionism, and which they had accepted during the debates. The lecture notes and sermon outlines of Marius Robinson, written in December, 1834, clearly present the theological basis for the students' antislavery evangelicalism.[106]

On December 15, one of the students lectured on the question, "What is the glory of God?" All of God's creation, of which theology is a part, is designed to exhibit the glory of God. The glory of God is the "benevolence of God." God glorifies Himself, not "by increasing the amount of his benevolence or glory ... but by exhibitions of himself, by the communication of good--the practical exercise of his benevolence." God glorifies Himself by His creatures in three ways. The first way is in the creation and governance of the universe. Second, God glorifies Himself in His creatures by His perfect creation of them in design and execution. For example, the hand is an "instrument perfect in its parts--perfect as a whole--perfect in the adaptation to its intended use which is to minister to happiness in a specified way." Similarly, the human mind exemplifies the manner in which God glorifies Himself in the creation of man.

> God designed that the mind of man should be free & accountable, capable of communicating & recieving [sic] happiness as the result of its own voluntary action. Accordingly he has perfectly adapted mind itself & all the circumstences [sic] that surround it, to this end.

Finally, "God is glorified by the voluntary action of his creatures," which "is manifest, if their action tend to the attainment of their destined end."107

The relationship between evangelical theology and the students' abolitionism is apparent in these lecture notes. God created man's mind "free & accountable, capable of communicating & recieving [sic] happiness as the result of its own voluntary action." By denying the slave this freedom, slaveholders not only sinned against their fellow human beings, but also sinned against God by rejecting His benevolence in creating the mind free and accountable. Most important, slavery was truly sinful because it rejected God's end and design in the world, the exhibition of His own glory.

Also in December, Robinson preached a sermon which expressed the same theological framework and impulse on which the students had based their abolitionism. The sermon had four main points. The first was that "Christians can save the world." Second, Christians could save the world using four methods: the first was the presentation of the truth, or "correct principles"; the second was the presentation of pious Christians as role models; the third included the practices of prayer and revivalism; the fourth was the practice of brotherly love. The third major point of Robinson's sermon concerned the ways in which Christians could lose the power of saving the world. One of these ways was the adoption of "any other rules of action than the bible." For example, "Expediency" was such a nonbiblical rule of action or principle. The practice or even countenance of sin, such as slavery, was a second way. The last three ways included "Moral cowardice," "Opposing benevolent efforts" because of prudence, and "Indolence." Robinson's closing point emphasized the Christian's "Responsibility." The urgency in his final appeal is apparent in his brief notes: "World perishing--C. can save it--God calls them to save it ... Guilt of not helping."108

The most significant example of the relationship between the students' evangelicalism and their antislavery was
A Statement of the Reasons Which Induced the Students of
Lane Seminary, to Dissolve Their Connection with That Institution, which was published in January, 1835 (although it was
written in November and dated December 15, 1834). Before
the trustees had met to pass the new regulations on October
6, Weld had "been engaged for several days in arranging and
pasting in some facts upon the subject of Abolition So as to
be ready for an emergency. "109 After the students had left
the Seminary, Weld and several others were "appointed" a
committee by the seceders "to prepare an expose of the whole
matter, and present it to the public. "110 By November 10,
it was nearly completed, but was later withheld from publication, apparently at the faculty's request. 111 After much anti-
cipation, the Statement of Reasons appeared in early January,
1835. 112

Signed by fifty-one students, the Statement of Reasons
contained an exposition of the right of free discussion. It
chronicled the events of the past year, and presented arguments against the regulations passed on October 6. It defended the students' actions and severely criticized the trustees and faculty for preferring "the triumph of expediency
over right" and for bowing to public pressure. 113

The Statement of Reasons was significant because of
its clear delineation of the issues and the relation between
free discussion and abolitionism. Equally important, the
rights of free speech and antislavery action were built on a
theological foundation that was evangelical, and appropriated
from Finney.

On entering the Seminary, the Statement of Reasons
said, the students had adopted the "principle, that free discussion, with correspondent effort, is a DUTY, and of course
a RIGHT. "

We believe free discussion to be the duty of every
rational being. It is the acting out of the command
"Prove all things. " It is inquiry after immutable
truth, whether embodied in the word, or hid in the
works of God, or branching out through the relations
and duties of man. We are bound to conduct this
search, wherever it may lead, and to adopt the conclusions to which it may bring us. And, whereas,
the single object of ascertaining truth is to learn

> how to act, we are bound to do at once, whatever
> truth dictates to be done. [114]

The duty of the students to search for the truth and act upon
it was the same duty which Finney urged upon all sinners
and converted Christians: one must act because one is responsible. [115]

Because one has the duty to act, one is able to act,
but also, one must not be impeded from acting. Free discussion is a right, one of those rights which "are not derived from man ... they are inseparable from accountable
agency, and inalienable, and, of course, are neither surren-
dered nor forfeited by membership in a theological seminary."
Free discussion is a right conferred by God, and its pro-
scription would be "sacrilege!"[116]

Regarding the trustees' and faculty's preference for
"expediency" and bowing to public pressure, the Statement
of Reasons noted, "He that moves with the tide of public
sentiment, is a part of it, augments it, and cannot absolve
himself from the responsibility of its effects."[117] This was
a complete rejection of Beecher's tactic never to push for
reform until public sentiment was ready for it. [118] In a
statement reminiscent of Finney's idea of "duty,"[119] the
Statement of Reasons described the proper stance of the individual regarding public sentiment. If public sentiment is
wrong, the individual must do more than

> silently withdraw his original contribution, leaving
> the remainder to sweep on unresisted. It is not
> enough that he neither vote for iniquity himself,
> nor solicits the votes of others. If he would be
> guiltless of blood, he must do his utmost to unite
> against it the suffrages of the world. A moral
> agent cannot determine duty by proxy. [120]

The theological basis of the Statement of Reasons was
evangelical. The stress on the responsibility of the moral
agent to act in total commitment was Finney's legacy to the
students' antislavery evangelicalism. That the students felt
an affinity with the revivalist is apparent in letters between
the students at Cumminsville and Finney about the time of
the publication of their Statement of Reasons. [121] The students had considered asking Finney to come west to teach
them privately, but, having learned that Finney would be asked
to become Professor of Theology at Oberlin Collegiate Institute,

in northeastern Ohio, they encouraged him to accept the post.
If he did, "nearly or quite all the theological students who
left Lane, would place themselves at once under your instruction." Finney was needed in the West. Indeed, the area was
in dire need of a revival-oriented theological seminary "from
whose professors young men can catch that high toned moral
feeling & that practical energy, which are so essential for
ministers at this crisis." Lane Seminary was

> governed by a time serving expediency, --by a sub-
> serviency to popular prejudices, & opinions, ill
> adapted to fit its pupils for warring with the sins
> & enormous evils of a corrupt & corrupting age. [122]

The entire letter of the Cumminsville students stressed
the importance of a new revival ministry. The total lack of
reference to antislavery would seem peculiar were it not for
the fact that the Lane students considered antislavery to be a
natural result of a revivalistic evangelicalism. Antislavery
was not a new application of evangelical theology but the logical effect of it. Lyman Beecher's acceptance of "expediency"
and his refusal to see an inherent relationship between evangelicalism and antislavery made his own evangelicalism seem
counterfeit. Beecher, however, saw things differently.

The Faculty

After the secession of students, the Lane faculty was
faced with the problem of insuring the Seminary's existence.
Beecher and Stowe assumed the task of maintaining Lane's
credibility and reputation as an institution free of party animosity and conflict. They convinced the trustees to amend
the new regulations, obtained new students, issued a statement
to justify their own actions, and defended Lane's course in the
press.

On October 25, the Executive Committee, with Beecher
and Stowe present, resolved that it was "inexpedient for them
to exercise the power conferred them" to expel students, and
recommended that Order 2 be repealed. [123] On November 5,
the entire Board accepted Beecher's and Stowe's recommendations to make changes in the "phraseology" of the new laws
in order to "make their intention more obvious. "[124]

The Standing Rules were incorporated into the "Laws"
of the Seminary under the heading "Deportment of Students. "

They stated that all student absences, lectures, meetings, and societies were to be subject to the "consent" and "direction" of the faculty. [125] Order 2 was amended to read that the Executive Committee could expel any student "on reccommendation [sic] of the Faculty. "[126] The revised laws appeared less oppressive, especially the change in Order 2, although the intent remained the same: to insure faculty control of the students.

With the change in the laws secured, Beecher attempted to attract students to his nearly empty Seminary. He was faced with the prospect of teaching only about a dozen students where there had been over one hundred. To enlarge the student body, Beecher personally sought out prospective students. "If students would not offer themselves, he would go after them, even to the highways and hedges, and compel them to come in.... "[127] Near the end of 1834, Calvin Stowe claimed that the number of students had increased to forty. [128]

Beecher also tried to win back some of the students at Cumminsville. At a meeting with "a number of the most discreet among them," he placed the blame for the entire conflict on Biggs, and encouraged them to work "to form a reaction" among the seceders. [129] He denied any complicity in the laws, and said that he had supported their execution only to placate public sentiment and protect the Seminary from mob violence. [130] Although at least two students admitted their "misapprehension respecting some of the laws of the institution," expressed "their entire concurrence in the laws as explained by" the faculty, and re-entered the Seminary, [131] most of the seceders rejected Beecher's explanation. John T. Pierce wrote, "The faculty have done what they could to reclaim us, but all in vain; we are a reckless set and will take no wholesome advice, even from our best friends. "[132]

Increasing the number of students was one way of minimizing the harm done to the Seminary by the student secession. To minimize further the damage, the trustees closed the Literary Department (twenty-five out of fifty-eight of its students had left because of the laws) at the end of October. [133] The firing of Morgan, the major teacher in the Department, the lack of endowment funds from which to pay instructors, and the competition for students from other colleges constributed to this decision, but it seems likely that the trustees closed the Literary Department primarily to give the impression that the Seminary's losses due to the student withdrawal were only in the Theological Department. Regarding the latter department, the faculty estimated "that after all the hue and cry ... not more than 20 theological students have left on account of the late regulations of the trustees."[134] By attracting new and regaining former students, by eliminating the Literary Department, and by minimizing the number of theological students who had withdrawn, the faculty and trustees gave the impression that the conflict had not been crippling to the Seminary.

Nevertheless, even the loss of twenty students under such circumstances had to be explained. On January 2, the Cincinnati Journal published the "Statement of the Faculty, concerning the late Difficulties in the Lane Seminary."[135] This was intended to present the viewpoint of the faculty and counteract the students' Statement of Reasons, published the same week. The faculty declared that the trustees had abolished the students' antislavery society because of "the spirit and manner" of the students in "doing a few things not necessary to the prosperity of the society itself, against the advice of the faculty, and reckless of the consequences in doing violence to public sentiment." The "Statement of the Faculty" then asserted that the students had consistently ignored faculty advice, first in refusing to postpone the debate on slavery, and then, on several occasions, in lacking discretion in the practice of their doctrine of "immediate intercourse irrespective of color...."[136]

The faculty's "Statement" contended that the issue was the right of students to discuss and act "entirely at their own discretion, and unregulated by the discretion of the faculty." The faculty and trustees could not concede this right, since, in the words of the faculty "Declaration" of October 17, all student activities had to be "in subordination to the great ends of the institution" as determined by the faculty. The conflict over the students' right to free discussion and activities had occurred because the students had misused that right "by pressing upon public sensibility the doctrine, and countenancing and justifying the practice of intercourse irrespective of color." Such a doctrine was viewed by the faculty as "not necessarily associated with abolition principles...."[137]

A concluding paragraph, added by Beecher after the rest of the "Statement of the Faculty" was in type, accused Weld of coming to Lane "with the express design of making the institution subservient to the cause of abolition." Weld's zeal for antislavery and his rejection of caution and others' advice presented "an eminent instance of the monomania, which not unfrequently is the result of the concentration of a powerful intellect and burning zeal upon any one momentous subject to the exclusion of others;... "[138]

Beecher's remark about Weld indicates the faculty's lack of understanding of the students' theologically grounded antislavery evangelicalism. The students' Statement of Reasons had been a theological treatise on the freedom and duty of discussion and action. It held that these rights could not be limited legitimately by anyone, not even the students themselves. Their fanatic adherence to principle the faculty could only regard as "monomania."

On their side, the students and their supporters were unable to perceive that the faculty's and trustees' major concern was the continuation of the Seminary. For the faculty and trustees, Lane occupied a place of importance greater than the students' rights to free discussion and action. The Fifth Annual Report of the trustees presented the "sentiment"

> that the salvation of our country and the world, is intimately connected with the intellectual and moral elevation of the West; and that this school of the prophets, under God, is destined to exert a leading influence in accomplishing this important result. [139]

The passage of the regulations by the trustees was an attempt to preserve Lane for its great purpose. The faculty members' insistence that the Standing Rules and Orders of October 6, and the more mildly phrased laws of November 5 were the same in intention underscored their dedication to that same purpose. [140] In published letters in the New York Evangelist, the Boston Recorder, and the Cincinnati Journal, Calvin Stowe labored to explain that the issue was not free speech or antislavery, but who should control the Seminary and guide it in its great task. [141] In his exchange of letters with John Rankin, an antislavery minister, in the Cincinnati Journal, Stowe never brought up the issue of slavery itself, and he discussed it in his last letter only when Rankin specifically asked him to do so. [142]

Almost a year after the student withdrawal, Beecher delivered a lecture at Miami University entitled A Plea for Colleges. [143] "I trust it may do good" he stated, "in these ultra days of flippant genius and insubordination. "[144] In the Plea, Beecher expressed the same concern as Stowe for the

proper regulation of educational institutions. He noted the
importance of education for the West, the nation, and the
world, and expressed dismay at the increasing "tendency of
personal liberty to the subversion of laws," which he saw as
"the epidemic of the day." Colleges and seminaries had experienced this same tendency among their students, and
Beecher regarded this as extremely dangerous. In a bitterly
sarcastic passage, obviously referring to Lane, Beecher emphasized that the maintenance of order, "heaven's first law,"
could be properly maintained only by faculty, not students or
the press. In another passage reminiscent of the Lane controversy, he stated that education should be "regarded as a
preparation for public action [not] the commencement of it."[145]

The Plea also revealed Beecher's own set of concerns.
He desired the universal spread of the Gospel and the propagation of reform. The completion of this gigantic task required the training of individuals in educational institutions,
and any threat to the good order and functioning of these
schools was a threat to the entire cause. Viewed from
Beecher's perspective, the secession of students from his
Seminary was an example of insubordination and the subversion of good order, and not a protest concerning free speech
and antislavery. His students had misunderstood him as
much as he had misunderstood them.

Characteristically, Beecher looked for and found the
bright side in the Lane controversy. He admired the academic excellence of his first theological class, and admitted
that he and the students had never quarrelled.[146] All things
considered, however, he was glad that such troublesome students had chosen to leave. One of his daughters-in-law described Beecher's attitude in a letter written about two weeks
after the secession. "Father is very well and is making 'old
shears cut' all around." The secession of students, "with
Weld at their head," was

> a proceeding on their part, which Father says "has
> purged out the old leaven" better than it could have
> been done in any other way--& he accordingly re-
> joices over it....

Nevertheless, Beecher was a little wistful. Although he was
glad the "old leaven" had been purged, his daughter-in-law
added that "he would have been glad to retain some of [the
students] at his own selection."[147]

The Wider Context: The Lane Rebellion in Perspective

The students' withdrawal from Lane generated widely
different reactions locally and in the East.   The local papers,
if they noted the conflict at all, generally approved the actions of the faculty and trustees.   The Cincinnati Journal
highly approved of the passage of the regulations of October
6, and stated:

> Parents and guardians may now send their sons
> and wards to Lane Seminary, with a perfect con-
> fidence, that the proper business of a theological
> school will occupy their minds; and that the dis-
> cussion and decision of abstract questions, will
> not turn them aside from the path of duty. [148]

The Cincinnati Chronicle and Literary Gazette concurred in
this sentiment.   When the students left the Seminary, it
noted:

> The existence of such troubles [at Lane] was a
> source of regret to all the friends of the Institu-
> tion; and we are happy to hear that they have been
> in a great part quieted; most of those students,
> whose conduct was injuring the Seminary, having
> left it. [149]

The Catholic Telegraph was the only local paper to
criticize openly (and satirically) the trustees and faculty.
For once, Protestants could be justly accused of the charge
they most often leveled against Catholicism: despotism.
The Telegraph could not resist proclaiming the irony of the
Lane situation.   The students, it declared, had only been
following the great principle of the Reformation: to interpret
and act on one's beliefs without the interposition of an inter-
mediary.

> Has not the right of every man to interpret the
> Bible for himself been gloriously asserted?   Are
> not these sons of the Prophets guaranteed the in-
> alienable privilege of expounding and carrying into
> effect the charitable enactments of the sacred code
> in the spirit in which they understand them and in
> the manner in which they prefer? ... If they have
> been abridged of their rights ... they may well
> complain of their arbitrary rulers' displeasure,
> for having acted in accordance with the axioms

laid down by Calvin and faithfully adhered to by
his disciples since the blessed Reformation. [150]

From other cities came word of the public response
to the controversy. Papers that supported the students included the Friend (published at the Western Theological Seminary), the Standard (published by the trustees of South Hano-
ver Theological Seminary), the Lowell Observer, the Salem
Landmark, the Cortland Republican, the Ohio Observer, the
Emancipator, the Liberator, and the New York Evangelist. [151]
The Liberator, more vocal than most, responded to the passage of the laws by calling Lane "a Bastile of Oppression--
a Spiritual Inquisition. "[152]

Joshua Leavitt, editor of the New York Evangelist,
mounted the most sustained and informed attack against the
actions of the trustees and faculty. Kept apprised of developments in the situation by the students at Cumminsville, [153]
Leavitt charged the trustees with despotism and the faculty
with duplicity. He asserted that the trustees had acted without faculty advice and had ended the proper "paternal system"
of governing educational institutions. Further, the faculty
members had acquiesced in the trustees' laws, and had even
denied that the trustees' regulations had usurped their own
administrative powers. The regulations of the trustees and
the faculty's "Declaration" concerning those regulations had
been published without regard to principles. The regulations
were intended "to appease a community excited to madness
against the designs of abolitionists" while the faculty's "declaration" was intended "to gain the confidence of students and
young men who are becoming generally tinctured with abolitionism. " Finally, Leavitt accused the trustees and faculty
of deliberately deceiving the public by passing regulations to
limit discussion when their real reason was to stop the students' equal treatment of blacks. [154]

On the trustees' side during the dispute were papers
such as the Cincinnati Journal, the New York Observer, the
New York Christian Intelligencer, the Connecticut Observer,
the Vermont Chronicle, the Boston Recorder, the Portland
Christian Mirror, the Western Recorder, the Christian Gazette of Philadelphia, the Southern Religious Telegraph, and
the Southern Christian Herald. [155] The Boston Recorder expressed the common conviction that the issue was the control
of the Seminary, and not antislavery. After the student debate on slavery, the faculty had "pursued a lenient course--
perhaps too lenient; and by argument and remonstrance, suc-

ceeded in regaining, to a good degree, the control of the Seminary." The trustees had passed the regulations of October 6 in order to "finish the work of reform" insuring the governance of the Seminary by the faculty.[156]

Besides showing support for the trustees and faculty, papers like the Recorder, the Christian Mirror, and the Cincinnati Journal raised other issues. The first concerned the deliberate intervention into the internal affairs of Lane Seminary by supporters of the antislavery movement. The Recorder accused Leavitt and "his coadjutors" of attempting "to carry their various projects for 'reform,' by enlisting young men who are preparing for the ministry" with or without the compliance or permission of the faculty.[157] The Christian Mirror suggested to Leavitt, among other things, that Lane's faculty were better able to judge how to govern the Seminary than newspaper editors six hundred miles away.[158] Thomas Brainerd raised the issue of interference in the management of his own paper, the Cincinnati Journal, by the abolitionists. He reported that during his trip to the East in the spring of 1834, the existence of the Journal had been threatened if he would not openly support abolitionism.[159] Finally, the Cincinnati Journal accused the antislavery press of biased reporting and the deliberate distortion of the facts of the controversy.[160]

In addition to comments in the press, individuals connected with Lane expressed their opinions of the conflict. J. R. Barbour, of Philadelphia, who collected subscriptions for the Seminary, wrote, "I have no doubt that the trustees, & faculty will be sustained by public sentiment in the course they have taken."[161] George A. Avery, another collections agent whose brother, Courtland, was one of the seceders, expressed the opposite view. He wrote, "in view of the adoption of certain regulations which have obtained some notoriety I feel constrained to decline any further agency in behalf of the Institution...."[162] Nine months, later, in August, 1835, Avery expressed his views more fully:

> I look upon the conduct of the Trustees as arbitrary tyrranical [sic] & wicked & that of the faculty as indicating a great amount of confidence in God as time-serving as governed entirely too much by a desire to please men rather than God in a word as leaving the high & consecrated ground of strait-forward & unbending obedience to God for the low grounds the fogs & quicksands of muddy wisdom & timeserving expediency.[163]

Major donors of the Seminary also expressed their disapprobation of the measures. "Mr. Lane" objected to the actions of the trustees and faculty. [164] Arthur Tappan requested clarification of the measures; [165] and although he continued to pay Beecher's salary until bankruptcy in the Panic of 1837 forced him to stop, he was disappointed in the Seminary's course. In 1838 he wrote to Beecher,

> I thank you for the particulars respecting your Seminary and regret that I cannot feel any sympathy in the happiness you express in the present and anticipated prosperity. The past history will explain the cause of this. [166]

Abolitionists disavowed any animosity towards Lane Seminary, but were pleased nevertheless at the turn of events there. Lewis Tappan had predicted, early in October, that, if the regulations were passed,

> the students will swing their packs, and be voluntary agents all over the country. As the death of Stephen spread Christianity over the world so the extinction of free discussion & the right of free association in Lane Sem. may spread our doctrines far & wide. [167]

Elizur Wright, Jr., exclaimed, "Who knows what mighty benefits, too, may grow out of this persecution."[168]

The "benefits" for the antislavery movement which grew out of the Lane controversy were substantial. The conflicts concerning the relationship between students and faculty, and over the role of education in society demonstrated the extent to which slavery had insinuated itself into the major institutions of American society. Indeed, during the 1830's many colleges and seminaries were confronted with these same issues because of slavery. Students often debated the merits of colonization and antislavery. At times, as at Miami University in the summer of 1834, the faculty cancelled discussions about slavery to prevent threatened violence.[169] At Kenyon College, Illinois College, and Miami University, regulations similar to those of Lane were enacted.[170] At Amherst, the faculty severely restricted the activities of the students' antislavery society.[171] At Andover Theological Seminary the students, when requested by faculty, disbanded their society to avoid "endangering the spirit of piety and brotherly love among them, and essentially interfering with that intellectual and moral improvement, which it is the grand object of the Institution to promote. "172 However, students at Marietta College, Western Reserve, and Phillips Academy withdrew rather than forsake their abolitionism. 173 All of these incidents highlighted the fact that slavery was perceived as a serious problem.

The Lane conflict stood out from all the other debates, gag laws, and student withdrawals. First, Lane preceded and provided a point of reference for most of the antislavery controversies in other schools. 174 In addition, the Seminary's location on the border of a slave state, its talented student body, and its nationally known president provided a dramatic setting and cast for the Lane rebellion. Within this setting, the evangelicalism expressed by the students provided a theological framework and religious impulse for antislavery. The Lane rebels had not "revived"175 the idea of the sin of slavery, but their rebellion served to place slavery within the framework of an evangelical theology which demanded immediate emancipation. Finally, the antislavery careers of the Lane rebels provided examples of the power--and limits--of antislavery evangelicalism.

Notes

1. Lane Theological Seminary General Catalogue, pp. 7-8, lists twenty-seven, but two of these, Rev. James Challen and Rev. James Thompson (mistakenly identified as John Thompson in the Catalogue) had been removed by the other Board members in September, 1830, because neither had ever attended any Board meetings. Lane Seminary, Trustees Formal Minutes, Meeting of 20 September 1830, LTS.

2. Occupations and biographical information on the members of the Board can be found in: Cincinnati Directory for the Year 1834, passim; Greve, History of Cincinnati, passim; History of Cincinnati and Hamilton County, Ohio, passim; Memorial Association, In Memoriam, pp. 110-11, 222-23; Edna Ritzi Nicholai, "Groesbeck, Ohio: The Olive Branch Church Cemetery," Bulletin of the Historical and Philosophical Society of Ohio 16 (April 1958): 183; Conteur [pseud.], "Interesting Facts Concerning a Prominent Family in Early Cincinnati," Cincinnati Enquirer, 9 December 1923; Smithson E. Wright, comp., "Obituaries of Cincinnatians" (scrap-

book), Cincinnati Historical Society, Cincinnati; Cincinnati, Cincinnati Historical Society, Nathaniel Wright Diary, Journal & Miscellaneous Papers (hereafter cited as Nathaniel Wright Papers, CHS); and Fletcher, History of Oberlin, 1:155, n. 14. I differ from Fletcher's conclusions regarding the trustees' occupations mainly on minor points (e. g. Neff had been trained as a lawyer but did not practice law; instead, he was a hardware merchant and something of a financier). More important, Fletcher omitted from his list Ephraim Robbins, an insurance agent; and included D. W. Fairbank, a publisher and bookseller, who did not join the Board until after the Lane rebellion. Lane Seminary, Trustees Formal Minutes, Meeting of 30 October 1834, LTS.

3. Cincinnati Directory for the Year 1834, pp. 240-45; New York Evangelist, 9 and 16 November 1833; Cincinnati Advertiser and Ohio Phoenix, 8 February 1834; Cincinnati Journal, 19 April 1833, 24 January, 14 and 28 February, 4 April 1834; and "Intelligence," African Repository 9 (May 1833): 89.

4. See above, p. 21.

5. "Rail Road from Cincinnati to Charleston, S. C. ," Western Monthly Magazine 4 (November 1835): 327-33; and Rail Road Proceedings and Address of Fulton and Vicinity, to the People of Ohio (Cincinnati: Kendall & Henry, 1835).

6. "The Great Rail Road," Western Monthly Magazine 4 (December 1835): 415-18. Neff's interest in this railroad is noted in Rail Road Proceedings, pp. 19, 30; and in Memorial Association, In Memoriam, p. 223.

7. The Cincinnati Journal, 25 July 1834, devoted two and one-half columns to the July 4 riot in New York city.

8. Beecher, Biggs, and Stowe, "Statement of the Faculty," pp. 36-42. The Western Christian Advocate, a Methodist paper published in Cincinnati, printed a letter which said that the New York riots had been caused specifically by the abolitionists' demand for amalgamation (reprinted in the Emancipator, 19 August 1834). Undoubtedly, this would have increased the trustees' apprehensions.

9. Huntington Lyman to James A. Thome, 17 August 1834, File 16/5, Box 19, OCA.

10. On Crothers, see above, p. 76.

11. "Intelligence," African Repository 9 (May 1833): 88. At the November 5, 1834 meeting of the Cincinnati Colonization Society, three weeks after the student withdrawal, five trustees, including Nathaniel Wright, President of the Board, were made officers of that organization. Cincinnati Journal, 28 November 1834.

12. "Report of the Committee on Slavery," 20 August 1834, Lane Papers, Folder 15, MTS.

13. Thomas J. Biggs to Franklin Y. Vail, 23 July 1834, Lane Papers, Folder 26, MTS.

14. Theodore D. Weld to James G. Birney, 7 August 1834, in Dumond, ed., Letters of Birney, 1:128; and Huntington Lyman to James A. Thome, 17 August 1834, File 16/5, Box 19, OCA.

15. Huntington Lyman to James A. Thome, 17 August 1834, File 16/5, Box 19, OCA; and Cincinnati Journal, 15 August 1834.

16. Biggs wrote a total of four letters in favor of colonization, which were published in the Cincinnati Journal, 8 and 29 August, 5 and 12 September 1834.

17. The students at Lane informed Elizur Wright that Stowe had been asked to review Birney's Letter on Colonization, to which the professor replied, " 'if I review him, I shall agree with him.' " Quoted in Elizur Wright to Amos A. Phelps, 20 August 1834 (typed copy), Elizur Wright Papers, v. 2, Library of Congress, Washington, D. C. (hereafter cited as Elizur Wright Papers, LC). See also Theodore D. Weld to James G. Birney, 7 August 1834, in Dumond, ed., Letters of Birney, 1:129; and Henry B. Stanton to James A. Thome, 11 September 1834, File 16/5, Box 19, OCA.

18. Lane Seminary, Minutes of Meetings of the Executive Committee of the Board of Trustees, Meeting of 9 August 1834, Lane Papers, Folder 15, MTS.

19. Lane Seminary, Minutes of Meetings of the Executive Committee of the Board of Trustees, Meeting of 16 August 1834, Lane Papers, Folder 15, MTS.

20. Ibid.; Mahan, Autobiography, pp. 176-77.

21. Thomas J. Biggs to Lyman Beecher, 18 August 1834, Lane Papers, Folder 15, MTS.

22. Lane Seminary, Minutes of Meetings of the Executive Committee of the Board of Trustees, Meeting of 20 August 1834, Lane Papers, Folder 15, MTS.

23. Lane Seminary, Minutes of Meetings of the Executive Committee of the Board of Trustees, Meeting of 23 August 1834, Lane Papers, Folder 3, MTS. The Committee members had first discussed firing Morgan at the meeting on the twentieth. Any hesitation they may have felt was apparently removed by a report, entitled "Effects, upon the Students of Lane Seminary, arising from a discussion of the Slavery question." Probably written by Nathaniel Wright, this report stated the "Prof. Morgan is not less the life Blood of this matter than T. D. Weld for if he has not so much power he plies it more constantly; for he first pays such attention to the students both as a Teacher & an associate as to win them, then the duty of Abolition is pressed, so that every student here is obliged to make due confession to some body on the subject of Slavery." Nathaniel Wright Family Papers, Box 61, Library of Congress, Washington, D.C. (hereafter cited as Nathaniel Wright Papers, LC).

24. Lane Seminary, Minutes of Meetings of the Executive Committee of the Board of Trustees, Meeting of 25 August 1834, Lane Papers, Folder 3, MTS. This was the only business discussed at the quarterly meeting of the Executive Committee.

25. Cincinnati Daily Gazette, 30 August 1834.

26. New York Evangelist, 20 September 1834.

27. Boston Recorder, 19 September 1834.

28. Cincinnati Cross and Baptist Journal of the Mississippi Valley, 5 September 1834.

29. Hudson Ohio Observer, 11 September 1834.

30. "Report of the Committee on Slavery," 20 August 1834, Lane Papers, Folder 15, MTS.

31. Henry B. Stanton to James A. Thome, 11 September 1834, File 16/5, Box 19, OCA.

32. Thomas J. Biggs to Lyman Beecher, 18 August 1834, Lane Papers, Folder 15, MTS; Mahan, Autobiography, p. 177; and Nathaniel Wright Papers, Letterbook 4, LC.

33. Lyman Beecher to Nathaniel Wright, 3 September 1834, Vertical File, Western Reserve Historical Society, Cleveland (hereafter cited as Vertical File, WRHS). Beecher's most recent letter to Wright had been concerned primarily with Beecher's denial of responsibility for the burning of the Ursuline Convent in Charlestown, Massachusetts, by a mob on August 11. It had been rumored that Beecher's anti-Catholic speeches in the East had incited the mob. Beecher feared that the Roman Catholics in Cincinnati might take advantage of the "temporary odium about abolition" at the Seminary and thus "accomplish mischief." Lyman Beecher to Nathaniel Wright, 15 August 1834, Nathaniel Wright Papers, Box 18, LC.

34. Ibid.

35. Lyman Beecher to Nathaniel Wright, 7 September 1834, Vertical File, WRHS.

36. Ibid.

37. Ibid.

38. Ibid. Beecher's ideas of cooperation of all antislavery advocates were shared by others, and in January, 1835, the American Union for the Relief and Improvement of the Colored Race was organized in Boston. Cincinnati Journal, 17 April 1835.

39. Wright's cautiousness is noted in an undated obituary in Smithson E. Wright, comp., "Obituaries of Cincinnatians," Cincinnati Historical Society. Wright had been chairman of the special committee, and later wrote

the most objectionable Order 2, which gave the
Executive Committee the power to expel any student
without cause. Lane Seminary, Minutes of Meetings
of the Executive Committee of the Board of Trustees,
Meeting of 9 August 1834, Lane Papers, Folder 15,
MTS; and Mahan, Autobiography, p. 182.

40. Nathaniel Wright to Lyman Beecher, 13 September 1834,
in Cross, ed. , Autobiography of Beecher, 2:245-46;
and Nathaniel Wright Papers, Letterbook 4, LC.
The attribution of Wright's authorship of this letter
is my own.

41. Morgan Neville was passing by the Seminary when he
saw the blacks enter the grounds, and, because he
knew the actions of the students were of interest to
the trustees, "I observed them more particularly. "
Morgan Neville to Jacob Burnet, 5 September 1834,
Nathaniel Wright Papers, Box 18, LC. Neville was
one of the leaders of the meeting which incited the
mob that destroyed Birney's press in Cincinnati in
July, 1836. Executive Committee of the Ohio Anti-
Slavery Society, Narrative of the Late Riotous Proceedings against the Liberty of the Press, in Cincinnati. With Remarks and Historical Notices, Relating
to Emancipation (Cincinnati: n. p. , 1836), pp. 24-25.

42. Henry B. Stanton to James A. Thome, 11 September
1834, File 16/5, Box 19, OCA; and Theodore D.
Weld to James G. Birney, 10 September 1834, in
Dumond, ed. , Letters of Birney, 1:134.

43. Theodore D. Weld to James G. Birney, 10 September
1834, in Dumond, ed. , Letters of Birney, 1:133.

44. Lane Seminary, Trustees Formal Minutes, Meeting of
the Executive Committee, 6 September 1834, LTS.
It was also voted that all matters of the Executive
Committee be considered "as confidential, " and that
a meeting of the entire Board be called for October 6.

45. Stanton believed that "The act which brought the matter
to a focus" was the visit by the blacks on the thir-
tieth. Henry B. Stanton to James A. Thome, 11
September 1834, File 16/5, Box 19, OCA.

46. [Tappan], Life of Arthur Tappan, pp. 228-31; quotations

from pp. 228, 230. Elizur Wright wrote, "we have just learned that Dr. Beecher is coming on, with great and mighty resolution to hush up the controversy between Abo. & Col. by another 'New Lebanon Convention.' He has succeeded in blinding the eyes of one of the delegates from England, it is said. But Anti Slavery men have been too well acquainted with the quagmires of Expediency and policy heretofore, to leave firm ground and plunge into them now." Elizur Wright to Amos Phelps, 20 August 1834, Elizur Wright Papers, v. 2, LC.

47. Lewis Tappan to Theodore D. Weld, 29 September 1834, Slavery Manuscripts, Box 2, New York Historical Society, New York.

48. Ibid.

49. Mahan, Autobiography, p. 178.

50. Lyman Beecher to Theodore D. Weld, 8 October 1834, in Barnes and Dumond, eds., Letters of Weld, 1:172-73.

51. Theodore D. Weld to James G. Birney, 6 October 1834, in Dumond, ed., Letters of Birney, 1:136-37; and Robert Boal to Franklin Y. Vail, 15 September 1834, Lane Papers, Folder 2, MTS. Boal added that he believed that the trustees "have (as we think) in this matter acted admirably & not untill [sic] it was absolutely necessary."

52. Henry B. Stanton to James A. Thome, 11 September 1834, File 16/5, Box 19, OCA.

53. Huntington Lyman to James A. Thome, 4 October 1834, File 16/5, Box 19, OCA.

54. Lane Seminary Trustees Formal Minutes, Meeting of 6 October 1834; LTS; Huntington Lyman to James A. Thome, 4 October 1834, File 16/5, Box 19, OCA; and Mahan, Autobiography, pp. 178-81.

55. Robert H. Bishop to Nathaniel Wright, 16 September 1834, Lane Papers, Folder 3, MTS.

56. Hudson Ohio Observer, 7 August 1834.

57. Lane Seminary, Trustees Formal Minutes, Meeting of 6 October 1834, LTS.

58. Ibid.; what appear to be rough drafts of the Standing Rules and Orders are in the Lane Papers, Folder 15, MTS.

59. Mahan, Autobiography, pp. 180-81; and Lane Seminary, Minutes of Meetings of the Board of Trustees, Meeting of 6 October 1834, Lane Papers, Folder 2, MTS. These minutes were notes taken by Wright on which the Formal Minutes were based. Wright's concern with Order 2 is evident in his remark to the Recording Secretary that "The Faculty should have a copy Immediately. Others will be filling their heads."

60. This "explanation" follows the Orders and Standing Rules in both the Lane Papers, Folder 15, MTS; and Lane Seminary, Trustees Formal Minutes, Meeting of 6 October 1834, LTS.

61. Ibid.

62. Ibid. Weld recognized this aspect of the new regulations. Statement of Reasons, p. 15.

63. Thomas J. Biggs to Franklin Y. Vail, 23 July 1834, Lane Papers, Folder 26, MTS.

64. Henry B. Stanton to James A. Thome, 11 September 1834, File 16/5, Box 19, OCA.

65. Lyman Beecher to Nathaniel Wright, 7 September 1834, Vertical File, WRHS.

66. Theodore D. Weld to James G. Birney, 6 October 1834, in Dumond, ed., Letters of Birney, 1:140.

67. Lane Seminary, Minutes of Meetings of the Executive Committee of the Board of Trustees, Meeting of 10 October 1834, Lane Papers, Folder 3, MTS.

68. Quoted in Cross, ed., Autobiography of Beecher, 2:246.

69. Mahan, Autobiography, p. 182; Cross, ed., Autobiography of Beecher, 2:247; and Cincinnati Journal, 15 May 1835.

70. Henry B. Stanton to James A. Thome, 11 September 1834, File 16/5, Box 19, OCA.

71. Tappan predicted to Amos Phelps that the students would leave if the laws were passed. Lewis Tappan to Amos Phelps, 10 October 1834, Phelps Papers, Ms. A. 21. 4, p. 62, BPL. Tappan may have told Beecher at their meeting on September 29. Beecher's statement to Weld that he was glad to learn that the students would decide what to do after the trustees had acted indicates that Weld had told him of the options the students were considering. Lyman Beecher to Theodore D. Weld, 8 October 1834, in Barnes and Dumond, eds. , Letters of Weld, 1:172.

72. Henry B. Stanton to James A. Thome, 11 September 1834, File 16/5, Box 19, OCA.

73. The number of students present on the first day of the term can only be estimated. A comparison of student lists, student requests for dismission, and Weld's statement that there were seventeen prospective students, indicates a total of sixty-three (forty-six from the previous year). Lane Seminary, Fourth Annual Report, pp. 25-28; Lane Seminary, Fifth Annual Report, pp. 31-32; student requests for dismission, 15, 16, and 17 October 1834, Lane Papers, Folder 15, MTS; Lane Seminary, Faculty Minutes, Meetings of 10 April through 17 October 1834, LTS; and Theodore D. Weld to James G. Birney, 20 October 1834, in Dumond, ed. , Letters of Birney, 1:146.

74. Mahan, Autobiography, pp. 182-83. This student was probably not Weld, who refused to request a dismission until the trustees had decided whether or not to expel him.

75. Theodore D. Weld to James G. Birney, 20 October 1834, in Dumond, ed. , Letters of Birney, 1:146.

76. Student requests for dismission, dated 15 and 16 October 1834, Lane Papers, Folder 15, MTS.

77. Emancipator, 4 November 1834.

78. Quoted in the Lowell Observer, and reprinted in the Emancipator, 18 November 1834.

79. The resolution was "discussed at some length" before it was withdrawn. Lane Seminary, Minutes of Meetings of the Executive Committee of the Board of Trustees, Meeting of 16 October 1834, Lane Papers, Folder 3, MTS.

80. Weld's request for dismission is in the Lane Papers, Folder 15, MTS.

81. Lane Seminary, Minutes of Meetings of the Executive Committee of the Board of Trustees, Meeting of 17 October 1834, Lane Papers, Folder 3, MTS; and "Declaration of the Faculty of Lane Seminary," Cincinnati Daily Gazette, 22 October 1834. This document was widely circulated and was included in Lane Seminary, Fifth Annual Report, pp. 44-45.

82. Emancipator, 28 October 1834.

83. George Clark to Theodore D. Weld, [January 1835] and 10 October 1884, Weld-Grimké Papers, Boxes 17 and 16, WLCL.

84. Statement of Reasons, p. 28. Stone received his dismission on November 13. Also on the thirteenth, Henry Cherry asked for and received another dismission (the first was on July 14), and Samuel F. Porter asked that his be dated in August. Earlier, on October 21, Henry P. Thompson requested a dismission, and gave as his reason his intention of entering Centre College in Danville, Kentucky. Lane Seminary, Faculty Minutes, Meetings of 13 November and 21 October 1834, LTS.

85. Ibid. Butts's request for dismission is dated December 9, and is in the Lane Papers, Folder 15, MTS. His request was granted the following day. Lane Seminary, Faculty Minutes, Meeting of 10 December 1834, LTS.

86. These figures were determined by consulting the student lists in Lane Seminary, Fourth Annual Report, pp. 25-28; Lane Seminary, Fifth Annual Report, pp. 31-32; and also Lane Seminary, Faculty Minutes, Meetings of 4 March through 10 December 1834, LTS.

87. Lane Seminary, Fourth Annual Report, pp. 25-28; Lane

Seminary, Fifth Annual Report, pp. 31-32; and Lane
Seminary, Faculty Minutes, Meeting of 11 June 1834,
LTS. Five of the students who entered had been of-
ficers of the Seminary's colonization society formed
in July. They were Lewis Bridgman, James H.
Mattison, Samuel C. Masters, Henry H. Spalding,
and Lewis L. G. Whitney. Cincinnati Journal, 11
July 1834. One, Hiram Babcock, was named a
colonizationist in a letter from Henry B. Stanton to
James A. Thome, 11 September 1834, File 16/5,
Box 19, OCA.

88. Apparently, four students, John M. Boal, Carlos Brainerd, Talbot Bullard and John E. Finley, with prominent relatives in the city, left because of the antislavery activities of the students. In addition, two
avowed colonizationists, Zerah K. Hawley and Enoch
S. Huntington, decided over the summer not to return. Cincinnati Journal, 11 July 1834; and Huntington Lyman to James A. Thome, 4 October 1834,
File 16/5, Box 19, OCA. Ten had left school in
the spring or summer because of illness, to teach
school, or other reasons. They were John C. Alexander, George W. Ames, Myron A. Gooding, Barton
Lee, Jacob Parsons, Josiah Porter, David Rowe,
Calvin H. Tate, H. St. John Van Dake, and Thomas
S. Williamson. Lane Seminary, Faculty Minutes,
Meetings of 4 March through 14 July 1834, LTS; on
Porter, see A. T. Norton, History of the Presbyterian Church, in the State of Illinois (St. Louis: W.
S. Bryan, 1879), p. 314; on Williamson, see Cincinnati Journal, 15 August 1834. Augustus Wattles had
left to work with the blacks in the city, and although
he signed a request for dismission, he was not considered a student by the Executive Committee, which
noted that he had not recited during the entire spring
term. Lane Seminary, Minutes of Meetings of the
Executive Committee of the Board of Trustees, Meeting of 20 October 1834, Lane Papers, Folder 3, MTS.
Another student, Burritt Hitchcock, had been in the
East for some time and learned of the rebellion
through the papers. Burritt Hitchcock to Samuel F.
Dickinson, 19 February 1835, Lane Papers, Folder
8, MTS. Isaac H. Wright had left the Seminary "before the explosion" and was "astonished" to see his
name attached to the students' Statement of Reasons.
Isaac H. Wright to Samuel F. Dickinson, 11 April

1835, Lane Papers, Folder 8, MTS. Finally, Edwin
Hutchinson had shot himself to death on September
20. Cincinnati Journal, 10 October 1834.

89. See student requests for dismission, 15, 16, and 17
October, and 9 December 1834, Lane Papers, Folder
15, MTS; Lane Seminary, Faculty Minutes, Meetings
of 17 and 21 October, 13 November, and 10 December 1834, LTS; and Statement of Reasons, p. 28.
The list of students who signed the Statement of Reasons is partially inaccurate. "Nearly one-half who
have authorised their names to be appended to the
document, have never seen it. " Cincinnati Journal,
2 January 1835. There may have been others like
Wright, who did not give permission to have his
name attached to the document, and Gooding, who
had received a dismission and left five and one-half
months before the rebellion.

90. These men were Henry Cherry, Samuel Fuller Porter,
and Joseph Warren. E. D. Morris, "The Foreign
missionary alumni of Lane Seminary, " Lane Papers,
Folder 10, MTS; File on Samuel Fuller Porter,
Alumni Records Office, Oberlin College, Oberlin,
Ohio; and Norton, Presbyterian Church in Illinois,
pp. 633-34.

91. Statement of Reasons, p. 23.

92. The following is a list of the "Lane rebels": James
M. Allan, William T. Allan, John W. Alvord, Ben-
jamin F. Arnold, Courtland Avery, Lewis Barnes,
Enoch N. Bartlett, Andrew Benton, James Bradley,
Lewis Bradley, Charles P. Bush, Lorenzo D. Butts,
Christopher C. Cadwell, William W. Caldwell, Ebe-
nezer B. Chamberlain, Uriah T. Chamberlain, Henry
Cherry, George Clark, John Clark, James S. Cook,
Charles Crocker, Amos Dresser, Amasa Frissell,
Jr. , Joseph D. Gould, Isaac Griffith, William Hamil-
ton, Aaron M. Himrod, Coleman S. Hodges, Augustus
Hopkins, David S. Ingraham, Deodat Jeffers, Russell
J. Judd, Elisha Little, Huntington Lyman, Alexander
McKellar, Charles W. McPheeters, Enoch R. Martin,
Israel S. Mattison, John J. Miter, James Morrison,
Abraham Neely, Lucius H. Parker, Joseph H. Payne,
Samuel Payne, Samuel Penny, Jr. , Algernon S.
Pierce, John T. Pierce, Ezra A. Poole, George G.

Porter, Samuel F. Porter, Marius R. Robinson,
Munson S. Robinson, Abner S. Ross, Charles Sexton,
Henry B. Stanton, Robert L. Stanton, James Steele,
Asa A. Stone, Sereno W. Streeter, James A. Thome,
Henry P. Thompson, Samuel H. Thompson, J. C.
Tibbils, John A. Tiffany, Giles Waldo, Josiah J.
Ward, Joseph Warren, Calvin Waterbury, Matthew
Watson, Edward Weed, Joseph Weeks, Theodore D.
Weld, Samuel T. Wells, George Whipple, and Hiram
Wilson.   Fletcher includes among the rebels Hiram
Foote, C. Stewart Renshaw, and Elisha B. Sherwood.
History of Oberlin, 1:183, n. 15.   Although Foote
and Renshaw may have been on the Seminary grounds
when the rebellion occurred, there is little evidence
to indicate that either was enrolled as a student at
Lane.   Evidence for Renshaw's having been enrolled
include the following: Lucy Wright to Elizur Wright,
3 April 1834, Elizur Wright Papers, v. 3, LC, where
Renshaw is described as "formerly student of Lane";
Theodore D. Weld to Gerrit Smith, 6 August 1839,
in Barnes and Dumond, eds. , Letters of Weld, 2:
780-81, which states that Renshaw "had just entered
at Lane when driven away by the laws"; and an obituary of Renshaw, Oberlin Evangelist, 29 February
1860, which states that he "studied at the Oneida
Institute, at Lane Seminary, we believe, and at Oberlin. "   Neither Foote nor Renshaw is mentioned in
Lane Seminary, Faculty Minutes, LTS, and the Executive Committee's instructions to the Steward to pay
"strict attention to the rules regulating the admission
of students" would seem to indicate that neither was
a student.   Lane Seminary, Minutes of the Executive
Committee of the Board of Trustees, Meeting of 10
October 1834, Lane Papers, Folder 3, MTS.   Sherwood did not even leave home to attend Lane Seminary
until October 15, 1834, and he admitted that he did
not leave Lane, where he was very happy, until "near
the close of the seminary year, " on May 19, 1835.
Elisha B. Sherwood, Fifty Years on the Skirmish
Line (Chicago and New York: Fleming H. Revel Co. ,
1893), pp. 23-25.   Both Foote and Renshaw were
very active in the antislavery movement.   See Myers,
"Agency System, " pp. 495-97, 525-28.

93.   Students went to schools such as Yale Divinity School,
Auburn Theological Seminary, Western Theological
Seminary, Miami University, Oneida Institute, Centre

The Lane Rebellion / 159

College, and, later, Oberlin Collegiate Institute.
Fletcher, History of Oberlin, 1:164-65; Huntington
Lyman, Sereno W. Streeter, Henry B. Stanton,
William T. Allan, James A. Thome, Samuel Wells,
Benjamin Folts, and George Whipple to Theodore D.
Weld, 8 January 1835, in Barnes and Dumond, eds.,
Letters of Weld, 1:185, 188 (hereafter cited as Folio
letter to Theodore D. Weld, 8 January 1835); and
Theodore D. Weld to James G. Birney, 23 January
1835, in Dumond, ed., Letters of Birney, 1:173.

94. Four students who requested re-admission included
     Robert L. Stanton (brother of Henry B.), Charles
     Sexton, Samuel Payne, and John A. Tiffany. Robert
     L. Stanton and Charles Sexton to the Faculty, 21
     October 1834, Lane Papers, Folder 8, MTS; Lane
     Seminary, Faculty Minutes, Meeting of 21 October
     1834, LTS; and Lane Seminary, Fifth Annual Report,
     pp. 31-32. When Sexton asked for re-admission,
     the faculty "resolved that he be advised to direct his
     attention to another pursuit." Lane Seminary, Facul-
     ty Minutes, Meeting of 21 October 1834, LTS.

95. Theodore D. Weld to James G. Birney, 20 October
     1834, in Dumond, ed., Letters of Birney, 1:146.
     The students were in Cumminsville by November 1.
     Diary of Benjamin Foltz, Entry of 1 November 1834,
     Robert S. Fletcher Papers, Box 17, Oberlin College
     Archives, Oberlin, Ohio (hereafter cited as Fletcher
     Papers, OCA); see also Cincinnati Journal, 7 Novem-
     ber 1834. Students at Cumminsville at one time or
     another included William T. Allan, John W. Alvord,
     Andrew Benton, William W. Caldwell, Uriah T.
     Chamberlain, George Clark, Russell J. Judd, Hunting-
     ton Lyman, Lucius H. Parker, John T. Pierce, Sam-
     uel F. Porter, Marius R. Robinson, Henry B. Stan-
     ton, Serono W. Streeter, James A. Thome, Edward
     Weed, Samuel Wells, and George Whipple. Augustus
     Wattles may have been present at times, as well as
     several prospective students who had refused to enter
     Lane. Emancipator, 23 December 1834; Samuel
     Wells, James A. Thome, William T. Allan, Marius
     R. Robinson, and John T. Pierce to Theodore D.
     Weld, 15 December 1834, in Barnes and Dumond,
     eds., Letters of Weld, 178-84 (hereafter cited as
     Folio letter to Theodore D. Weld, 15 December 1834);
     and Folio letter to Theodore D. Weld, 8 January 1835,

in Barnes and Dumond, eds., Letters of Weld, 1:184-94; and Uriah T. Chamberlain to Samuel F. Dickinson, 13 March 1837, Lane Papers, Folder 8, MTS. Cumminsville was a village which had grown up at the intersection of St. Clair's and Wayne's Trails. It is described as it was in the 1830s in H. W. Felter, "History of Cumminsville, 1811-1873,' in History of Cumminsville, 1792-1914, ed. John A. Herbert (n. p. : Raisbeck & Co., [1914]), no pagination.

96. Felter, "History of Cumminsville, 1811-1873," no pagination. That the students probably stayed at the "Hall of Free Discussion" is indicated by a letter of George Clark to Theodore D. Weld, [January 1835], Weld-Grimké Papers, Box 17, WLCL, in which he wrote: "Brother Weld be of good cheer the cause is going on here steadily. I am at last settled down in Lib. [erty] Hall. " Ludlow's daughter married Salmon P. Chase in 1846. Albert Bushnell Hart, Salmon Portland Chase, American Statesmen (Boston: Houghton Mifflin & Co., 1899), p. 40.

97. Theodore D. Weld to Lewis Tappan, 1 January 1870, in [Tappan], Life of Arthur Tappan, p. 236.

98. Folio letters to Theodore D. Weld, 15 December 1834, and 8 January 1835, in Barnes and Dumond, eds., Letters of Weld, 1:178-94. One of the former students found time to circulate a petition in the city asking Congress to abolish slavery and the slave trade in the District of Columbia. Emancipator, 14 April 1835.

99. Harrold, "Cincinnati Abolitionist," p. 175; and Oberlin Evangelist, 6 July 1859.

100. Folio letter to Theodore D. Weld, 8 January 1835, in Barnes and Dumond, eds., Letters of Weld, 1:193.

101. Volume of notes on theology, 1834-1840, Robinson Papers, Folder 6, WRHS.

102. Folio letter to Theodore D. Weld, 8 January 1835, in Barnes and Dumond, eds., Letters of Weld, 1:190.

103. Ibid., 1:193.

104. Ibid., 1:190-91.

105. In Fletcher Papers, Box 17, OCA.

106. Robinson Papers, Folders 2, 3, and 6, WRHS.

107. Ibid., Folder 2.

108. Ibid., Folder 3.

109. Huntington Lyman to James A. Thome, 4 October 1834, File 16/5 Box 19, OCA.

110. Emancipator, 28 October 1834.

111. Emancipator, 23 December 1834; and Folio letter to Theodore D. Weld, 15 December 1834, in Barnes and Dumond, eds., Letters of Weld, 1:181.

112. Ibid. The Statement of Reasons was published in the Emancipator, 6 January 1835, in numerous other papers, and in pamphlet. I have used the latter because it is paginated. By February, 1835, abolitionists in the East had circulated 4,000 extra copies of the Statement of Reasons. Emancipator, 3 February 1835.

113. Statement of Reasons, p. 28.

114. Ibid., pp. 3, 5.

115. Finney, "Sinners Bound to Change Their Own Hearts," pp. 18, 38.

116. Statement of Reasons, p. 5.

117. Ibid.

118. Beecher was reputed to have said, "Boys, you are right in your views, but most impracticable in your measures. Mining and quiet strategy are ordinarily better as well as safer methods of taking a city, than to do it by storm. It is not always wise to take a bull by the horns." Quoted in Greve, History of Cincinnati, 1:594. Cf. Beecher's comments on public opinion in "Resources of the Adversary, and Means of Their Destruction," in Sermons, pp. 433-35.

119. Finney, Lectures on Revivals, pp. 403-4, 457.

120. Statement of Reasons, p. 9.

121. Henry B. Stanton and George Whipple to Charles G. Finney, 10 January 1835, Finney Papers, Roll 3.

122. Ibid. Finney replied that he had seen the need for "a new race of ministers" and the necessity of a school to train them. "I hoped a good deal from Lane, but alas that expectation has failed." Charles G. Finney to George Whipple and Henry B. Stanton, 18 January 1835, Finney Papers, Roll 3.

123. Lane Seminary, Minutes of Meetings of the Executive Committee of the Board of Trustees, Meeting of 25 October 1834, Lane Papers, Folder 3, MTS.

124. Lane Seminary, Trustees Formal Minutes, Meeting of 5 November 1834, LTS; and New York Evangelist, 29 November 1834. A set of revised "Laws" was included in Lane Seminary, Fifth Annual Report, pp. 21-28.

125. "Laws," p. 24. Cf. Lane Seminary, Laws of the Cincinnati Lane Seminary (n. p., [1833]), p. 7.

126. Lane Seminary, Trustees Formal Minutes, Meeting of 30 October 1834, LTS.

127. Stowe, "Sketches," p. 233.

128. Boston Recorder, 5 December 1834. A year later there were only thirty students at the Seminary. Lane Seminary, Sixth Annual Report of Trustees of the Lane Theological Seminary, Cincinnati: and a Catalogue of the Officers and Students. December, 1835 (Cincinnati: Corey & Webster, 1835), pp. 23-24.

129. Cross, ed., Autobiography of Beecher, 2:247.

130. Emancipator, 11 November 1834. The students were not as "discreet" as Beecher had hoped, because his attempt to reclaim them was soon reported to the Emancipator.

131. Robert L. Stanton and Charles Sexton to the Faculty, 21 October 1834, Lane Papers, Folder 8, MTS.

132. Folio letter to Theodore D. Weld, 15 December 1834, in Barnes and Dumond, eds. , Letters of Weld, 1:183.

133. Lane Seminary, Trustees Formal Minutes, Meeting of 30 October 1834, LTS; and Cincinnati Journal, 7 November 1834.

134. Cincinnati Journal, 2 January 1835.

135. This was later printed in Lane Seminary, Fifth Annual Report, pp. 33-47.

136. Ibid. , p. 37.

137. Ibid. , p. 45, 44, 47, 42-43.

138. Ibid. , p. 47.

139. Lane Seminary, Fifth Annual Report, pp. 3-4. The faculty emphasized that "free inquiry and associated action can be enjoyed only in subordination to the great ends of the institution, and in consistency with its prosperity, of which it belongs to the faculty, and not the students, to judge. " Beecher, Biggs, and Stowe, "Statement of the Faculty, " p. 37.

140. Cincinnati Journal, 15 May 1835.

141. New York Evangelist, 29 November 1834; Boston Recorder, 5 December 1834; and Cincinnati Journal, 15 May, 19 June, and 24 July 1835. "The whole amount of our claim is this: that the faculty ought to have the control of the proceedings of the students, with the authority to interpose and direct, when they are satisfied that the interests of the institution and of the public demand it; and that when a difference of opinion arises as to the propriety of any measure, the opinion of the students is to yield to that of the faculty, and not the opinion of the faculty to that of the students. " Boston Recorder, 5 December 1834.

142. Cincinnati Journal, 24 July 1835.

143. 2d ed. (Cincinnati: Truman & Smith, 1836).

144. Lyman Beecher to Edward Beecher, December 1835,
     in Cross, ed., Autobiography of Beecher, 2:277-78.

145. Beecher, Plea for Colleges, pp. 89, 80-83.

146. Beecher, Biggs, and Stowe, "Statement of the Faculty,"
     p. 33; and Cross, ed., Autobiography of Beecher,
     2:241.

147. Mrs. William H. Beecher to Mr. and Mrs. Thomas
     Perkins, 3 November 1834 (copy), Cincinnati His-
     torical Society, Cincinnati. Beecher's son, Henry
     Ward, a student at Lane, called the seceding stu-
     dents "a little muddy stream of vinegar...." Quoted
     in Paxton Hibben, Henry Ward Beecher: An Ameri-
     can Portrait (New York: George H. Doran Co.,
     1927), p. 69.

148. Cincinnati Journal, 10 October 1834.

149. Cincinnati Chronicle and Literary Gazette, 1 November
     1834.

150. Cincinnati Catholic Telegraph, 30 January 1835.

151. Cincinnati Journal, 5 December 1834; Emancipator,
     25 November and 9 December 1834; and Hudson
     Ohio Observer, 1 January 1835.

152. Liberator, 3 January 1835.

153. Regarding the "Statement of the Faculty," Henry B.
     Stanton wrote, "Thinking that brother Leavitt would
     probably publish parts of their statement with com-
     ments, at the suggestion of the brethren, I gave
     him a big sheet full of new facts,..." Folio letter
     to Theodore D. Weld, 8 January 1835, in Barnes
     and Dumond, eds., Letters of Weld, 1:188.

154. New York Evangelist, 1, 8, and 29 November, and 27
     December 1834.

155. Cincinnati Journal, 5 December 1834; and Liberator,
     14 March 1835.

156. Boston Recorder, 7 November 1834.

157. Ibid.

158. Reprinted in the Cincinnati Journal, 17 October 1834.

159. Ibid. , 19 December 1834.

160. Ibid. , and 9 January 1835. Stowe complained of the unquestioned acceptance of the students' accounts of what had occurred over those given by the faculty. Cincinnati Journal, 15 May 1835.

161. J. R. Barbour to Franklin Y. Vail, 10 January 1835, Lane Papers, Folder 5, MTS. See also the letters from Daniel Noyes and Henry Herrick to Franklin Y. Vail, 27 January and 16 April 1835, Lane Papers, Folder 5, MTS.

162. George A. Avery to Franklin Y. Vail, 17 November 1834, Lane Papers, Folder 5, MTS. Avery was also the brother-in-law of Henry B. and Robert L. Stanton. Fletcher, History of Oberlin, 1:24.

163. George A. Avery to Franklin Y. Vail, 15 August 1835, Lane Papers, Folder 5, MTS.

164. Emancipator, 30 December 1834. It is not clear which of the Lane brothers this refers to.

165. Arthur Tappan to Franklin Y. Vail, 16 October 1834, Lane Papers, Folder 5, MTS. At a meeting of the Executive Committee on October 20, Wright and Vail were given the unenviable task of informing Tappan "of the true character & objects of the special laws [and] orders recently proposed for the government of Lane Seminary. " Lane Seminary, Minutes of Meetings of the Executive Committee of the Board of Trustees, Meeting of 20 October 1834, Lane Papers, Folder 3, MTS. Wright told Tappan that the Board had acted without the faculty because "the excited state of the populace here occasioned apprehensions of violence. " Nathaniel Wright to Arthur Tappan, 21 October 1834 (copy), Nathaniel Wright Papers, Box 61, LC.

166. Cross, ed. , Autobiography of Beecher, 2:316-17; and Arthur Tappan to Lyman Beecher, 20 January 1838, Lane Papers, Folder 5, MTS.

167. Lewis Tappan to Amos A. Phelps, 10 October 1834, Phelps Papers, Ms. A. 21. 4, p. 62, BPL.

168. Elizur Wright, Jr. to Theodore D. Weld, 9 January 1835, in Barnes and Dumond, eds., Letters of Weld, 1:194. When Wright saw the Statement of Reasons, he exclaimed, "O" what an advantage there is in truth and Straightforwardness!" Elizur Wright, Jr. to Elizur Wright, Sr., 5 January 1835, Elizur Wright Papers, v. 2, LC.

169. Hudson Ohio Observer, 7 August 1834.

170. Cincinnati Journal, 10 October 1834.

171. Emancipator, 20 January 1835.

172. Liberator, 21 February 1835; quotation from a letter of Leonard Woods, President of Andover.

173. Feuer, Conflict of Generations, pp. 323-24; Cutler, History of Western Reserve, pp. 24-30; Leonard, Story of Oberlin, p. 249; Waite, Western Reserve University, pp. 96-111; Sherlock Bristol, The Pioneer Preacher: An Autobiography, Introduction by J. H. Fairchild (New York: Fleming H. Revell, 1887), pp. 40-53; and Fletcher, History of Oberlin, 1:184-86.

174. New York Evangelist, 17 January 1835. Reference was made to Lane when the students of Bangor Seminary organized an antislavery society in the summer of 1837. Calvin Montague Clark, American Slavery and Maine Congregationalists: A Chapter in the History of the Development of Anti-Slavery Sentiment in the Protestant Churches of the North (Bangor, Maine: Published by the Author, 1940), p. 102.

175. Barnes, Antislavery Impulse, p. 103.

CHAPTER V

THE LANE REBELS

Overview

Of the seventy-five Lane rebels, little or nothing is
known about twenty-one, other than that they did not return
to the Seminary in the fall of 1834. Four students who withdrew recanted and re-entered the Seminary, but two of these
were later active in the antislavery movement. [1]* Of the fifty-
four rebels for whom some information is available, forty-
two engaged in antislavery activities after 1834. [2] From the
time of the Lane rebellion to the end of the Civil War, the
Lane rebels took part in--and sometimes led--numerous and
different antislavery endeavors.

Eighteen rebels worked as paid agents for antislavery
societies between 1834 and 1859, and served in that capacity
from as briefly as six months to as long as seven years. [3]
All these agents served during the mid and late 1830's. In
1835-1836 over half of the agents of the American Anti-Slavery
Society were Lane rebels, and the famous "Seventy," that
group of agents largely recruited and trained by Theodore
Weld in 1836, included ten rebels. [4] Some of these men,
such as William T. Allan, Marius R. Robinson, Sereno W.
Streeter, and Edward Weed, were also employed as agents
by state antislavery societies, as were a few men, such as
Lorenzo D. Butts, who had not been agents for the national
society. [5] It is possible that others may have acted as agents,
such as Augustus T. Hopkins and Andrew Benton, who were
active in the Ohio Anti-Slavery Society. [6]

In addition to working as professional agents for antislavery societies, many Lane rebels engaged in many organized activities which directly supported antislavery. These
activities included the leadership of local, state, regional,

---

*Notes to Chapter V begin on page 199.

and national antislavery societies. Uriah T. Chamberlain and Charles Crocker were officers in local societies. [7] Lorenzo D. Butts, Augustus T. Hopkins, John J. Miter, Marius R. Robinson, Henry B. Stanton, and George Whipple held responsible positions in antislavery organizations on the state, regional, or national level. [8]

Some of the rebels engaged in the preparation of antislavery propaganda. Theodore Weld's The Bible against Slavery (1837) and American Slavery as It Is (1839) were the best known publications. James A. Thome assisted Weld with Slavery and the Internal Slave Trade (1841), was responsible for most of Emancipation in the West Indies (1838), and prepared numerous speeches and pamphlets for the antislavery movement, such as "Address to the Ladies of Ohio" (1836), and Prayer for the Oppressed (1859). Henry B. Stanton published articles and lectures, as well as his testimony before the state legislature of Massachusetts, Remarks of Henry B. Stanton (1837).

Many of the rebels combined their antislavery with other religious and reform endeavors. At least fifteen were connected with the American Missionary Association (a society formed in 1846 to aid churches and missions which were explicitly antislavery), and its predecessors or auxiliaries. [9] George Whipple was Corresponding Secretary for the Association. [10] David S. Ingraham ministered to the free blacks of Jamaica and Hiram Wilson to runaways in Canada, while Uriah T. Chamberlain performed exceptional work as a home missionary to white churches in Pennsylvania. [11]

Lane rebels also participated in antislavery conventions. Thirty-three were delegates or officers at state or national antislavery societies' conventions, occasional political conventions, and special religious meetings which had slavery as their major focus. [12] For example, Andrew Benton was on the committee that convened a Christian antislavery convention in 1850. [13]

Lastly, Lane rebels encouraged other reform societies to denounce slavery. Lucius H. Parker wrote to the American Home Missionary Society, an organization which supported Congregational and Presbyterian churches on the frontier, but which had not taken a stand against slavery, that "God is in the movement in releasing us from slavery; & may it be found that we labor together with him. "[14]

Of the fifty-four Lane rebels for whom some biographical information is available, at least forty-eight became ordained ministers. [15]   As ministers, many of them worked informally for antislavery as part of their ministerial duties. The fact that so many of the rebels became clergy even after leaving Lane indicates the basis from which they supported antislavery.   The majority remained evangelical Christians throughout their lives, although there were a few who discarded evangelicalism, such as William T. Allan, and others who stretched evangelicalism to its limits, such as Edward Weed, who espoused perfectionism. [16]

Despite the differing kinds and degrees of antislavery involvement and eventual religious convictions, all of the rebels began their lives after 1834 with two common characteristics: evangelicalism and antislavery.   The relationship between these two characteristics changed over time, and varied among the rebels, but this changing relationship demonstrates some of the complexities of the antislavery movement. Some of these complexities will be examined in the following sections.

Antislavery or Evangelicalism

The students who congregated at Cumminsville in the winter of 1834-1835 had made no firm plans for continuing their theological studies after the spring of 1835. [17]   They had been given funds by Arthur Tappan, who had also approached Charles G. Finney about going to Ohio to teach them. [18]   A rumor had circulated since November that a new theological seminary would be established in the West which would guarantee free speech. [19]

Into this situation rode Rev. John J. Shipherd, one of the founders and the general agent for the newly established Oberlin Colony, located in Lorain County about thirty miles southwest of Cleveland. [20]   In December, 1833, two months before the Lane debate, Shipherd opened the Oberlin Collegiate Institute, an ambitious undertaking which included plans for an academic school, a collegiate department, and a theological department.   At the end of its first year of operation, over one hundred students were enrolled.   However, by June, 1834, primarily because Shipherd's financial ability did not equal his educational aspirations, the Institute "was in a more than precarious financial state. "[21]

When Shipherd arrived in Cincinnati on a fund-raising tour, about December 1, he made the acquaintance of the rebels and Mahan. He was impressed with Mahan, partly because Weld and the " 'glorious good fellows' " at Cummins-ville highly recommended him, and partly because the Cumminsville students stated that they would go to Oberlin and bring Arthur Tappan's financial support if Mahan were appointed President and John Morgan a professor. Little wonder that Shipherd believed his journey to Cincinnati had been providential. [22] In mid-December, he wrote to the Board of Trustees of Oberlin Institute requesting that it appoint Mahan President and Morgan a professor. He also requested the Board to pass a resolution, in accordance with the demands of Mahan and the rebels, granting freedom of speech to the students and the admittance of students without regard to race. [23]

Shipherd, accompanied by Mahan who had eagerly accepted the offer of Oberlin's Presidency, journeyed east to raise funds and to obtain the services of Charles G. Finney, recommended by Weld, as professor of theology. [24] In New York, Finney agreed to accept the appointment if the trustees would agree to "never interfere with the internal regulation of the school" and "that we should be allowed to receive colored people on the same conditions that we did white people;..." Arthur Tappan and others agreed to subscribe funds to endow and sustain the Institute if Finney accepted. [25]

From the point of view of the Oberlin trustees and students, Oberlin's future rested on the Institute's willingness to accept black students. Mahan, the rebels, Finney, and also Morgan[26] were forcing the trustees to make a commitment. At first they postponed action on the acceptance of blacks, which effectively signalled their rejection of it. [27] The majority of students already at Oberlin did not want blacks in the school, nor did some of the Colony's and Institute's leaders, including Philo P. Stewart, one of the founders. However, the awareness of the advantages which the accession of the rebels and others would bring, Shipherd's insistence on accepting the conditions laid down by Finney and his backers, and the work of leaders in Oberlin such as John Keep finally prevailed. In a dramatic meeting of the Board of Trustees, Keep cast the deciding vote to accept the proposed conditions. [28]

Although many of the Oberlin trustees and students were alarmed by the demand that black students be admitted,

Finney himself did not consider the race question the central issue. He believed that the most important goal for Oberlin was not antislavery, nor the acceptance of blacks as students, nor freedom of speech; instead Finney felt that it was the training of "a new race of ministers" which would promote revivalism and an activist practical theology. [29] For Finney, the issues of equal treatment irrespective of race and freedom of speech were subsidiary to the major goals of securing non-believers' conversions and Christians' acceptance of duty. Regarding the issue of slavery, Finney wanted the trustees to "let that subject alone for the faculty to manage," because interference with the faculty on any issue could harm Oberlin's major purpose: the training of a revival ministry. [30] Finney's intent was to insure control by those who knew best how to train the new ministry.   Free speech and antislavery were to be subsidiary to the creation of a revival ministry which would evangelize the West and, eventually, the world.

With proper assurances given, Oberlin's new faculty and prospective students made preparations to move to the new community in the spring of 1835.   Mahan returned from New York to Cincinnati in March, resigned his pastorate on May 1, and moved his family to Oberlin. [31]   Finney and Morgan arrived by early summer. [32]

On the trip north to their new school, the Cumminsville rebels attended the organization of the Ohio Anti-Slavery Society, April 22 through 24.   Those present included George Clark, Huntington Lyman, John T. Pierce, Henry B. Stanton, Sereno W. Streeter, Theodore D. Weld, and George Whipple, who were among the delegates from Hamilton County.   Hiram Wilson attended from Morgan County.   James A. Thome and William T. Allan were admitted as corresponding members representing Augusta, Kentucky, and Huntsville, Alabama, respectively.   Enoch N. Bartlett, Uriah T. Chamberlain, and Lucius H. Parker were also present to sign the "Declaration of Sentiments," written by Weld. [33]

The first major statement of the "Declaration" set forth the evangelical basis of antislavery.   "We believe Slavery to be a sin--always, every where, and only sin. " It was sin because it

> holds and uses men, as mere means for the accomplishment of ends, of which ends their own interests are not a part, --thus annihilating the sacred and eternal distinction between a person and a thing, a

> distinction proclaimed an axiom by all human con-
> sciousness--a distinction created by God ... This
> distinction slavery contemns, disannuls and tram-
> ples under foot. This is its fundamental element,--
> its vital principle, that which makes it a sin in it-
> self under whatever modification existing. [34]

The "Declaration" asserted that the sin of slavery had insinuated itself into all aspects of American life. The slave was a victim, but so also were the slaveholders, the nation, and the churches which compromised themselves by overt or tacit acceptance of slavery. The only responsible response to this sin was the immediate emancipation of the slaves, "the sacred right of the slaves and the imperative duty of their masters." Immediatism did not mean "that the slaves shall be deprived of employment and turned loose to roam as vagabonds." Instead, "they shall receive the protection of law...." The means of convincing people of the sin of slavery and the necessity of immediatism would be "by ceaseless proclamation of the truth upon the whole subject" and a dependence on God. [35]

Weld based the ideas of the sin of slavery, the duty of immediatism, and the means of obtaining an end to slavery on an evangelical theological foundation. Slavery was a sin because it contradicted God's universal decree that a person was a moral agent distinct from a thing. Slaveowners had the ability and duty to quit slavery immediately, just as they should leave off all other sins. The means of ending slavery was the proclamation of the truth, combined with the belief that "For success in this sacred enterprise, we cease from man, and look to God alone."[36]

After Weld closed the Ohio convention with prayer on Friday, April 24, the majority of the rebels in attendance travelled north to Oberlin, where they had been expected since the beginning of the month. [37] Upon their arrival, they built a one story, barracks-type dormitory, known as "Cincinnati Hall."[38] In June they participated in the formation of the Oberlin Anti-Slavery Society. [39]

In mid-July, five of the rebels at Oberlin, on Weld's recommendation, were commissioned agents by the American Anti-Slavery Society. [40] Some of them may have joined Weld as he toured northern Ohio after his return from the annual meeting of the Presbyterian Church in Pittsburgh in May. [41] Others journeyed to towns and villages near Oberlin to deliver

lectures against slavery. [42] In December, after attending a
series of lectures given by Weld at Oberlin and his course
of instruction at Cleveland, these Oberlin agents toured Ohio
and western New York. [43] Like Weld, all of them faced mobs,
and John W. Alvord had "such a mob-raising tendancy [sic]
that he needs some guardians. "[44] When the rebels ended
their agencies, about the time of the annual meeting of the
Ohio Anti-Slavery Society in Granville in late April, 1836,
those in Ohio had lectured over one hundred and sixty times
in at least fifty villages and towns. [45] During the year, the
number of local antislavery societies in Ohio had grown from
about twenty to one hundred and twenty, primarily because of
the activities of the agents in the state. [46] Allan, Alvord,
Streeter, Thome, and Weld, along with Augustus Wattles,
"were very largely responsible for creating antislavery sentiment in many areas of the state ... and thus in the last anal-
ysis, for abolitionizing Ohio. "[47]

Following the Ohio Anti-Slavery Society convention,
which ended April 28, most of the eleven rebels in attendance
returned to Oberlin. Thome first went home to Augusta, Kentucky, while Allan attended the anniversary meeting of the
American Anti-Slavery Society in New York. [48] On the whole,
the antislavery activities of the rebels during the summer of
1836 were minimal. At Oberlin the respective proponents of
antislavery and revivalism engaged in a conflict which demonstrated that evangelicalism was both a foundation of as well
as a limitation for antislavery.

James G. Birney was one of the antislavery advocates
who was disappointed that the Oberlin agents were leaving the
field. In late April, 1836, he wrote to Lewis Tappan,

> I greatly lament that our Oberlin agents have deter-
> mined to quit their field of labor till Autumn. They
> were doing well and advancing the cause with emi-
> nent success. We shall feel their loss during the
> approaching summer. They seemed to have looked
> to a temporary return to Oberlin with so much cer-
> tainty that I could not insist on their continuing their
> agency at this time. [49]

Weld had known that the Oberlin agents intended to lecture only during the winter vacation. Thome wrote that Weld
had even advised him "to spend the summer at Oberlin. "[50]
However, neither Birney nor Weld were aware that even the
agents' "temporary" labors in the antislavery field would be

contested by Finney, who wanted the agents, and Weld, to join him in conducting revivals. [51] The conflict which ensued between Finney and the advocates of antislavery revealed the tensions which existed in the relationship between evangelicalism and antislavery.

Although Finney had signed a letter to the American Colonization Society in 1833 critical of that Society's program for alleviating slavery, he had not signed a later, more immediatist statement. [52] Similarly, although he had denied communion to slaveholders and slave traders in December, 1833, his failure to endorse unconditionally the antislavery movement dismayed and angered others in the cause. [53]

Finney's first major public expression giving his reasons for holding antislavery views appeared in his Lectures on Revivals, published in 1835. In listing "hindrances to Revivals," he included poeple who "take wrong ground in regard to any question involving human rights" such as slavery. The providence of God had "brought it distinctly before the eyes of all men," and the church "is under oath to testify, and ministers and churches who do not pronounce it sin, bear false testimony for God. "[54]

The "low state of religion" in the country could be attributed, in part, to some churches taking "the wrong side on the subject of slavery...." To maintain and encourage a revival of religion, Finney presented ten "things which ought to be done," one of which was that the "churches must take right ground on the subject of slavery." Taking the "right ground" meant that Christians must "inform themselves on this subject," and that Christians and the churches "should meekly, but FIRMLY take decided ground" and "express before the whole nation and the world, their abhorrence of this sin. "[55]

Finney set very definite limits upon the extent to which the churches and Christians should advocate antislavery and rebuke slavery's defenders. The subject of slavery had to be introduced, but it should be done "meekly," "with discretion, and with great prayer," and once the church had decided to condemn slavery, it should "express her opinion upon the subject, and be at peace. "[56] Under no circumstances should slavery or any "diversion of the public mind" be introduced to such an extent that it would "hinder" a revival. [57]

Finney objected to such "diversions" because he believed only revivalism could promote religious conversion, which was the starting point for the individual's reception of the "whole gospel." An individual's conversion would be followed by the inculcation of "fundamental principles" which would enable him to act correctly on every moral and social issue. [58] An overemphasis on specific aspects of the gospel would cause the "Christian character" to lose its "symmetry."[59] The antislavery concern with the sin of slavery dealt with a portion of the gospel, but a portion which, if overemphasized, would be counterproductive to the "whole gospel," and, incidentally, to antislavery itself.

In the winter of 1836, Finney slightly modified his stance on the limits of antislavery agitation. Because of the Southern interference with antislavery materials in the mails, Finney began leaving out references to the "meekness" with which one should rebuke defenders of slavery, and he announced that Christians must continually bear witness against slavery.

> We will speak of it [the sin of slavery] and bear
> our testimony against it, and pray over it, and
> complain of it to God and man. --Heaven shall know
> and the world shall know, and hell shall know, that
> we protest against the sin and will continue to re-
> buke it, till it is broken up. [60]

Nevertheless, in spite of the increased severity of his remarks against slavery, Finney maintained the conviction that antislavery agitation should not be allowed to interfere with revivals of religion.

In addition, and in relation to the boundaries which he set on antislavery agitation, Finney believed that the sin of slavery did not include racial prejudice, which he claimed to be a matter of "constitutional taste," and not "a wrong 'per se.' or a wrong in itself."[61] This belief was based on "the reasonableness and utility of benevolence."[62] Benevolence towards others was "the exercise of the same regard to, and desire for their happiness, as we have for our own."[63] The happiness of each individual, and the total of all had a "relative importance" in relation to God's happiness, which was infinitely greater and more important. [64] Likewise, there were distinctions to be made in one's desire for the happiness of others based on the total amount of happiness which one's actions could achieve through benevolence.

> That you should regard your neighbor's happiness
> according to its real value, and the happiness of
> all mankind, according to the relative importance
> of each one's individual happiness, and the happi-
> ness of the whole, as much above your own, as the
> aggregate amount of theirs is more valuable than
> yours, is right in itself. [65]

Finney believed that antislavery activities increased
the total amount of happiness of mankind by working to free
slaves from slavery and slaveholders from the sin of slavery.
However, he believed the advocation of "amalgamation," or
the intermingling of blacks and whites, did not increase the
total amount of happiness in the world, but decreased it in
several ways. First, "to bring forward & insist upon Amalgamation just now would do infinite mischief to" abolition.
The cause "has already been greatly embarrassed by partially
bringing this subject forward," and the New York riots of
1834 and 1835 had been the results of the abolitionists' insistence on the doctrine of amalgamation. [66]

The introduction of a "collateral point," such as amalgamation, "is certainly unwise & unphilosophical" and "distract[s] the public attention with two questions at the same
time in stead [sic] of one. " "The true Philosophy of promoting & consummating an excitement & public action upon any
subject," a revival, for example, "is to confine the publick
[sic] mind to a point. "[67]

Besides hurting the cause of emancipation by diverting
public attention from the sin of slaveholding, the abolitionists'
insistence upon amalgamation raised the possibility of free
blacks suffering at the hands of mobs. "I am unwilling,"
Finney wrote, "to see the indignation & rage of the lawless
mob excited against" free blacks. [68]

Finally, Finney was concerned about the effect which
the principle of amalgamation would have on the spiritual
prosperity of the churches. [69] More than any other controversial subject, antislavery had the potential to cause dissen-
sion on the local and national levels. Indeed Finney experienced some conflict in his own church; Lewis Tappan's mixing
of black and white choirs in the Chatham Street Chapel in
May, 1835, caused some conflict after the riots in New York
in July. "And the first thing br [sic] Finney heard, when he
returned [from Oberlin], was this slander, " wrote Tappan.
Finney counseled moderation, which angered Tappan, who

stated, "After all, the choirs sat separately on the orchestra, the whites on one side and the colored on the other!"[70]   Finney wrote to Tappan's brother Arthur that the disagreement with Lewis about amalgamation "has destroyed my influence with him. "[71]

Weld found himself in the middle of this disagreement. While in Oberlin in November, 1835, he expressed a sympathetic understanding of Finney's position, and defended the revivalist against Tappan's accusations.   Although Weld believed that Finney had not done enough against the sin of slavery which Weld considered "Omnipresent, " he understood that it was Finney's "great business, aim and absorbing passion to promote" revivals.

> God has called some prophets, some apostles, some teachers.   All the members of the body of Christ have not the same office.   Let Delavan drive Temperance, McDowell moral Reform, Finney Revivals, Tappan antislavery, etc.   Each of these is bound to make his own peculiar department his main business, and to promote collaterally as much as he can the other objects.

Finney had not done as much as he should have for antislavery, but Weld admitted that neither he nor Tappan had done enough for other reforms, such as temperance. [72]

Weld agreed with Finney that a distinction had to be made between fundamental and secondary principles.   As Weld told the Grimké sisters, "the only common sense method of conducting a great moral enterprise is to start with a fundamental plain principle,... "[73]   Once the fundamental principle was admitted,

> then the derivative principles which radiate in all directions from this main central principle have been held up in the light of it and the mind having already embraced the central principle, moves spontaneously outward over all its relations.   No moral enterprise when prosecuted with ability and any sort of energy EVER failed under heaven so long as its conductors pushed the main principle and did not strike off until they got to the summit level. [74]

In November, 1835, Weld and Finney apparently came to an understanding.   Both admitted the necessity of emphasiz-

ing the major principle instead of secondary ones, that each
had his own major concern, and that each did not spend
enough time on collateral concerns. [75] Finney, however,
further believed that he and Weld had agreed on the necessity of minimizing the emphasis on amalgamation, a course
which would maintain peace in the churches. [76]

Finney probably informed Tappan of this understanding
during the winter. This, coupled with the information that
Weld had advised blacks not to attend the convention of the
Ohio Anti-Slavery Society the previous April, convinced Tappan that Weld had been swayed by Finney on the importance
of moderation on the issue of amalgamation. Tappan accused
Weld of racial prejudice, and Weld replied in exasperation,
"Really, after so long a time I must forsooth solemnly avow
my principles on this subject!!"[77] Weld had treated blacks
as equals all of his life. [78] It is clear that, although Weld
and Finney might have agreed that fundamental principles
should be promoted before secondary ones, Weld certainly
did not consider amalgamation a collateral or subsidiary issue. His explanation for sounding like a moderate showed
connections both with Finney, who believed antislavery and
amalgamation were separate, and with Tappan, who believed
that they were the same. The open social treatment of
blacks, Weld wrote,

> would be in its inevitable effect upon all classes
> and parties an ostentatious display of superiority
> to prejudice and a blustering bravado defiance,
> which would produce an entire misconstruction of
> motives, and turn public attention violently from
> the main point to a collateral one, which is true
> as really involves the principle of the main point,
> but which will be far more rapidly advanced as an
> appendage of the main point, than by making it the
> main point, and that the appendage. Crowd ahead
> the hub and you crowd ahead the spokes.... [79]

Strategically, amalgamation was a collateral point for Weld,
though ideally it "involves the principle of the main point" of
antislavery, which was "HUMAN rights. "[80]

Finney's and Weld's respective views on antislavery
provided the background for their controversy over whether
or not to promote revivalism or antislavery. Finney's major
objection to Tappan's antislavery was based on the belief that
the energies of reform-minded people should go into the pro-

motion of revivals of religion, which created the greatest
amount of happiness and dealt with the "whole gospel," and
that other reforms should be subsidiary to that.   Amalgamation was the issue which demonstrated to Finney that abolitionists were willing to sacrifice revivalism, and therefore
evangelical religion, for their cause.   This belief led Finney,
after trying unsuccessfully to moderate abolitionists' activities, to oppose his students' continued full-time antislavery
work to the detriment of religion. [81]

The first indication of Finney's opposition was a letter from Sereno W. Streeter, one of the Oberlin antislavery
agents, written to Weld in July, 1836.   "Mr. Finney,"
Streeter wrote, "is making a strong effort to have us Evangelize instead of abolitionizing ... He wants to take us out
and train us in the field. "[82]

One day after Streeter wrote, Finney addressed Weld
on the issue more fully.

> Br. Weld is it not true, at least do you not fear
> it is, that we are in our present course going fast
> into a civil war? ... Nothing is more manifest to
> me than that the present movement will result in
> this, unless your mode of abolitionizing the country
> be greatly modified.

Few of the abolitionists, he continued, were "wise men,"
and some had become "reckless," "denunciatory," and were
unwilling to cooperate.   The only way "to save our country
and affect [sic] the speedy abolition of slavery" was to make
abolition "an append[a]ge of a general revival of religion...."[83]

In early August, Allan, Alvord, Streeter and Thome
wrote to Weld to ask "Whether we should lecture [for anti-
slavery], or engage in protracted meetings and promote revivals of religion."   Finney had held two meetings with the
students to discuss this subject, "and speaks of himself as
being agonized about it."   Finney had said that he had come
to Oberlin specifically to train the students from Lane for a
new type of ministry, and that the part of the church which
favored revivals was waiting for those students "to enter upon
the work of Evangelists" and would be disappointed if they did
not do so.   Further, he had said emancipation would be effected "much sooner" if promoted through revivals.   The "only
hope of the country, the church, the oppressor and the slave
was in wide spread revivals. "[84]

Finney's arguments, "accompanied by his fervent earnestness," did not convince Thome or Allan to leave the antislavery field for revivalism, although Allan was "not fully at ease."[85] However, Alvord, Streeter, and Lyman at first sided with Finney.[86] Streeter gave his reasons for his own change in plans, which reflect both Finney's emphasis on the "whole gospel" and the evangelical foundation of antislavery. Christ had commissioned his disciples, wrote Streeter, "to observe all things...." Abolitionists charge that "ministers have not fulfilled their comission" because slavery still exists.

> But if we become Anti-Slavery lecturers merely,
> do we now lay ourselves open to the same charge?
> If we keep back faith and repentance, are we doing
> all for which Jesus Christ Commissioned us?

Second, when "full grown christians" are made, "upon them must our main reliance be placed for the Salvation of the world," which includes slavery's abolition. Third, Streeter expressed the view that slaveholders would not respond to the appeals and rebukes of antislavery advocates, but would only "relinquish their grasp" through "fear of God's eternal displeasure--yea thro' fear of eternal burnings."[87] To all of this, Alvord added, "In a word, can we not save souls, and save the slave too?"[88]

In early September, Weld wrote to the students at Oberlin trying to convince them to work for the antislavery cause, probably as members of the new group of agents Weld was then recruiting. Thome replied that "the influence of your letter with the Brethren, so far as I can discover ... has been to stagger them greatly in their new notions."[89]

Weld arrived in Oberlin about October 20 to counter Finney's influence and to recruit students for antislavery agencies. A dozen students were selected to become agents, and Weld "had a long talk with brother F.--" Finney had not been trying to make converts to his views "about Negro seats," and it appeared to Weld that Finney "is beginning to come right" on the amalgamation issue.[90]

Even though some students accepted antislavery agencies and Finney modified his stand on amalgamation, the revivalist's position on the promotion of revivals and the "whole gospel" eventually predominated over the advocacy of antislavery. Allan, Lyman, Streeter, and Thome again took agencies, as did six others.[91] However, only eleven rebels who attended

Oberlin were antislavery agents, out of a total of twenty-eight. Of those eleven, only Allan engaged in antislavery activities full-time after the 1830's.[92]

Because of what he considered to be the radicalization of antislavery to the detriment of evangelical religion, Finney became estranged from antislavery. This estrangement forced many of the rebels at Oberlin to make an "either-or" decision between evangelicalism and antislavery, something which Finney, and Weld, would rather have avoided. Finney preferred to incorporate antislavery into evangelicalism and, eventually, this was the position which most of the rebels assumed, including those not directly influenced by Finney after the rebellion. The transition from antislavery to evangelicalism incorporating antislavery is apparent in the later careers of those rebels who were antislavery agents.

From Antislavery to Evangelicalism

The Lane rebels had experienced a heightened awareness of the sinfulness of slavery because of the events which had transpired on Walnut Hills in 1834. This sentiment made antislavery the major preoccupation of about one-fourth of the rebels, those who were paid agents for antislavery societies, until the 1840's. [93]

With the establishment of a truce between Weld and Finney late in 1836, Weld recruited his former classmates to become agents as members of the famous "Seventy. " William T. Allan, Amos Dresser, Samuel F. Porter, James A. Thome, and Hiram Wilson were recruited by Weld before or during his visit to Oberlin in October, 1836.[94] Henry B. Stanton already had been active in the movement since the spring of 1835.[95] Edward Weed and Marius R. Robinson began agencies for the national society in Ohio in late summer, 1836, and John J. Miter began his work with the free blacks in the East in the fall.[96]

These rebels, along with those who held agencies for the state societies, operated in nine states, including Virginia, and in Canada.[97] Their activities included lecturing, debating, forming anti-slavery societies, soliciting funds, helping to educate and train free blacks, and collecting and disseminating information. All faced opposition and, occasionally, violence.

Because of the Lane debate and rebellion, all of the

rebels were familiar with the arguments and facts necessary
for lecturing and debating for antislavery. Some had received
additional training, such as that given by Weld in Cleveland
in 1835, during which prospective agents were led in "an investigation of the whole subject in all its relations" including
a "chapter on chemistry ... which was confined to the readi-
est way to deterge tar and feathers. "[98]

Lecturing, debating, and forming antislavery societies
were closely related activities, because the first two, if successful, usually led to the third. The intent of the lectures
was to convince, or "convert" the listeners to immediatism.
For example, Allan wrote, "The people are generally anxious
to hear and ready to be converted. "[99] After Weld's series
of lectures was concluded in Utica, New York, in 1836, Weed
wrote, "many of the good people seemed to feel as though
they had experienced a new conversion; and that an important
revival of religion had occurred among them. "[100] After one
of his own lectures, Weed stated that the "religious portion"
of his audience "felt as though their views of love to God and
man had been much enlarged, and their souls instructed in
righteousness. "[101]

The content of the lectures varied, depending on circumstances, but usually the rebels included their theological
understanding of man's place in God's universe as the basis
of their antislavery plea. Allan stated:

> The cruelty of which I complain, is the first, main
> principle of slavery; taking man from the position
> which God assigned him, and placing him among
> the things that may be owned as property. This is
> the crowning act of cruelty, the source, the fountain
> head of all the other horrors of slavery. [102]

At times, an indirect approach enabled the lecturer "to
do more for the cause I am pleading, than would have been
accomplished by a more direct effort. "[103] By beginning with
evangelicalism and then demonstrating the relationship of slavery to it, the lecturer could make a greater impact on church
members. For example, Weed "framed all my discourses so
as to bear more or less upon this great question [of slavery]. "
In his sermons,

> I have usually discussed great principles of action, --
> the power of truth, our duty to our fellow men, its
> perfect union and harmony with our duty to God, "and

the impossibility of separating in practice, the one from the other, ["]--the utter absurdity, and hypocrisy of the doctrine of piety, or love to God, whilst we "hate our brother, " ... [104]

Debates with anti-abolition advocates were welcomed by the Lane rebels, because their opponents were rarely as well-informed as they were, and a clear defeat of the anti-abolitionists made a great impression on the audience. Allan reported that he debated a "young man" who was "almost totally ignorant, not only of slavery, but of the principles of abolition which he had come to oppose. " He was forced to agree with Allan that the Bible controverted slavery. Then he asserted, in front of an audience which included many Christians, "that it [slavery] was not a question of right, but merely one of political expediency. " Allan wrote, "The result was good for the truth as usual, " and an antislavery society was formed. [105]

Besides lecturing, debating, and organizing societies, the Lane agents solicited funds. Some of them were particularly talented at raising money. Stanton was the financial agent for the American Anti-Slavery Society from 1837 to 1840. [106] Weed and Robinson were appointed financial agents in 1836, and Weed, although criticized for being too optimistic in his reports of the advance of the movement, was appreciated as an excellent fund raiser. [107]

Educating, aiding, and preaching to free blacks were other activities in which Lane rebels engaged. Robinson and Weed worked with Augustus Wattles in the Cincinnati black schools until they became agents in 1836. [108] Wilson was commissioned as an agent to work with blacks, mostly fugitive slaves, in Canada. He spent the rest of his life there feeding, clothing, teaching and preaching to blacks, and was supported only by the beneficence of friends after his commissions from the American Anti-Slavery Society and, later, the American Missionary Association were terminated in 1838 and 1853, respectively. [109] Miter was commissioned to work "among the free people of color" in Troy, New York, and in Newark, New Jersey. [110]

Some of the rebels were active in the propagandizing of the movement. James Thome was second only to Weld among the Lane rebels as a propagandist for antislavery. After serving as agent for the national society, he spent the summer of 1836 resting and completing the theological course

at Oberlin.[111] In the middle of July, Thome asked Weld if
he should go "to the West Indies, and act as correspondent
for some of the Anti-Slavery Papers?"[112] The idea of sending someone to report on the effects of emancipation in the
West Indies had been suggested before, even by Weld.[113]
Thome's willingness and his recognized ability made for a
combination of availability and opportunity for the antislavery
movement to prove the safety of immediatism.[114]

In late November, 1836, Thome and Joseph H. Kimball, former editor of the Herald of Freedom, sailed for the
West Indies. They stopped first at St. Thomas and spent a
short time observing slavery there. From St. Thomas they
sailed to Antigua, which had experienced immediate emancipation; Barbadoes, where the government had established a
successful apprentice program for its blacks; and Jamaica,
where the government had not succeeded in its own apprentice
program. The two men interviewed hundreds of people, including governors and public officials, missionaries, and former slaves, and they mailed back numerous reports for publication in the United States.[115]

Thome and Kimball returned to New York after six
months, in June, 1837, and were requested by the Executive
Committee of the American Anti-Slavery Society to prepare
a report for publication.[116] Because of Kimball's ill health
(he died in 1838), most of the work fell to Thome.[117] By
December the manuscript of nearly one thousand pages was
nearly completed, and Thome returned to his father's home
in Kentucky.[118] Weld edited the report "with an unsparing
hand," and reduced it to one-half of its original length.[119]

Emancipation in the West Indies was considered influential because it convincingly demonstrated, for the abolitionists, the safety of immediate emancipation. Henry B. Stanton said the book was "doing wonders" and contained "truth
enough to convert the nation."[120] Weld believed that the book,
"more than any other published in the Country, has advanced
the Anti Slavery Cause."[121] The Executive Committee of the
American Anti-Slavery Society thought Emancipation was so
important that it ordered a second printing of one hundred
thousand copies.[122]

Writing for the antislavery cause did not free Thome
from the dangers faced by those in the movement. In 1839
he fled Oberlin, where he was a professor, because of a rumor that he would be extradited to Kentucky for advising a

slave to flee. [123]   Other Lane rebels who advocated antislavery found themselves in occasional jeopardy.   While lecturing,
they often experienced the "usual paraphernalia" of noise,
eggs, and threats from people trying to disrupt their meetings,
and several rebels suffered greatly at the hands of mobs. [124]
Weld faced mobs more often than the others. [125]   Dresser,
before he became an agent, was publicly whipped in Nashville,
Tennessee, for possessing abolitionist materials. [126]   Alvord
awoke one night and discovered "the mob was entering my
room." He was kidnapped and threatened with tar and feathers. [127]   None of these men was injured as seriously as Robinson, who, in 1837 in Berlin, Ohio, was beaten, tarred and
feathered, driven ten miles out of town, and told never to
return.   In spite of his wounds and his abductors' threats,
Robinson returned to Berlin seven days later to give another
scheduled lecture. [128]

Robinson's dedication to antislavery is representative
of that of about one-fourth of the Lane rebels in the 1830's.
During the 1830's and 1840's, however, a transition occurred
among most of the rebels who considered themselves full-
time antislavery advocates.   Although their zeal for the cause
did not decline, the amount of time they devoted to antislavery
did.

There were numerous reasons for this transition.   Part
of it can be attributed to the change in tactics that occurred
with the decentralization of the movement which greatly reduced the number of agents.   There were fewer agencies
which the Lane rebels could fill.   Likewise, the politicizing
of the antislavery movement provided few roles for most of
the rebels, who objected to politicians because of the latters'
willingness to compromise principles. [129]   Evangelicalism's
demand that all connection with sin be discontinued made politics an illicit enterprise, and the attitude of most of the rebels towards lawyers and politicians was like that of Weed,
who wrote a close friend, "I am afraid if you become a lawyer and a politician you will lose your soul."[130]   Another
reason for the decrease in antislavery activities among the
rebels was the necessity of making a living and providing for
their families.

Nevertheless, changes such as decentralization, politics, and family responsibilities do not account completely for
the decline in antislavery activities among the most active
rebels.   It was still possible to remain committed to the
movement full-time, in spite of changes, as the careers of

Wilson and Robinson suggest.[131] It appears that a resurgence of evangelicalism displaced antislavery as the major focus of concern. Whether the result of discouragement because of the difficulties of antislavery, an increased theological awareness, or, in some cases, an interest in Oberlin perfectionism, some of the rebels moved from antislavery to the "whole gospel" of evangelicalism in which antislavery was a part.

Sixteen of the rebels most involved in antislavery (i. e. those who were agents) were ordained ministers, and fifteen of these pastored churches during the 1840's and 1850's.[132] Their later involvement with antislavery was more sporadic, and was usually conducted in the context of evangelical enterprises, such as working to insure the official condemnation of slavery by religious conventions or reform societies, preaching antislavery sermons, and writing and publishing antislavery tracts.

This transition from antislavery to evangelicalism is illustrated most clearly in the careers of James A. Thome and Edward Weed, who typified the Lane rebels who were full-time advocates for antislavery. Between them they engaged in most of the activities of antislavery agents. Both had taught in the black schools of Cincinnati, both became agents because of their evangelicalism, and both remained involved in antislavery, after the completion of their agencies, as part of their normal ministerial duties.

In the fall of 1836, during the conflict between Finney and Weld regarding the relationship of antislavery to evangelicalism, Thome wrote ecstatically of his love for the antislavery cause.

> For the past 3 years, I have walked in a new world. My path has turned with delight. Every foot-tread has touched some spring and revealed fresh treasures of happiness. Life has been rapture. I have scarcely felt trouble; when it has come, it has fallen upon me like the tender snow-flake--so gently. If God should now give me a thorn in the flesh, surely I should not murmur.[133]

Sometime during the autumn, and before his fact-finding tour to the West Indies, Thome experienced another conversion. He told Finney that "I feel daily that Christ is precious--unutterably precious ... I think I have felt a new spirit, & lived a new life." In referring to his preparation of Emancipation in the West Indies, Thome expressed his sentiments regarding the relationship between antislavery and evangelicalism, which clearly illuminate the change which the rebels experienced. He hoped that Emancipation "will promote the general cause of Christ as well as the immediate interests of the oppressed. " Although his views regarding the antislavery movement had not changed materially, "I can no longer feel satisfied to labor in a partial enterprise. I want to know nothing but Christ crucified. --"[134] This was a considerable turnabout for the man who had written to Weld regarding his opposition to Finney's attempts to have his students evangelize instead of lecture, "As for myself. I am firm. "[135]

Earlier, Thome said, he had doubted the "propriety" of any efforts to end slavery "in any associated capacity distinct from that of the church. " By February, 1839, he recognized that his hopes that the church, ministry, and religious press would work to end slavery were unrealistic. Nevertheless, he still disagreed with Weld and other abolitionists, and believed that Christians "would further the interests of the oppressed more effectually by preaching the Cross--the whole Cross I mean--than by forming Anti Slavery Societies composed indiscriminately of Christians, worldlings and infidels. "[136]

Thome continued to engage in antislavery activities after 1839, but, except for a period when he fled from rumored prosecution, these efforts were part-time and often in connection with other religious concerns. For example, from 1843 to 1848 he was secretary of the Western Evangelical Missionary Society. This society had been organized, in part, because of the refusal of the American Board of Commissioners for Foreign Missions to take a stand against slavery, and it eventually merged with the antislavery American Missionary Association. [137] Thome preached the major sermon at the annual meeting of the American Missionary Association in Chicago in 1855, was offered a Secretaryship in that society in 1863 (which he declined), and went to England and Scotland to raise funds for it in 1867-68. [138] He also helped organize and attended Christian Antislavery Conventions. [139] In his church, in the Western Reserve General Association, and in the Cleveland Congregational Conference Thome urged the adoption of antislavery resolutions. [140] Finally, he preached antislavery sermons and wrote essays for numerous occasions, such as the execution of John Brown, and on many antislavery topics, such as the church's relationship with the sin of slavery. [141]

In addition to Thome, Edward Weed illustrates the
transition from antislavery to evangelicalism as the major
focus of concern of the full-time advocates from the Lane
rebellion. After the students had left the Seminary in 1834,
Weed had gone from working in the black schools of Cincinnati to lecturing for antislavery. [142] While touring Ohio in
1836, as an agent for the American Anti-Slavery Society, he
lectured near Mansfield, where his growing belief that antislavery was an integral part of the gospel message was reinforced by the responses of "the religious portion" of his audience. "I am more than ever convinced," he wrote to his
wife, "that pleading the cause of the poor and needy is not
inconsistent with preaching the gospel, but that it is an indispensable part of the minister's duty."[143]

By February, 1838, Weed had "decided to leave my
agency as soon as possible consistent with the good of the
cause."[144] Despite entreaties from both Weld and Stanton
to remain in the field, he accepted a call from the Free
Presbyterian Church of Mt. Vernon, Ohio, in May.[145]

There were several reasons for his decision to leave
his full-time antislavery activities. Physical exhaustion was
one, although he remonstrated with himself for his weak-
ness.[146] Another reason was his desire to have more time
for study and for "the blessedness of sweet silence of mind
and loneliness, where none but God is present."[147] He was
also coming under the influence of the holiness movement,
which was leading him, through its insistence on self-exami-
nation, to an awareness and appreciation of the content of the
"whole gospel."[148]

Weed maintained an interest in antislavery during the
next twelve years, until his death in 1851. He lectured occasionally at black Sabbath schools, lectured and debated for
the movement, and attended conventions.[149] For a short
time he solicited funds for Gamaliel Bailey's National Era, the
semi-official paper of the American and Foreign Anti-Slavery
Society.[150] He was also on the first Executive Committee
of the American Missionary Association.[151] Finally, Weed
wrote articles, such as the "Report on Antislavery Memorials," which criticized the American Board of Commissioners
for Foreign Missions for its implicit support of slavery.[152]

Like Thome, Weed moved from antislavery to the
"whole gospel." His career indicates that he still believed
that antislavery was "an indispensable part of a minister's

duty, " but where the emphasis was on "indispensable" in July, 1836, by February, 1838, the emphasis was on "part. " Though antislavery was a part of a minister's duty, it was not the only, or even the major part of that duty. Evangelicalism, which had provided the impetus and groundwork for the antislavery of the Lane rebels, limited further antislavery endeavors by asserting its own demands.

Antislavery a Part of Evangelicalism

Thome and Weed illustrate the eventual position of nearly all of the Lane rebels regarding the relationship between evangelicalism and antislavery. Most emphasized an evangelicalism which contained antislavery, but the degree to which antislavery was asserted as a part of evangelicalism differed greatly, and was mirrored in the kinds of antislavery activities in which the rebels participated after the 1830's.

The American Missionary Association and its antecedents and auxiliaries provided opportunities for fifteen rebels to express their antislavery within the framework of evangelicalism, and Lane rebels played significant roles in each of the societies which formed that Association. [153]

In 1837, David S. Ingraham established an independent, self-supporting mission for the freed slaves in Jamaica, West Indies. In this he was aided by, among others, Amos Dresser. In addition to preaching and itinerating, Ingraham supervised a day school, an evening school, and a Sabbath school. Never in good health, he returned to the United States in July, 1841, and died at Weld's home, appropriately, on August 1, the anniversary of the emancipation of blacks in the West Indies. [154] Ingraham's mission was not able to sustain itself, and in 1844 a "Committee for West Indies Mission" was formed to continue his work. [155]

Another antecedent of the American Missionary Association was the Union Missionary Society. In 1842, James Steele headed an expedition to Sierra Leone in Africa. Supported by the Union Missionary Society, the mission's purposes were to return the survivors of the slaveship Amistad to their homes, and to establish mission stations in Africa. After unsuccessfully attempting to buy lands from the local chiefs (who wanted payment in liquor and tobacco), Steele became ill and had to return to the United States, but the mission was established. [156]

A third antecedent of the American Missionary Association was the Western Evangelical Missionary Society. Formed at the annual meeting of the Western Reserve Association in 1843, this Society's purpose was "to prosecute missionary operations among the western Indians, and in other parts of the world,... " It differed from the American Board of Commissioners for Foreign Missions in its decision not to "solicit or knowingly receive the wages of oppression, especially the price of the bodies and souls of men, for the prosecution of the work of the Lord. " George Whipple was elected Chairman of the Executive Committee and James A. Thome was its Secretary. Rebels who became members of the Board of Managers included Sereno W. Streeter, Ebenezer B. Chamberlain, Uriah T. Chamberlain, and Whipple. U. T. Chamberlain and Israel S. Mattison were the Society's agents, and George Clark was its "General Missionary. "157

At the Second Convention for Bible Missions, held in Albany, New York, in September, 1846, representatives of these organizations and other "friends of missions" formed the American Missionary Association. Its primary object "shall be to send the Gospel to those portions of our own and other countries which are destitute of it, or which present open and urgent fields of effort. " Requirements for membership in the new society included the profession of "evangelical sentiments, " faith in Jesus Christ, non-alignment with slavery "or in the practice of other immoralities, " and the contribution of funds. In all of its activities, the American Missionary Association would "endeavor particularly to discountenance slavery,... "158

Joseph H. Payne, a Lane rebel, was elected president of the Convention, and stated the reasons for organizing still another missionary society in the United States. The American Missionary Association was formed, Payne said, "for the propagation of a pure and free Christianity,... " A "pure" Christianity would exclude those who practiced or ignored all types of sin, including those sins of slaveholding, polygamy, and caste. A "free" Christianity, based on a Biblical model, would be able to exclude such sins because it would not be under a "practical Episcopal superintendency, " or closed Board of Managers, practiced by missionary societies such as the American Board of Commissioners for Foreign Missions. 159

Several Lane rebels were involved in the organization and administration of the American Missionary Association.

Payne, as noted, was president of the convention which organized the Association. Edward Weed was a member of its first Executive Committee. [160] Neither of these was as influential in the activities of the American Missionary Association as George Whipple, Principal of the Preparatory Department and Professor of Mathematics and Natural Philosophy at Oberlin. He became Corresponding Secretary of the Association shortly after its organization, and was reelected to a secretaryship at each annual meeting until his death in 1876. Besides editing the American Missionary, Whipple helped establish policy, selected missionaries, settled disputes, inspected missions, and even sent money out of his own pocket to aid missionaries in financial distress. [161]

Whipple believed that the way to effect reforms was through the application of evangelical principles. In 1865, for example, he objected to the circular sent out containing the "Constitution of the American Freedmen's Aid Commission" because "The responsible management of the society, [is] left in the hands & too limited a number of men and those of a business, rather [th]an Evangelical Xn [sic] character...."[162] "To every age," he wrote, "is given an opportunity to make its mark for God and humanity, and if it fails to see its time & opportunity, the prvilege [sic] passes to another." He saw that the duty for his own age had been working for the freedom of the slaves "thru the exercise of ch.[ristian] benevolence & the practical application of the blessed Gospel & the great truths universally applied of the Dec.[laration] of Independence."[163] As Secretary of the American Missionary Association, Whipple adhered to the idea that antislavery could be implemented best through, and as a part of, evangelicalism.

Besides Payne, Weed, and Whipple, twelve other rebels were involved directly with the American Missionary Association. Hiram Wilson was commissioned by the Association as a foreign missionary in Canada. [164] Andrew Benton was a member of the Executive Committee and agent of the Western Home and Foreign Missionary Association in Cincinnati, which was affiliated with the American Missionary Association. [165] Amos Dresser and Lucius H. Parker performed services as collecting agents for the national Association, and Parker was also agent and member of the Executive Committee for another affiliated society, the Illinois Home Missionary Society. [166] Thome spent a year in England as a collections agent. [167] Enoch N. Bartlett, Uriah T. Chamberlain, George Clark, Israel S. Mattison, Samuel F. Porter, James Steele, and

Samuel H. Thompson, as well as Payne, received support as home missionaries, and ministered either to small churches in the Old Northwest and the West, or to freedmen in the South. [168]

In addition to working as officials or missionaries of the American Missionary Association, Lane rebels supported antislavery in other ways. One of the most common activities was the attending of conventions which had antislavery as their focus. Thirty-three of the rebels attended such conventions, which ranged from Christian antislavery assemblies to Liberty Party conventions. [169] A few of the rebels, such as Stanton, Weld, Parker, and Lorenzo D. Butts were involved in politics. [170] Others participated in other reform activities which were the result of antislavery or were connected with it. Dresser became an avowed pacifist, partly because of the whipping he had received in Nashville in 1835 for being an abolitionist. [171] John W. Alvord became secretary of the Boston branch of the American Tract Society when it broke away from the New York branch in a dispute over the slavery issue. [172] Lane rebels also criticized benevolent societies for implicit support of slavery, and encouraged them to condemn that sin. Ingraham was one of the first to question publicly the policy of the American Board of Commissioners for Foreign Missions regarding slavery. [173] Other rebels, such as Lucius H. Parker, Joseph H. Payne, Samuel H. Thompson, and Christopher C. Cadwell, encouraged the American Home Missionary Society to condemn slavery. [174]

Most of the rebels performed antislavery work as part of their normal ministerial duties. [175] Slavery was considered a sin, but not the only sin, and was often spoken of in the context of other issues of the day. Enoch N. Bartlett, for example, once announced a series of meetings to be held in his church on topics such as war and peace, the Christian's relation to civil government, church polity, the morality of commercial transactions, and fellowship with slaveholders. "The whole design of these meetings will be to hold up prominently and in connection, some of the fundamental principles of Christian morality and to give their practical effect upon the heart and conscience. "[176]

The extent and character of the part-time antislavery work of the Lane rebels is best illustrated, not in the recounting of separate episodes, but in the careers of individuals. On the one hand, Christopher C. Cadwell represents those rebels whose careers included a minimal amount of antislavery activities. Uriah T. Chamberlain, on the other hand, was one of those who performed extensive antislavery work within the context of his ministry.

Following the rebellion, Cadwell had stayed at Cumminsville until late December, 1834, when he returned home to New York. He was licensed and then ordained by the Synod of Central New York, and preached in his home church in Lenox for eighteen months. [177] He was also a delegate to the annual meeting of the New York Anti-Slavery Society in October, 1836. [178] Later that year he moved to Kingston, Upper Canada, where he remained sixteen months. In the spring of 1838, he "started for the west. "[179] With commissions from the American Home Missionary Society from 1841 to 1870 he pastored churches in Wisconsin and Illinois. [180]

His interest in and support of antislavery were not very strong while he was in the west. This was due, partly, to his location on the frontier, where slavery appeared to be a sin far removed from the everyday problems with the environment, and the much more immediate issue of intemperance. In addition, Cadwell's dependence on the American Home Missionary Society for support may have inhibited his desire to aid the antislavery cause. Finally, Cadwell's determination to present the "whole gospel" decreased the amount of time and effort he could devote to antislavery. [181]

Nevertheless, he did aid the movement. Perhaps encouraged by memories of the Lane rebellion and the renewal of his acquaintance with George Whipple, Cadwell prodded his congregation to support the antislavery American Missionary Association. [182] He also distributed copies of the American Missionary, and even served as a collections agent for the Genius of Liberty, [183] the paper of the Illinois Anti-Slavery Society. Writing to George Whipple in 1860, Cadwell expressed the sentiments of one still dedicated to an antislavery based on evangelicalism:

> We must still keep up the war cry, & push the enemy to the wall[.] God is with us--the work must go on[.] Oppression has run mad & I fear will become its own hangman[.] The Lord reigns let the earth tremble. [184]

Uriah T. Chamberlain is illustrative of the rebels who performed a considerable amount of antislavery labor within their callings as ministers. After the rebellion, Chamberlain spent the winter of 1834-35 in Kentucky, then "resided for a season" in Cincinnati, and finally entered Oberlin. [185] There he was secretary of the Oberlin Anti-Slavery Society for two years. [186] In the fall of 1836 he experienced another conversion, began preaching a year later, and was ordained, after graduating from the Seminary, in February, 1838. [187] During the next fifteen years he pastored churches in seven different towns in central and northeastern Ohio, was "scribe" of the Congregational Association of Central Ohio, served as moderator of the Western Reserve Association, and participated in revivals, and "Christian conventions. "[188] His antislavery activities during this time included working as a manager and agent for the Western Evangelical Missionary Society, and working for resolutions of the Congregational Association condemning slavery. [189] More important, he "preached"

> ... in the region where I commenced as a pastor--
> and spent ten years of my ministry--Having preached
> in all the churches thereabouts. & been mobbed--
> and egged and scarred & wounded for having preached
> what the Lord annointed [sic] me to preach if he ever
> annointed [sic] me at all--viz. "deliverance to the
> captives, and the opening of gates to them that are
> bound, and that the oppressed should go free--&c. "
> When it cost something to be an antislavery man and
> minister. [190]

Beginning in late 1853, Chamberlain worked as a missionary under the auspices of the Western Home and Foreign Missionary Society (of which Andrew Benton was corresponding secretary) and the American Missionary Society. [191] For over eight years he pastored Congregational churches in six towns in Pennsylvania, and was an itinerant missionary for the Congregational Association of Western Pennsylvania. [192] Although he never had more than fifty-four members in any one church, at times he had five preaching stations. [193] Chamberlain was also a successful revival preacher, although denominations other than his own often benefitted from his work. In response to this he wrote, "But I do not so much care where they [i. e. converts] go to if they do not go to the Devil. "[194] In addition to his other extensive pastoral labors, Chamberlain superintended ten Sabbath schools which had six hundred and seventy-two pupils and ninety-four teachers. [195]

Chamberlain's antislavery activities were closely tied to his ministerial duties. This connection is apparent in the description of his work in the Annual Report of the American

Missionary Association, which, in 1857, referred to his success, under God's blessing, in the "salvation of souls," temperance and antislavery.[196] In revivals, Chamberlain included sermons on antislavery as a matter of course. During
one revival in Randolph, Pennsylvania, in 1856, he preached
two or three sermons which dealt wholly with slavery, and
these "seemed to deepen the work of revival." When the confession of faith was read to the new converts, some "inquired
if there was no article on antislavery. As there was none,
an article was proposed and adopted by the church, making
slavery a test before the new converts could unite."[197]

Chamberlain described himself as "an Antislavery minister," which, along with his Congregational affiliation, dis-
qualified him from the association of most ministers in his
area, particularly

> those who maintain that "slaveholding & slave buying
> & slave selling" "are no bar to christian communion
> and pulpit labor" And who "dont want the subject
> agitated in my church" & "would be sorry to have
> any thing said on the subject in my pulpit even in
> prayer" "Not even about the compromise & Nebras-
> ka enactments" and yet who are as "good antislavery
> men as anybody" &c--[198]

His ostracism from ministers such as those he described did
not bother him. In fact he relished having to "face the Devil"
whenever he had the opportunity.[199] When other preachers
failed to condemn slavery, Chamberlain spoke out. In 1856
when Preston Brooks assaulted Charles Sumner in the United
States Senate, Chamberlain responded by giving condemnatory
sermons in a half dozen towns. He wrote, "As there is no
other minister (as the people express it) who will speak out
fully" on such important issues, "I have many calls."[200]

One of his calls was not an invitation to lecture. On
one occasion Chamberlain was sued for harboring a fugitive
slave, and was fined $50,000. On appeal the fine was re-
duced to one cent and court costs, and on further appeal the
decision was reversed.[201]

Chamberlain's antislavery activities and Cadwell's less
numerous ones illustrate the degrees which antislavery evangelicalism took among the rebels. Both men considered themselves to be evangelicals first, and antislavery advocates second. Chamberlain's reference to himself as an "antislavery

minister" was an accurate one, because antislavery was a quality of evangelicalism, and not its central element. In his self-assessment, Chamberlain was typical of the majority of the Lane rebels who were ordained.

Evangelicalism had provided the framework and impulse for the rebels' antislavery in 1834. As evangelicalism asserted its demand to spread the gospel, this antislavery was absorbed and subordinated, as the nature of the later antislavery activities of the rebels suggests. A minority of Lane rebels, however, were unable or unwilling to subjugate their antislavery to evangelicalism, and therefore gave up one, or the other, or both.

Evangelicalism, Antislavery, or Neither

In the years between 1834 and 1861, Lane rebels engaged in a variety of antislavery activities, most of which had connections with evangelicalism. There were some rebels, however, who were unable to cement or to maintain the relationship between evangelicalism and antislavery.[202] Some eliminated one element of the relationship, antislavery, by removing themselves, sometimes physically, from a context in which antislavery was an issue. For these, antislavery did not maintain the importance that it had had at Lane Seminary in 1834. A few rebels were unable to maintain the relationship between evangelicalism and antislavery because of what they perceived to be evangelicalism's connection with the churches, institutions corrupted by their toleration and support of slavery. All of these different responses of the Lane rebels illustrate the tensions between evangelicalism and antislavery in America.

Some of the rebels did not become involved in antislavery, or ended their connection with antislavery, because evangelicalism overshadowed such involvment. Henry Cherry and James Warren went to India as missionaries for the American Board of Commissioners for Foreign Missions.[203] Men such as Charles Crocker and Enoch R. Martin, who were supported by the American Home Missionary Society, did nothing for antislavery.[204] Deodat Jeffers moved to Michigan where he preached, farmed, and was a colporteur for the American Bible Society.[205]

A few rebels left the movement in dismay and were pessimistic of its eventual success. James M. Allan, for

example, went to Danville, Kentucky, after the rebellion.
There he signed the "Declaration" of the Kentucky Anti-Slavery
Convention in March, 1835, [206] and returned home to Alabama.
Within half a year he had decided that slavery would lead to
racial violence regardless of the appeals of abolitionists. [207]
Thus, he condemned slaveholders and "renounced the abolitionists," and moved to Illinois where he engaged in a number
of pursuits, none of which had any connection with antislavery. [208] From about 1845, Allan was believed to be leaning
towards the religious views of his brother, William, who was
one of three rebels whose conceptions of the relationship between antislavery and evangelicalism changed most radically. [209]

Marius R. Robinson, William T. Allan, and Theodore
D. Weld rejected much of evangelicalism because those in the
churches who tolerated and endorsed slavery claimed it as
their own. All three men rejected the church as a corrupt
institution, and the consequent awareness that the churches'
doctrines were temporal freed them from adherence to those
doctrines and the evangelicalism they expressed.

Robinson was ordained in 1836, and was commissioned
"to labor in and with the churches to arouse them to a sense
of their responsibility in the institution of American slavery."[210]
Less than a year later he asked for a dismission from the
Presbyterian Church because of its unwillingness to condemn
slavery, and, correspondingly, because of that denomination's
adherence to man-made creeds which substituted flawed human
regulations for God's moral laws. [211] Because the doctrines
of the church took no cognizance of slavery, they, along with
the church itself, were deficient and therefore illegitimate.
As editor of the Anti-Slavery Bugle, Robinson published articles condemning the church's support of slavery, [212] and in
his last editorial expressed his position regarding the church
and its doctrines. The publication of the Bugle, he wrote,

is a standing protest against that time serving expediency, which atheistically, in the church as well
as in the world, ignores the existence of a fixed
moral law in the universe, and established anarchy
in its place--by substituting as a moral standard
prejudices, wishes, or mistaken and conflicting policy and interests of ignorant and erring individuals
in the community. The interests of a true humanity,
the prevalent influence of a pure religion, and the
triumphs of freedom and justice over slavery and
outrage, require that the uncompromising protest

of at least one paper in the great West, should be
regularly maintained. [213]

Robinson's emphasis on "fixed moral law" and "pure religion"
indicates his adherence to the social content and moral rigor
of the evangelicalism which had urged the Lane rebels to embrace immediatism in 1834. In accusing the church of "expediency," he admitted his disenchantment with much of evangelicalism's theological content, and he eventually became a
Unitarian. [214]

William T. Allan, like Robinson, became disenchanted
with evangelicalism because of the church's refusal to condemn
slavery.   Probably influenced by the difficulties of preaching
antislavery in Peoria, Illinois, Allan became more radical,
and by 1850 he was known as "a Garrisonian no-government
and no-Sabbath man of some talent and education. "[215]   His
radicalization in antislavery roughly paralleled that in religion.
After 1845 he did not pastor a church, but worked as a merchant, village clerk, postmaster, and justice of the peace. [216]
By the late 1850's, his Lane classmate, James A. Thome,
mourned "A Sad Reverse":   Allan had become "an open preacher of infidelity at the West. "[217]   Allan continued to lecture on
all reforms, including antislavery, temperance, and free religion, and operated a station on the Underground Railroad. [218]

Robinson and Allan illustrate a movement which can be
described as from evangelicalism to antislavery.   Dismayed
by the "expediency" and sinfulness of the churches on the
slavery issue, both discarded much of evangelicalism while
retaining an interest, more marked in Robinson, in antislavery.   Neither, however, discarded the moral fervor and social aspect of the evangelicalism which had led them to antislavery in the first place.

Unlike Robinson and Allan, Theodore Weld, who was
distressed at the sinfulness of all institutions, including reform societies, completely rejected the social and doctrinal
elements of evangelicalism, as well as the antislavery which
it had precipitated.   By the 1840's, disturbed by the controversies within the antislavery movement, pessimistic about
political action, sceptical of ministers and churches, and resigned to the wicked power of public sentiment, Weld reduced
the scope of his religious beliefs and reform activities. [219]
He emphasized "personal religion" which relied on one's personal relationship with God. [220]   He downplayed the importance
of the Bible, and told Birney that "creeds have lost all hold

upon me,... "[221] Influenced by perfectionism and Swedenborgianism, Weld eventually joined a Unitarian society, far removed from his evangelicalism of the 1830's. [222] Regarding reform societies, Weld believed that they were flawed because they left "branches, trunk, and deep shot roots, to propogate [sic] anew with a vigor of production vastly increased by the pruning. "[223] Reform could only occur with and in the individual who aligned himself with "Truth. " In both his religious and reform views, Weld retreated into a quietism which had very little connection with evangelicalism. [224] More than any of the other Lane rebels, he had moved furthest from evangelicalism and antislavery.

It is apparent that the conflict in the relationship between evangelicalism and antislavery had several ramifications. Some of the rebels gave up the antislavery of the Lane debate and rebellion for evangelicalism. Others discarded much of evangelicalism in favor of antislavery and reform. Weld, and perhaps others, gave up both.

Notes

1. Robert L. Stanton and Charles Sexton were the two who re-entered Lane and later supported the antislavery movement. Reilly, "Robert L. Stanton, " p. 37; and New York Anti-Slavery Society, Proceedings of the First Annual Meeting of the New-York Anti-Slavery Society, Convened at Utica, October 19, 1836 (Utica: New York Anti-Slavery Society, 1836), p. 13.

2. The rebels who engaged in antislavery activities after 1834 included: James M. Allan, William T. Allan, John W. Alvord, Courtland Avery, Enoch N. Bartlett, Andrew Benton, Charles P. Bush, Lorenzo D. Butts, Christopher C. Cadwell, Ebenezer B. Chamberlain, Uriah T. Chamberlain, Henry Cherry, George Clark, Amos Dresser, Amasa Frissell, Augustus T. Hopkins, David S. Ingraham, Huntington Lyman, Alexander McKellar, Israel S. Mattison, John J. Miter, Abraham Neely, Lucius H. Parker, Joseph H. Payne, John T. Pierce, Samuel F. Porter, Marius R. Robinson, Charles Sexton, Henry B. Stanton, Robert L. Stanton, James Steele, Asa A. Stone, Sereno W. Streeter, James A. Thome, Samuel H. Thompson, Giles Waldo, Calvin Waterbury, Edward Weed, Theodore D. Weld, Samuel Wells, George Whipple, and Hiram Wilson.

Regarding the remaining rebels about whom something
is known, some of them may have engaged in antislavery activities but left no records. For example,
Russell J. Judd was pastor of the Free Church of
Brooklyn, New York. There is no evidence that he
worked in the antislavery movement, but he was one
of those circularized by Weld for information about
slavery in 1839. Lane Theological Seminary General
Catalogue, p. 18; and Theodore D. Weld to Russell
J. Judd, 16 September 1839, Weld-Grimké Papers,
Box 6, WLCL. Henry P. Thompson freed his two
slaves after the Lane debate, and entered Centre
College in Danville, Kentucky, after the rebellion.
While in Danville, he lived with James G. Birney,
so it is possible that Thompson did some antislavery
work of which there is no record. However, it is
also possible that he may have succumbed to pressure
to do nothing. Birney noted that Thompson had been
"greatly tormented and persecuted" for freeing his
slaves. Dumond, ed., Letters of Birney, 1:155,
n. 1; Centre College, General Catalogue of the Centre
College of Kentucky. 1890 (Danville: Kentucky Advocate Printing Co., 1890), p. 28; and Diary entry,
14 September 1834, James G. Birney Papers, Library
of Congress, Washington, D.C.

3. See above, pp. 181-89.

4. American Anti-Slavery Society, Third Annual Report of
the American Anti-Slavery Society; with the Speeches
Delivered at the Anniversary Meeting, Held in the
City of New-York, on the 10th of May, 1836, and the
Minutes of the Meetings of the Society for Business
(New York: William S. Dorr for the American Anti-
Slavery Society, 1836), p. 36; and Myers, "Agency
System," pp. 401-402, passim.

5. Allan was agent for the Illinois Anti-Slavery Society until
about 1845. Muelder, Fighters for Freedom, p. 145.
Robinson, Weed, Butts, and Streeter were employed
by the Ohio Anti-Slavery Society. Ohio Anti-Slavery
Society, Report of the Second Anniversary of the Ohio
Anti-Slavery Society, Held in Mt. Pleasant, Jefferson
Co., Ohio, on the Twenty-seventh of April, 1837 (Cin-
cinnati: Ohio Anti-Slavery Society, 1837), p. 56; Ohio
Anti-Slavery Society, Report of the Fourth Anniversary
of the Ohio Anti-Slavery Society, Held in Putnam,

Muskingum County, Ohio, on the 29th of May, 1839 (Cincinnati: Ohio Anti-Slavery Society, 1839), p. 25; and Philanthropist, 19 November 1839.

6. Ohio Anti-Slavery Society, Report of the Second Anniversary, 1837, p. 21.

7. Ohio Anti-Slavery Society, Report of the First Anniversary of the Ohio Anti-Slavery Society, Held Near Granville, on the Twenty-seventh and Twenty-eighth of April, 1836 (Cincinnati: Ohio Anti-Slavery Society, 1836), pp. 13-14.

8. Butts, Hopkins, Robinson, and Stanton held offices in the Ohio Anti-Slavery Society. Ohio Anti-Slavery Society, Report of the Second Anniversary, 1837, p. 10; Ohio Anti-Slavery Society, Report of the Third Anniversary of the Ohio Anti-Slavery Society, Held in Granville, Licking County, Ohio, on the 30th of May, 1838 (Cincinnati: Ohio Anti-Slavery Society, 1838), p. 11; Ohio Anti-Slavery Society, Report of the Fourth Anniversary, 1839, p. 20; and Ohio Anti-Slavery Society, Proceedings, 1835, p. 47. In 1839 Miter was the Corresponding Secretary for the Illinois Anti-Slavery Society. Philanthropist, 26 November 1839. Robinson was also involved with the Western Anti-Slavery Society, a pro-Garrison organization based in Ohio. Western Anti-Slavery Society, Minute Book, Western Reserve Historical Society, Cleveland. Stanton was very prominent in the American Anti-Slavery Society until 1840. Rice, "Henry B. Stanton," pp. 58-107. Whipple was on the Executive Committee of the American and Foreign Anti-Slavery Society. American and Foreign Anti-Slavery Society, The Annual Report of the American and Foreign Anti-Slavery Society, Presented at the General Meeting, Held in Broadway Tabernacle, May 11, 1847, with the Addresses, Resolutions, and Treasurer's Report (New York: William Harned for the American and Foreign Anti-Slavery Society, 1847), p. 3. Though active in the American Anti-Slavery Society, Weld refused all official leadership positions.

9. See above, pp. 189-192.

10. Clifton Herman Johnson, "The American Missionary Association, 1846-1861: A Study of Christian Abolitionism"

(Ph. D. dissertation, University of North Carolina at Chapel Hill, 1958), pp. 107-109.

11. Oberlin Evangelist, 7 October 1840, 18 August 1841; Pease and Pease, "The Clerical Do-Gooder: Hiram Wilson"; and American Missionary Association, The Thirteenth Annual Report of the American Missionary Association, and the Proceedings at the Annual Meeting, Held at Chicago, Illinois, October 19 and 20, 1859. Together with a List of Life Members (New York: American Missionary Association, 1859), p. 44.

12. See above, p. 192.

13. Folio letter to Theodore D. Weld, 8 January 1835, in Barnes and Dumond, eds., Letters of Weld, 1:192-93; and Christian Anti-Slavery Convention, Minutes, 1850, pp. 3, 17, 18.

14. Lucius H. Parker to the Secretaries of the American Home Missionary Society, [1851], American Home Missionary Society Papers, Amistad Research Center, Dillard University, New Orleans (Glen Rock, N. J.: Microfilming Corporation of America, 601112, 1975), Roll 28 (hereafter cited as AHMS Papers).

15. See above, pp. 186-89, 192-96.

16. Oberlin Evangelist, 22 June 1859; and [Lillie], Faith and Works, pp. 52-53.

17. Henry B. Stanton and George Whipple to Charles G. Finney, 10 January 1835, Finney Papers, Roll 3. The students' lease on their quarters expired April 1.

18. John J. Shipherd to John Keep, 13 December 1834, John J. Shipherd Papers, Box 1, Oberlin College Archives, Oberlin, Ohio (hereafter cited as Shipherd Papers, OCA); and Finney, Memoirs, p. 332.

19. Cincinnati Journal, 14 November 1834.

20. The history of Oberlin is recounted in Fletcher, History of Oberlin.

21. Ibid., 1:121, 131, 139.

22. John J. Shipherd to John Keep, 13 and 15 December 1834, Shipherd Papers, Box 1, OCA.

23. Ibid.; John J. Shipherd to Nathan P. Fletcher, 15 December 1834, Letters Received by Oberlin College, 1822-1866, Oberlin College Archives, Oberlin, Ohio (microfilm), Roll 2.

24. Mahan's willingness to leave Cincinnati was due, in part, to his support of the students, which had made his own position in the community tenuous. The conflict in his own church is reflected in Vine Street Congregational Church, Minutes of the Board of Trustees, Meetings of 17 and 27 November 1834, Cincinnati Historical Society, Cincinnati; see also Mahan, Autobiography, p. 184. The two agents left Cincinnati in late December, stopped at Hillsboro to talk with Weld, and then travelled up the Ohio and to the East. Weld was offered the professorship of theology, but declined in favor of Finney. John J. Shipherd to Fayette Shipherd, 22 December 1834 (copy), Fletcher Papers, Box 13, OCA; and Mahan, Autobiography, pp. 192-93.

25. Charles G. Finney to Trustees of the Oberlin Collegiate Institute, 30 June 1835, Finney Papers, Roll 3; Fletcher, History of Oberlin, 1:175; and Finney, Memoirs, p. 333.

26. John Morgan to Theodore D. Weld, 13 January 1835, in Barnes and Dumond, eds., Letters of Weld, 1:198.

27. Fletcher, History of Oberlin, 1:172.

28. Ibid.

29. Charles G. Finney to George Whipple and Henry B. Stanton, 18 January 1835, Finney Papers, Roll 3. Both Shipherd and Keep recognized that the issue was not race but who would manage the theological studies program. Fletcher, History of Oberlin, 1:176-78.

30. Ibid.

31. Mahan, Autobiography, p. 163; and Fairchild, Oberlin, p. 66.

32. Fletcher, History of Oberlin, 1:182.

33. Ohio Anti-Slavery Society, Proceedings, 1835, pp. 1-2,
    5-11.

34. Ibid., p. 6.

35. Ibid., pp. 6-8, 9.

36. Ibid., p. 9. Weld's method was that of "moral suasion,"
    which combined human means of persuasion with a
    reliance on God. Finney's idea of the true meaning
    of "moral suasion" was given in a letter to Joshua
    L. Leavitt, 26 February 1832. "As you use it the
    term 'moral suasion' ... it is all true, but find
    some other phraseology, & then show that you do
    not intend by it what heretics intend by moral sua-
    sion, to the exclusion of the Holy Ghost." Finney
    Papers, Roll 3.

37. Ohio Anti-Slavery Society, Proceedings, 1835, p. 47;
    and Fairchild, Oberlin, p. 348. Some of the rebels
    travelled to Oberlin via the Ohio Canal. A. L. Shum-
    way and C. deW. Brower, Oberliniana. A Jubilee
    Volume of Semi-Historical Anecdotes Connected with
    the Past and Present of Oberlin College, 1833-1883
    (Cleveland: Home Publishing Co., [1883]), p. 17.
    Those rebels who attended Oberlin included: William
    T. Allan, John W. Alvord, Courtland Avery, Lewis
    Barnes, Enoch N. Bartlett, James Bradley, Lorenzo
    D. Butts, Ebenezer B. Chamberlain, Uriah T. Cham-
    berlain, George Clark, Charles Crocker, Amos Dres-
    ser, David S. Ingraham, Deodat Jeffers, Huntington
    Lyman, Alexander McKellar, Israel S. Mattison,
    Lucius H. Parker, Joseph H. Payne, John T. Pierce,
    Samuel F. Porter, Munson S. Robinson, James Steele,
    Sereno W. Streeter, James A. Thome, Samuel H.
    Thompson, George Whipple, and Hiram Wilson.
    There are files concerning most of these in the
    Alumni Records Office, Oberlin College; see also
    Oberlin College, General Catalogue of Oberlin Col-
    lege, 1833-1908. Seventy-Fifth Anniversary. Includ-
    ing an Account of the Principal Events in the History
    of the College, with Illustrations of the College Build-
    ings (Oberlin: Oberlin College, 1909), passim; and
    "List of Unrecorded Students, 1834-1845. Supple-
    mentary to Catalogue," Fletcher Papers, Box 14, OCA.

James Bradley did not attend Oberlin itself but the
Sheffield Manual Labor Institute, a school organized
to handle some of the overflow of students desiring
to attend Oberlin.

38. A description of "Cincinnati Hall" is in Leonard, Story
of Oberlin, pp. 413-14.

39. Constitution of the Antislavery Society of Oberlin, File
16/5, Box 19, OCA.

40. Elizur Wright, Jr. to Theodore D. Weld, 16 July 1835,
in Barnes and Dumond, eds., Letters of Weld, 1:227.

41. Thomas, Theodore Weld, pp. 95-96. Huntington Lyman
accompanied Weld when the latter lectured, with some
opposition, in Painesville, Ohio. Lyman's account is
in Barnes and Dumond, eds., Letters of Weld, 1:238,
n. 4.

42. James H. Fairchild to "Dear Aunt," 12 October 1835,
James H. Fairchild Papers, Box 21, Oberlin College
Archives, Oberlin, Ohio, described a lecture given
by William T. Allan in Brownhelm; see also John L.
Myers, "Antislavery Activities of Five Lane Seminary
Boys in 1835-36," Bulletin of the Historical and Philo-
sophical Society of Ohio 21 (April 1963): 99.

43. Theodore D. Weld to Lewis Tappan, 17 November and
22 December 1835, in Barnes and Dumond, eds.,
Letters of Weld, 1:244-45, 248-49; John W. Alvord,
Theodore D. Weld, Lucius H. Parker, and William
T. Allan to Marius R. Robinson, 23 November 1835,
File 16/5, Box 18, OCA; Huntington Lyman to Wil-
liam Goodell Frost, 28 January 1882, in File on
Huntington Lyman, Alumni Records Office, Oberlin
College; and Myers, "Antislavery Activities of Five
Lane Seminary Boys." Unlike modern colleges and
universities, Oberlin's major vacation occurred dur-
ing the winter months, a time when most of Oberlin's
students were able to earn money by teaching school.

44. James A. Thome and John W. Alvord to Theodore D.
Weld, 9 February 1836, in Barnes and Dumond,
eds., Letters of Weld, 1:258.

45. Myers, "Antislavery Activities of Five Lane Seminary
Boys," passim.

46. Ohio Anti-Slavery Society, Report of the First Anniversary, 1836, p. 20.

47. Myers, "Antislavery Activities of Five Lane Seminary Boys," p. 111.

48. Those rebels who attended the convention included: William T. Allan, John W. Alvord, Uriah T. Chamberlain, George Clark, Amos Dresser, Israel S. Mattison, Joseph H. Payne, John T. Pierce, Sereno W. Streeter, James A. Thome, and Hiram Wilson. Ohio Anti-Slavery Society, Report of the First Anniversary, 1836, pp. 3-6; James A. Thome to Theodore D. Weld, 2 May 1836, in Barnes and Dumond, eds., Letters of Weld, 1:298; and American Anti-Slavery Society, Third Annual Report, 1836, p. 23.

49. James G. Birney to Lewis Tappan, 29 April 1836, in Dumond, ed., Letters of Birney, 1:319.

50. Theodore D. Weld to James G. Birney, 30 October and 19 December 1835, in Dumond, ed., Letters of Birney, 1:254, 284; and James A. Thome to Theodore D. Weld, 31 March 1836, in Barnes and Dumond, eds., Letters of Weld, 1:285.

51. Charles G. Finney to Theodore D. Weld, 21 July 1836, in Barnes and Dumond, eds., Letters of Weld, 1:319. Finney had been very anxious that Weld enter Oberlin and become a revivalist. As early as January, 1835, Finney had written the rebels about Weld: "Will he surely be at Oberlin? Why dont [sic] he write to me? I fear he will destroy his health lecturing so much. Dont [sic] let him delay to get into the ministry." Charles G. Finney to George Whipple and Henry B. Stanton, 18 January 1835, Finney Papers, Roll 3.

52. Emancipator, 25 June 1833.

53. See above, p. 84.

54. Finney, Lecture on Revivals, pp. 287, 288.

55. Ibid., pp. 288, 293, 299; see also p. 302.

56. Ibid., pp. 300, 303.

57. Ibid., p. 286.

58. Ibid., pp. 424-25.

59. Ibid., p. 203.

60. Charles G. Finney, Lectures to Professing Christians. Delivered in the City of New-York, in the Years 1836 and 1837 (New York: John S. Taylor, 1837), p. 55. Southern interference with the mails is examined in Nye, Fettered Freedom, pp. 32-69.

61. Charles G. Finney to Arthur Tappan, 30 April 1836, Finney Papers, Roll 3.

62. Finney, "Sinners Bound to Change Their Own Hearts," p. 41.

63. Ibid.

64. Ibid., p. 42.

65. Ibid., pp. 42-43.

66. Charles G. Finney to Arthur Tappan, 30 April 1836, Finney Papers, Roll 3.

67. Ibid.

68. Ibid.

69. Charles Stuart to Charles G. Finney, 19 August 1836, Finney Papers, Roll 3.

70. Lewis Tappan to Theodore D. Weld, 15 March 1836, in Barnes and Dumond, eds., Letters of Weld, 1:276.

71. Charles G. Finney to Arthur Tappan, 30 April 1836, Finney Papers, Roll 3; and Wyatt-Brown, Lewis Tappan, p. 177.

72. Theodore D. Weld to Lewis Tappan, 17 November 1835, in Barnes and Dumond, eds., Letters of Weld, 1:243.

73. Theodore D. Weld to Sarah and Angelina Grimké, 26 August 1837, in Barnes and Dumond, eds., Letters of Weld, 1:434.

74. Ibid.; see also Theodore D. Weld to J. F. Robinson, 1 (?) May 1836, in Barnes and Dumond, eds., Letters of Weld, 1:296.

75. Theodore D. Weld to Lewis Tappan, 17 November 1835, in Barnes and Dumond, eds., Letters of Weld, 1:242-44; and Charles G. Finney to Arthur Tappan, 30 April 1836, Finney Papers, Roll 3.

76. Charles G. Finney to Arthur Tappan, 30 April 1836, Finney Papers, Roll 3.

77. Theodore D. Weld to Lewis Tappan, 9 March 1836, in Barnes and Dumond, eds., Letters of Weld, 1:270-74; quotation from p. 270. Tappan replied that he had heard that Weld and Finney opposed having James Bradley as a speaker at the anniversary meeting of the American Anti-Slavery Society. Lewis Tappan to Theodore D. Weld, 15 March 1836, in Barnes and Dumond, eds., Letters of Weld, 1:277.

78. See Catherine H. Birney, The Grimke Sisters: Sarah and Angelina Grimk[é]; the First American Women Advocates of Abolition and Woman's Rights (Boston: Lee & Shepard, 1885; New York: C. T. Dillingham, 1885; reprint ed., New York: Haskell House, 1970), p. 115, n. 1.

79. Theodore D. Weld to Lewis Tappan, 9 March 1836, in Barnes and Dumond, eds., Letters of Weld, 1:273-74.

80. Ibid.; Theodore D. Weld to Sarah and Angelina Grimké, 26 August 1837, in Barnes and Dumond, eds., Letters of Weld, 1:435; see also Charles Stuart to Charles G. Finney, 19 August 1836, Finney Papers, Roll 3.

81. Finney wrote to Arthur Tappan in April, to Charles Stuart in June, and to Weld in July, and tried to convince all of them to moderate their abolitionism. Charles G. Finney to Arthur Tappan, 30 April 1836, Finney Papers, Roll 3; Charles Stuart to Charles G. Finney, 19 August 1836, Finney Papers, Roll 3; and Charles G. Finney to Theodore D. Weld, 21 July 1836, in Barnes and Dumond, eds., Letters of Weld, 1:318-20.

82. Sereno W. Streeter to Theodore D. Weld, 20 July 1836, in Barnes and Dumond, eds., Letters of Weld, 1:317.

83. Charles G. Finney to Theodore D. Weld, 21 July 1836, in Barnes and Dumond, eds., Letters of Weld, 1:318, 319.

84. William T. Allan, Sereno W. Streeter, John W. Alvord, and James A. Thome to Theodore D. Weld, 9 August 1836, in Barnes and Dumond, eds., Letters of Weld, 1:323-39; quotations from pp. 323, 324, 327, 328.

85. Ibid., 1:328.

86. Ibid., 1:325-27, 329.

87. Ibid., 1:325-26.

88. Ibid., 1:326-27.

89. James A. Thome to Theodore D. Weld, 9 September 1836, in Barnes and Dumond, eds., Letters of Weld, 1:340.

90. Theodore D. Weld to Lewis Tappan, 24 October 1836, in Barnes and Dumond, eds., Letters of Weld, 1:345.

91. The other six who took agencies were: Courtland Avery, Lorenzo D. Butts, Amos Dresser, John T. Pierce, Samuel F. Porter, and Hiram Wilson. See above, pp. 181-89.

92. Allan was an agent for the Illinois Anti-Slavery Society until the mid-1840s. Muelder, Fighters for Freedom, p. 97.

93. Almost one-fourth of the Lane rebels became agents. Of those for whom there is some information (fifty-four), one-third became agents. The rebels who became agents for antislavery societies included: William T. Allan, John W. Alvord, Courtland Avery, Lorenzo D. Butts, Amos Dresser, Huntington Lyman, John J. Miter, John T. Pierce, Samuel F. Porter, Marius R. Robinson, Henry B. Stanton, Sereno W. Streeter, James A. Thome, Calvin Waterbury, Edward Weed, Theodore D. Weld, Samuel T. Wells, and Hiram Wilson. Myers, "Agency System," pp. 270-

71, 401-402, passim; and Dumond, ed., Letters of
Birney, 1:357, n. 2. It would be fortunate for this
study if thirty or thirty-two of the Lane rebels had
become agents, as Barnes and Dumond have stated,
but this does not appear to have been the case.
Barnes, Antislavery Impulse, p. 77; and Barnes
and Dumond, eds., Letters of Weld, 1:xxiii.

94. Myers, "Agency System," pp. 401-404. A discussion
of the "Seventy" is in ibid., pp. 397-459.

95. Rice, "Henry B. Stanton," pp. 58-62.

96. [Lillie], Faith and Works, p. 33; Nye, "Marius Robinson," p. 146; and Myers, "Agency System," pp.
404, 427-30.

97. The states in which Lane rebels served as agents included Rhode Island, Massachusetts, New York,
Pennsylvania, Ohio, Indiana, Illinois, Michigan,
and Virginia. Myers, "Agency System," passim;
Ohio Anti-Slavery Society, Report of the Fourth
Anniversary, 1839, p. 25; Gamaliel Bailey to James
G. Birney, 28 October 1838, in Dumond, ed., Letters of Birney, 1:474; Merton L. Dillon, "The Antislavery Movement in Illinois: 1809-1844" (Ph.D.
dissertation, University of Michigan, 1951), pp. 306-
309; and Emancipator, 5 August 1837. Robinson
worked in Virginia. Marius R. Robinson to Emily
R. Robinson, 19 November 1837, Robinson Papers,
Folder 1, WRHS.

98. Huntington Lyman to William Goodell Frost, 28 January
1882, in File on Huntington Lyman, Alumni Records
Office, Oberlin College.

99. Emancipator, 4 May 1837.

100. Edward Weed to "Dear Sisters," 7 March 1836, in
[Lillie], Faith and Works, pp. 35-36.

101. Edward Weed to "Dear Wife," 22 November 1836, in
[Lillie], Faith and Works, p. 44.

102. Emancipator, 26 May 1836. This passage followed a
long and descriptive scenario of the creation of man
which ends with the intrusion of the slaveholder,

who, "in the presence of God and all the earth,
seizes that husband and wife and these children,
and drags them down from their noble elevation,
the platform of manhood, and degrades them into
the condition of things, writing upon them: These
are mine. " Allan used this scenario more than
once, and probably with great success. See Emancipator, 5 August 1837.

103. Ibid. , 20 October 1836.

104. Ibid. See Stanton's remarks on sin and slavery in the
Liberator, 6 June 1835.

105. Emancipator, February 1836. See also ibid. , 10 November 1836; and James A. Thome to Theodore D.
Weld, 9 February 1836, in Barnes and Dumond,
eds. , Letters of Weld, 1:257.

106. Rice, "Henry B. Stanton, " pp. 94, 104, 231.

107. Emily Robinson to Marius R. Robinson, 3 December
1837, Robinson Papers, Folder 1, WRHS; and Gamaliel Bailey to James G. Birney, 19 December
1837, and 28 June 1838, in Dumond, ed. , Letters
of Birney, 1:434, 462.

108. Nye, "Marius Robinson, " p. 146; and [Lillie], Faith
and Works, p. 33.

109. Pease and Pease, "Clerical Do-Gooder: Hiram Wilson, " pp. 121, 134. Wilson is best understood
through his extensive correspondence, much of
which is in the Oberlin College Archives.

110. Emancipator, 22 December 1836; and Myers, "Agency
System, " pp. 426-30.

111. James A. Thome to Theodore D. Weld, 31 March and
9 September 1836, in Barnes and Dumond, eds. ,
Letters of Weld, 1:285, 339-42; and File on James
A. Thome, Alumni Records Office, Oberlin College.

112. James A. Thome to Theodore D. Weld, 16 July 1836,
in Barnes and Dumond, eds. , Letters of Weld, 1:313.

113. American Anti-Slavery Society, Third Annual Report,

1836, pp. 29-30; and Theodore D. Weld to Lewis Tappan, 5 April 1836, in Barnes and Dumond, eds., Letters of Weld, 1:289.

114. Regarding Thome's ability to complete such a project, William Lloyd Garrison wrote, "Thome would, I think, do admirably well...." William Lloyd Garrison to Henry E. Benson, 18 August 1836, in Louis Ruchames and Walter Merrill, eds., The Letters of William Lloyd Garrison, vol. 2: A House Dividing against Itself, 1836-1840, ed. by Louis Ruchames (Cambridge: Harvard University Press, the Belknap Press, 1971), p. 159.

115. Myers, "Agency System," p. 444; James A. Thome and J. Horace Kimball, Emancipation in the West Indies. A Six Months' Tour in Antigua, Barbadoes, and Jamaica, in the Year 1837 (New York: American Anti-Slavery Society, 1838), pp. iv, passim; letters were published in the Emancipator, 20 April, 18 May, 1 and 15 June, and 5 October 1837.

116. Emancipator, 8 June 1837.

117. Thome and Kimball, Emancipation in the West Indies, p. v; and James A. Thome to Theodore D. Weld, 30 November 1837, in Barnes and Dumond, eds., Letters of Weld, 1:484, and n. 2.

118. Theodore D. Weld to Sarah and Angelina Grimké, 27 January 1838, in Barnes and Dumond, eds., Letters of Weld, 2:526; and James A. Thome to Theodore D. Weld, 25 December 1837, in Barnes and Dumond, eds., Letters of Weld, 1:502.

119. Ibid.; and Theodore D. Weld to James A. Thome, 5 April 1838, in Barnes and Dumond, eds., Letters of Weld, 2:621.

120. Henry B. Stanton to Henry Cowles, 20 June 1838, Henry Cowles Papers, Box 1, Oberlin College Archives, Oberlin, Ohio.

121. Theodore D. Weld, "The Oberlin Institute" (typed copy), Oberlin College Archives, Oberlin, Ohio.

122. Theodore D. Weld to James A. Thome, 5 April 1838,

in Barnes and Dumond, eds. , Letters of Weld,
2:623. Emancipation in the West Indies was highly
praised in American Anti-Slavery Society, Fifth
Annual Report of the Executive Committee of the
American Anti-Slavery Society, with the Minutes of
the Meetings of the Society for Business, and the
Speeches Delivered at the Anniversary Meeting on
the 8th May, 1838 (New York: William S. Dorr
for the American Anti-Slavery Society, 1838), p. 46.

123. Thome recounted his flight to Weld, Gerrit Smith, and
Finney. James A. Thome to Theodore D. Weld,
27 August 1839, in Barnes and Dumond, eds. , Let-
ters of Weld, 2:793-95; James A. Thome to Gerrit
Smith, 4 October 1839 (photocopy), Fletcher Papers,
Box 18, OCA; and James A. Thome to Charles G.
Finney, 3 February 1840, Finney Papers, Roll 4.
Evidently, Weld did not believe it was necessary for
Thome to flee. See James A. Thome to Theodore
D. Weld, 22 November 1839, in Barnes and Dumond,
eds. , Letters of Weld, 2:815-16. While in the East
Thome assisted Weld in the preparation of Slavery
and the Internal Slave Trade in the United States of
North America; Being Replies to Questions Trans-
mitted by the Committee of the British and Foreign
Anti-slavery Society, for the Abolition of Slavery
and the Slave Trade throughout the World. Presented to the General Anti-Slavery Convention, Held
in London, June, 1840 (London: Thomas Ward &
Co. , 1841).

124. Emancipator, 4 May 1837.

125. Barnes, Antislavery Impulse, p. 86, quotes a statement
describing Weld as "the most mobbed man in the
United States. "

126. Amos Dresser, The Narrative of Amos Dresser, with
Stone's Letters from Natchez, --An Obituary Notice
of the Writer, and Two Letters from Tallahassee,
Relating to the Treatment of Slaves (New York:
American Anti-Slavery Society, 1836). The incident
was extensively reported. See, for example, the
Cincinnati Daily Gazette, 14, 15, and 18 August
1835; Cincinnati Journal, 28 August 1835; Philan-
thropist, 25 November 1836; and Emancipator, 25
May 1837. Dresser even related it to a convention

of abolitionists in 1874. Chicago Tribune, 10 and
11 June 1874.

127. Emancipator, January 1836.

128. Ibid. , 29 June, 13 July, 17 August 1837; and Nye,
      "Marius Robinson," pp. 147-48.

129. Myers, "Agency System," pp. 665-82 examines all of
      the reasons for the decline of the agency system.

130. Edward Weed to "Dear Brother," 23 May 1843, in
      [Lillie], Faith and Works, p. 116.

131. Pease and Pease, "Clerical Do-Gooder: Hiram Wil-
      son"; and Nye, "Marius Robinson. "

132. Weld and Stanton were the only ones of these rebels
      who were never ordained. Robinson was the only
      one of those who were ordained who did not pastor
      a church in the 1840's and 1850's. William T.
      Allan left the ministry probably during the 1850's.
      See above, p. 198.

133. James A. Thome to Theodore D. Weld, 9 September
      1836, in Barnes and Dumond, eds. , Letters of
      Weld, 1:341.

134. James A. Thome to Charles G. Finney, 3 June 1837,
      Finney Papers, Roll 3.

135. William T. Allan, Sereno W. Streeter, John W. Alvord,
      and James A. Thome to Theodore D. Weld, 9
      August 1836, in Barnes and Dumond, eds. , Letters
      of Weld, 1:328.

136. James A. Thome to Theodore D. Weld, 7 February
      1839, in Barnes and Dumond, eds. , Letters of
      Weld, 2:750, 751.

137. Oberlin Evangelist, 27 September 1843; and James A.
      Thome to George Whipple, 7 December 1847, and
      16 May 1848, AMA Archives, Ohio-Roll 1.

138. American Missionary Association, Ninth Annual Report,
      1855, pp. 103-127; James A. Thome to George
      Whipple, 18 October 1863, AMA Archives, Ohio-

Roll 12; and James A. Thome to M. E. Strieby,
1 February 1867 through 17 February 1868, AMA
Archives, United Kingdom-Roll 2.

139. Oberlin Evangelist, 23 June 1852, and 13 July 1859;
and Ohio State Christian Anti-Slavery Convention,
Proceedings of the Ohio State Anti-Slavery Convention, Held at Columbus, August 10th and 11th,
1859 (n. p., [1859]), pp. 2, 3.

140. Henry M. Tenney, "The History of the First Congregational Church of Cleveland," Papers of the Ohio
Church History Society 2 (1892): 40, 38; and Oberlin Evangelist, 27 April 1859, 31 July 1839.

141. Oberlin Evangelist, 9 November and 21 December 1859;
and James A. Thome, "Come-outism and Come-
outers," Oberlin Quarterly Review 2 (November
1846): 158-88. In 1859 Thome was co-winner of
a prize offered by the American Tract Society for
the best tract on the subject of "prayer for the oppressed." James A. Thome, Prayer for the Oppressed. A Premium Tract (Boston: American
Tract Society, [1859]).

142. Myers, "Agency System," p. 465. Weed had been licensed by the Chillicothe Presbytery in November,
1835, and appointed a missionary to work with
blacks in Ohio. Galbraith, History of the Chillicothe Presbytery, p. 131.

143. Weed was commissioned an agent by the national society on July 6, 1836. Myers, "Agency System,"
p. 404; and Edward Weed to "Dear Wife," 22 November 1836, in [Lillie], Faith and Works, p. 44.
The day before Weed had written to Gamaliel Bailey,
"The Lord is willing the subject upon the minds of
the people. Prejudice is giving way--truth entering--
and opposition faltering and waning. Dear brother,
let us be encouraged to go forward, nothing doubting.
Victory over this might bloody Moloch of our coun-
try--Slavery, shall soon crown our efforts. We are
fighting the battles of the Lord. On our banner is
inscribed--Glory to God, good will to men; truth and
love our weapons, offensive and defensive." Philanthropist, 16 December 1836.

144. Edward Weed to Phebe Weed (?), 3 February 1838, in [Lillie], Faith and Works, p. 62.

145. Edward Weed to "My Dear Wife," 27 February 1838, in [Lillie], Faith and Works, p. 64; also p. 66.

146. Edward Weed to Phebe Weed (?), 4 February 1837, in [Lillie], Faith and Works, p. 49.

147. Edward Weed to Phebe Weed (?), 3 February 1838, in [Lillie], Faith and Works, p. 62.

148. Weed wrote, "I feel that the standard of holiness must be set higher in the churches, or soon they will be only a mass of hypocrites, of dead putridity." Edward Weed to Phebe Weed (?), 4 March 1837 (?), in [Lillie], Faith and Works, pp. 52-53; see also Edward Weed to "My Dear Wife," 27 February 1838, in [Lillie], Faith and Works, pp. 64-65.

149. Edward Weed to Phebe Weed (?), 12 June 1842, in [Lillie], Faith and Works, p. 95; Edward Weed to "Brother B," February 1842, in [Lillie], Faith and Works, pp. 86-87; Theodore D. Weld to Gerrit Smith, 6 June 1841, in Barnes and Dumond, eds., Letters of Weld, 2:865; and Edward Weed to Hamilton Hill, 3 December 1844, Letters Received by Oberlin College, Roll 9.

150. Edward Weed to "My Dear Wife," 31 December 1846, in [Lillie], Faith and Works, pp. 157-58.

151. American Missionary Association, Proceedings, 1846, p. 5.

152. Edward Weed, "Report on Anti-Slavery Memorials, Adopted by the American Board of Commissioners for Foreign Missions, September, 1845," Oberlin Quarterly Review 1 (February 1846): 279-317.

153. These fifteen Lane rebels included: Enoch N. Bartlett, Andrew Benton, Uriah T. Chamberlain, George Clark, Amos Dresser, David S. Ingraham, Israel Mattison, Lucius H. Parker, Joseph H. Payne, Samuel F. Porter, James Steele, James A. Thome, Samuel H. Thompson, George Whipple, and Hiram Wilson. Their connections with the American Mis-

sionary Association are noted in the following:
American Missionary Association, Proceedings of
the Second Convention for Bible Missions, Read in
Albany, September Second and Third, MDCCCXLVI:
with the Address of the Executive Committee, of the
American Missionary Association, &c. &c. &c. (New
York: J. H. Tobitt for the American Missionary As-
sociation), p. 3; American Missionary Association,
The Third Annual Report of the American Missionary
Association. Held at Boston, Massachusetts. Sep-
tember 26, 1849 (New York: American Missionary
Association, 1849), p. 22; American Missionary Association, The Seventh Annual Report of the Ameri-
can Missionary Association, Presented at Worcester,
Mass., September 28th, 1853. And the Proceedings
at the Annual Meeting, Together with a List of Life-
Members (New York: American Missionary Association, 1853), pp. 56-57; American Missionary Association, The Eighth Annual Report of the American
Missionary Association, Presented at West Meriden,
Ct., September 27th, 1854: and the Proceedings at
the Annual Meeting, Together with a List of Life-
Members (New York: American Missionary Association, 1854), pp. 54-57; American Missionary Asso-
ciation, The Ninth Annual Report of the American
Missionary Association, Presented at Chicago, Ill.,
September, [sic] 26th, 1855: and the Proceedings
at the Annual Meeting, Together with a List of Life-
Members (New York: American Missionary Associa-
tion, 1855), p. 16; American Missionary Associa-
tion, The Eleventh Annual Report of the American
Missionary Association, and the Proceedings at the
Annual Meeting, Held at Mansfield, Ohio, October
14th and 15th, 1857, Together with a List of Life
Members (New York: American Missionary Association, 1857), pp. 56-57, 79; American Missionary
Association, The Fifteenth Annual Report of the
American Missionary Association, and the Proceedings at the Annual Meeting, Held at Norwich, Ct.,
October 23, 1861, Together with a List of Life Members (New York: American Missionary Association,
1861), pp. 35-37; American Missionary Association,
The Sixteenth Annual Report of the American Missionary Association, and the Proceedings at the Annual Meeting, Held at Oberlin, Ohio, October 15 &
16, 1862. Together with a List of the Life Members
Added during the Year (New York: American Missionary Association, 1862), p. 4; Oberlin Evangelist,

7 October 1840, 3 July 1850, 24 October 1855; Union Missionary, January 1846; and Johnson, "American Missionary Association," pp. 107-109, passim.

154. Oberlin Evangelist, 7 October 1840; Amos Dresser to John J. Shipherd, 5 December 1839, Letters Received by Oberlin, Roll 6; David S. Ingraham to Lewis Tappan, 27 June 1839, Lewis Tappan Papers, Library of Congress, Washington, D. C. (microfilm), Roll 6; Theodore D. Weld to Lewis Tappan, 31 July 1841, in Barnes and Dumond, eds., Letters of Weld, 2:870-72; an obituary of Ingraham is in Oberlin Evangelist, 18 August 1841. Ingraham also encouraged another Lane rebel, Alexander McKellar, to become a missionary to blacks in Central or South America. In 1841 McKellar, a native of Scotland, applied for a missionary post with the London Missionary Society. He was accepted and sent to the Brunswick Chapel Station in Berbice, British Guiana (present-day Guyana) in 1843; he died two years later. Alexander McKellar to John Arundel, 8 February 1841, Candidates Answers to Printed Questions, Box 26, London Missionary Society, London, United Kingdom; File on Alexander McKellar, Alumni Records Office, Oberlin College; and Oberlin Evangelist, 16 August 1843, 19 November 1845.

155. C. H. Johnson, "American Missionary Association," p. 61.

156. Ibid., p. 58; Augustus Field Beard, A Crusade of Brotherhood: A History of the American Missionary Association (Boston: Pilgrim Press, 1909), p. 30; Oberlin Evangelist, 8 December 1841, 27 April and 6 July 1842; Union Missionary, January 1846; and James Steele to Lewis Tappan, January through August 1842, AMA Archives, Sierra Leone-Roll 2. The Amistad had been a slaveship which was taken over by rebellious slaves who eventually landed in the United States in 1839. Actions by prominent abolitionists, as well as arguments by John Quincy Adams before the Supreme Court, prevented the blacks from being returned to slavery. Instead, accompanied by missionaries who hoped to establish a station in Africa, they were returned to their

homes in 1842. See Wyatt-Brown, <u>Lewis Tappan</u>, pp. 205-212, 215-17.

157. <u>Oberlin Evangelist</u>, 5 July 1843, 8 July 1846.

158. American Missionary Association, <u>Proceedings, 1846</u>, pp. 3-5.

159. <u>Ibid.</u>, pp. 3, 6-16; quotations from pp. 6, 13.

160. <u>Ibid.</u>, p. 5.

161. Fletcher, <u>History of Oberlin</u>, 2:689; and Johnson, "American Missionary Association," pp. 107-109, 253. Whipple's dedication is described in Beard, <u>Crusade of Brotherhood</u>, p. 209.

162. "Objections to the circular of the Am. Fre. A. Com. & its organization," [September 1865], AMA Archives, District of Columbia-Roll 2.

163. George Whipple to M. E. Strieby, 14 October 1865, AMA Archives, Connecticut-Roll 7; see also George Whipple to Hamilton Hill, 5 March 1847, Letters Received by Oberlin, Roll 11.

164. Pease and Pease, "Clerical Do-Gooder: Hiram Wilson"; and American Missionary Association, <u>The Fifth Annual Report of the American Missionary Association, Presented at Cleveland, Ohio, September 24th, 1851; and the Proceedings at the Annual Meeting, Together with a List of Life Members</u> (New York: American Missionary Association, 1851), p. 32.

165. Andrew Benton to George Whipple, 19 June 1850, AMA Archives, Ohio-Roll 2; and <u>Oberlin Evangelist</u>, 3 July, 23 October 1850.

166. Amos Dresser to George Whipple, 22 May 1847, AMA Archives, Ohio-Roll 1; Lucius H. Parker to George Whipple, 26 November 1847, AMA Archives, Illinois-Roll 1; Report of collecting agent, 1 November 1857, AMA Archives, Illinois-Roll 5; and American Missionary Association, <u>Eleventh Annual Report, 1857</u>, pp. 57, 79.

167. James A. Thome to M. E. Strieby, 1 February 1867 through 17 February 1868, AMA Archives, United Kingdom-Roll 2.

168. References to these men are in the AMA Archives and Annual Reports.

169. The Lane rebels who attended conventions included: James M. Allan, William T. Allan, John W. Alvord, Courtland Avery, Enoch N. Bartlett, Andrew Benton, Charles P. Bush, Lorenzo D. Butts, Christopher C. Cadwell, Uriah T. Chamberlain, George Clark, Amos Dresser, Amasa Frissell, Augustus T. Hopkins, Huntington Lyman, Israel Mattison, John J. Miter, Abraham Neely, Lucius H. Parker, Joseph H. Payne, John T. Pierce, Marius R. Robinson, Charles Sexton, Henry B. Stanton, Sereno W. Streeter, James A. Thome, Giles Waldo, Calvin Waterbury, Edward Weed, Theodore D. Weld, Samuel T. Wells, George Whipple, and Hiram Wilson. Information concerning some of the conventions, meetings, and gatherings in which Lane rebels participated is contained in the following: American Anti-Slavery Society, Second Annual Report of the American Anti-Slavery Society; with the Speeches Delivered at the Anniversary Meeting, Held in the City of New-York, on the 12th of May, 1835, and the Minutes of the Meetings of the Society for Business (New York: William S. Dorr for the American Anti-Slavery Society, 1835), pp. 24, 25, 27, 31; American Anti-Slavery Society, Third Annual Report, 1836, pp. 20, 22, 23; American Anti-Slavery Society, Fourth Annual Report of the American Anti-Slavery Society, with the Speeches Delivered at the Anniversary Meeting Held in the City of New York, on the 9th May, 1837. And the Minutes of the Meetings of the Society for Business (New York: William S. Dorr for the American Anti-Slavery Society, 1837), pp. 18, 19, 23; American Anti-Slavery Society, Sixth Annual Report of the Executive Committee of the American Anti-Slavery Society, with the Speeches Delivered at the Anniversary Meeting Held in the City of New-York, on the 7th of May, 1839, and the Minutes of the Meetings of the Society for Business Held on the Evening and the Three Following Days (New York: William S. Dorr for the American Anti-Slavery Society, 1839), pp. 33, 38; American Anti-

Slavery Society, Annual Report, Presented to the
American Anti-Slavery Society, by the Executive
Committee, at the Annual Meeting, Held in New
York, May 7, 1856. With an Appendix (New York:
American Anti-Slavery Society, 1856), p. 53; New
York Anti-Slavery Society, Proceedings, 1836, pp.
12-14; Ohio Anti-Slavery Society, Report of the
First Anniversary, 1836, pp. 4-6; Ohio Anti-Slavery
Society, Report of the Second Anniversary, 1837,
pp. 3-6; Ohio Anti-Slavery Society, Report of the
Third Anniversary, 1838, pp. 3-4; Ohio Anti-Slavery
Society, Report of the Fourth Anniversary, 1839,
p. 3; Ohio Anti-Slavery Society, Report of the Fifth
Anniversary of the Ohio State Anti-Slavery Society,
Held in Masillon, Stark County, Ohio, May 27, 1840
(n. p. , 1840), pp. 1, 3; Christian Anti-Slavery Convention, Minutes of the Christian Anti-Slavery Convention. Assembled April 17th-20th, 1850 (Cincinnati: Ben Franklin Book & Job Rooms for the
Christian Anti-Slavery Convention, 1850), pp. 17-
18; Christian Anti-Slavery Convention, Minutes of
the Christian Anti-Slavery Convention. Held July
3d, 4th, and 5th, 1851, at Chicago, Ill. (Chicago:
Western Citizen for the Christian Anti-Slavery Convention, 1851), pp. 3-5; Emancipator, 5 May 1835;
Lowell (Ill.) Genius of Liberty, 3 July 1841, 2
April 1842; Oberlin Evangelist, 3 July 1844, 25
May 1853, 9 November 1859; Philanthropist, 26
November 1839, 8 September 1840, 23 June 1841,
5 January and 15 June 1842; Dillon, "Antislavery
Movement in Illinois, " pp. 286-87, 294-95; Muelder,
Fighters for Freedom, p. 169; and Fletcher, His-
tory of Oberlin, 1:240-41.

170. Stanton was greatly involved with politics. Rice,
      "Henry B. Stanton, " pp. 229-384. Weld worked for
      a time with the political abolitionists in Washington.
      Abzug, "Theodore Dwight Weld, " pp. 272-88. Par-
      ker and Butts were involved with the Liberty Party.
      On Parker see Muelder, Fighters for Freedom,
      pp. 169-70; and File on Lucius H. Parker, Alumni
      Records Office, Oberlin College. On Butts see
      Philanthropist, 9 December 1840, 13 January 1841;
      and Fletcher, History of Oberlin, 1:387.

171. Amos Dresser, The Bible against War (Oberlin: Pub-
      lished for the Author, 1849), pp. 253-76, which
      contained his account of his Nashville experience.

172. Fletcher, History of Oberlin, 1:263-64. Alvord was later connected with the Freedmen's Bureau and was President of the ill-fated Freedman's Bank. See Carl R. Osthaus, Freedmen, Philanthropy, and Fraud: A History of the Freedman's Savings Bank (Urbana: University of Illinois Press, 1976). Alvord's role in the Bank's failure was "ambiguous." P. 165.

173. See the correspondence between Ingraham and the American Board of Commissioners for Foreign Missions begun in December, 1835, in the Emancipator, 11 May 1837.

174. Lucius H. Parker to the Secretaries of the American Home Missionary Society, [1851], AHMS Papers, Roll 28; Joseph H. Payne to Milton Badger, Charles Hall, and David B. Coe, 28 February 1852, AHMS Papers, Roll 29; Samuel H. Thompson to George Whipple, 12 April 1853, AMA Archives, Wisconsin-Roll 1; and Christopher C. Cadwell to Milton Badger, 7 October 1854, AHMS Papers, Roll 31.

175. The rebels who became ordained included: William T. Allan, John W. Alvord, Courtland Avery, Enoch N. Bartlett, Andrew Benton, Charles P. Bush, Lorenzo D. Butts, Christopher C. Cadwell, Ebenezer B. Chamberlain, Uriah T. Chamberlain, Henry Cherry, George Clark, Charles Crocker, Amos Dresser, Amasa Frissell, Augustus T. Hopkins, David S. Ingraham, Deodat Jeffers, Russell J. Judd, Huntington Lyman, Alexander McKellar, Charles S. McPheeters, Enoch R. Martin, Israel S. Mattison, John J. Miter, Lucius H. Parker, Joseph H. Payne, Samuel Payne, John T. Pierce, Ezra A. Poole, George G. Porter, Samuel F. Porter, Marius R. Robinson, Munson S. Robinson, Robert L. Stanton, James Steele, Sereno W. Streeter, James A. Thome, Henry P. Thompson, Samuel H. Thompson, John A. Tiffany, Josiah J. Ward, Joseph Warren, Calvin Waterbury, Edward Weed, Samuel T. Wells, George Whipple, and Hiram Wilson. At least thirty-one of these forty-eight participated in antislavery activities.

176. Oberlin Evangelist, 2 September 1846.

177. Christopher C. Cadwell to George Whipple, 21 November 1860, AMA Archives, Wisconsin-Roll 3; P. H. Fowler, Historical Sketch of Presbyterianism within the Bounds of the Synod of Central New York. Prepared and Published at the Request of the Synod (Utica, N. Y. : Curtiss & Childs, 1877), p. 741.

178. New York Anti-Slavery Society, Proceedings, 1836, p. 14.

179. Christopher C. Cadwell to George Whipple, 21 November 1860, AMA Archives, Wisconsin-Roll 3.

180. See Cadwell's correspondence in the AHMS Papers from 1841 through 1870, Rolls 19-23, 249-74; and Stephen Peet, History of the Presbyterian and Congregational Churches and Ministers in Wisconsin. Including an Account of the Organization of the Convention, and the Plan of Union (Milwaukee: Silas Chapman, 1841), pp. 90, 104, 126, 141, 145-46, 152, 156-57, 179.

181. Christopher C. Cadwell to Lewis Tappan, 1 November 1860, AMA Archives, Wisconsin-Roll 3; Christopher C. Cadwell to Milton Badger, 7 October 1854, AHMS Papers, Roll 31; see also statistics in AHMS Papers, Roll 1.

182. Christopher C. Cadwell to Lewis Tappan, 8 February 1853, 6 March 1854, 7 August 1855, and 1 November 1860, AMA Archives, Wisconsin-Rolls 1, 2, 3; and Christopher C. Cadwell to George Whipple, 21 November 1860, AMA Archives, Wisconsin-Roll 3.

183. Christopher C. Cadwell to George Whipple, 21 November 1860, AMA Archives, Wisconsin-Roll 3; and Lowell (Ill.) Genius of Liberty, 2 April 1842.

184. Ibid. When emancipation seemed assured, Cadwoll wrote to Whipple, on December 12, 1864, "In my judgment God will favor our cause by just so much as we obey the voices of providence requiring our most earnst [sic] endeavor to elevate the unshackled bond man [sic]. I thank the arbitrar [sic] of nations that I am permitted to see this day. " AMA Archives, Wisconsin-Roll 3.

185. Uriah T. Chamberlain to Samuel F. Dickinson, 13 March

1837, Lane Papers, Folder 8, MTS. Chamberlain believed that he owed the Seminary a small amount of money. He instructed the Steward that, if the money were not owed, the Steward should put it "into the treasury of the Lord through the channel of the Anti S. Socy [sic]. "

186. American Anti-Slavery Society, Third Annual Report, 1836, p. 98; and American Anti-Slavery Society, Fourth Annual Report, 1837, p. 139.

187. Uriah T. Chamberlain to Samuel F. Dickinson, 13 March 1837, Lane Papers, Folder 8, MTS; Uriah T. Chamberlain to S. S. Jocelyn, 9 November 1857, AMA Archives, Pennsylvania-Roll 2; and File on Uriah T. Chamberlain, Alumni Records Office, Oberlin College.

188. File on Uriah T. Chamberlain, Alumni Records Office, Oberlin College; Oberlin Evangelist, 25 September 1839, 7 June 1843; and Uriah T. Chamberlain, Jason Olds, Adrian Foote, and Martin Wilcox to Charles G. Finney, 12 December 1846, Finney Papers, Roll 4.

189. Oberlin Evangelist, 5 July 1843, 18 December 1839.

190. Uriah T. Chamberlain to S. S. Jocelyn, 9 November 1857, AMA Archives, Pennsylvania-Roll 2.

191. Uriah T. Chamberlain to George Whipple, 3 November 1853, AMA Archives, Pennsylvania-Roll 1.

192. Uriah T. Chamberlain to S. S. Jocelyn, 21 October 1854 through 11 April 1862, AMA Archives, Pennsylvania-Rolls 1, 2, 3.

193. American Missionary Association, Eighth Annual Report, 1854, p. 55; and American Missionary Association, Ninth Annual Report, 1855, p. 52.

194. American Missionary Association, Thirteenth Annual Report, 1859, pp. 39, 44, 72; and Uriah T. Chamberlain to S. S. Jocelyn, 3 January 1860, AMA Archives, Pennsylvania-Roll 2.

195. Ibid. , p. 72.

196. American Missionary Association, Eleventh Annual Re-
      port, 1857, p. 46.

197. American Missionary Association, The Tenth Annual
      Report of the American Missionary Association, and
      the Proceedings at the Annual Meeting, Held at Ful-
      ton, Oswego Co., N.Y., Together with a List of
      Life-Members (New York: American Missionary
      Association, 1856), p. 54; see also Uriah T. Cham-
      berlain to S. S. Jocelyn, 12 June and 3 July 1856,
      AMA Archives, Pennsylvania-Roll 2.

198. Uriah T. Chamberlain to Andrew Benton, 10 July 1854,
      AMA Archives, Pennsylvania-Roll 1.

199. Uriah T. Chamberlain to S. S. Jocelyn, 9 April 1861,
      AMA Archives, Pennsylvania-Roll 3.

200. Uriah T. Chamberlain to S. S. Jocelyn, 3 July 1856,
      AMA Archives, Pennsylvania-Roll 2. In May, 1856,
      Senator Charles Sumner of Massachusetts delivered
      a scathing attack on the South in a speech, "The
      Crime against Kansas." During this speech he
      also attacked the character of Senator Andrew P.
      Butler of South Carolina (among others). Two days
      later, Representative Preston S. Brooks of South
      Carolina, Butler's nephew, assaulted Sumner in the
      Senate chambers and beat him senseless with a
      cane. The incident greatly increased sectional ten-
      sion. See David Donald, Charles Sumner and the
      Coming of the Civil War (New York: Alfred A.
      Knopf, 1960), pp. 278-311.

201. Shumway and Brower, Oberliniana, p. 35; and I. T.
      Chamberlain to the "Clerk of Oberlin College,"
      2 August 1917, File 16/5, Box 19, OCA.

202. Those rebels unable or unwilling to cement or maintain
      the relationship between antislavery and evangeli-
      calism included: James M. Allan, William T. Al-
      lan, Henry Cherry, Charles Crocker, Deodat Jef-
      fers, Russell J. Judd, Enoch R. Martin, Samuel
      Payne, Ezra A. Poole, Marius R. Robinson, Mun-
      son S. Robinson, Henry B. Stanton, John A. Tif-
      fany, Giles Waldo, Josiah J. Ward, James Warren,
      and Theodore D. Weld. Russell J. Judd pastored
      the Free Church of Brooklyn until 1844 when he

was deposed and excommunicated for "grossly las-
civious conduct." To avoid prosecution he fled and
spent the next twenty-five years as a bookseller in
Wisconsin. Quoted in Oberlin Evangelist, 28 Feb-
ruary 1844; and letters from Lewis Tappan to
Charles G. Finney, Theodore D. Weld, and George
Whipple, 1 and 9 February 1844, Tappan Papers,
Roll 3. Samuel Payne was a missionary for the
American Home Missionary Society from 1836 until
his death in 1845. AHMS Papers, Roll 1. Munson
S. Robinson eventually became a fruit farmer in
California. File on Munson S. Robinson, Alumni
Records Office, Oberlin College. Henry B. Stanton
was never ordained and became a lawyer and politician. By the 1840's and 1850's he had given up
not only evangelicalism but his concern for black
freedom as well. Rice, "Henry B. Stanton," pp.
351, 359-60. John A. Tiffany was a missionary
for the American Home Missionary Society. AHMS
Papers, Roll 1. Giles Waldo became vice-counsul
to the Sandwich Islands. Yale University, Eighth
General Catalogue of the Yale Divinity School, Centennial Issue, 1822-1922 (New Haven: Yale University Press, 1922), p. 62. Josiah J. Ward always
maintained abolitionist principles, but he did no
work in the cause other than to become a life member of the American Missionary Association in 1858.
Josiah J. Ward to George Whipple, 6 January 1858,
AMA Archives, New York-Roll 8.

203. [John Q. Adams and William J. Hinke], General Biographical Catalogue of Auburn Theological Seminary,
1818-1918 (Auburn, N.Y.: Auburn Seminary Press,
1918), p. 61; and Norton, Presbyterian Church in
Illinois, pp. 633-34.

204. Letters from Crocker and Martin are in the AHMS
Papers, Rolls 181-202 and 17-41.

205. File on Deodat Jeffers, Alumni Records Office, Oberlin
College.

206. Emancipator, 5 May 1835.

207. James M. Allan, "Autobiography of One of County's
Original Settlers," undated newspaper clipping, Illinois State Historical Society Library, Springfield.

208. Ibid. The quotation is from William T. Allan, Sereno W. Streeter, John W. Alvord, and James A. Thome to Theodore D. Weld, 9 August 1836, in Barnes and Dumond, eds., Letters of Weld, 1:325.

209. A. Lyman to Milton Badger, 1 June 1850, AHMS Papers, Roll 26.

210. Ordination papers of Marius R. Robinson, 15 March 1836, Robinson Papers, Folder 8, WRHS.

211. Homer C. Boyle, "An Appreciation of Marius R. Robinson" (typed copy of an article in the Salem (Ohio) Daily News, 31 July 1927), Robinson Papers, Folder 7, WRHS.

212. Nye, "Marius Robinson," p. 153.

213. Salem (Ohio) Anti-Slavery Bugle, 26 February 1859.

214. Boyle, "An Appreciation of Marius R. Robinson," Robinson Papers, Folder 7, WRHS.

215. Dillon, "Antislavery Movement in Illinois," pp. 319-22; and A. Lyman to Milton Badger, 1 June 1850, AHMS Papers, Roll 26.

216. Lane Theological Seminary General Catalogue, p. 17; Allan, "Autobiography," Illinois State Historical Society Library; and Portrait and Biographical Album of Henry County, pp. 795, 326-27.

217. Oberlin Evangelist, 22 June 1859.

218. Notes on William T. Allan, Siebert Papers, Box 106, OHS.

219. Abzug, "Theodore Dwight Weld," pp. 290 98.

220. Ibid., p. 290.

221. Ibid., p. 299; and Theodore D. Weld to James G. Birney, 16 December 1848, in Dumond, ed., Letters of Birney, 2:1121. Weld's opinion of ministers is in [Weld], "Oberlin Institute," OCA.

222. Ibid., p. 352.

223. Theodore D. Weld to Lewis Tappan, 2 May 1844, in Barnes and Dumond, eds. , <u>Letters of Weld</u>, 2:1005.

224. Abzug, "Theodore Dwight Weld," pp. 290-98.

CHAPTER VI

SUMMARY AND CONCLUSION: EVANGELICALISM
AND ANTISLAVERY

Context: Cincinnati and Lane Seminary

The major purposes of this study were an investigation
of the role of evangelicalism in the formation of the antislavery of the Lane rebels, and an examination of the relationship
between that evangelicalism and antislavery over a period of
time. An evaluation of the origins of Lane Seminary, of the
Lane debate, of the ensuing rebellion, and of the lives of the
rebels leads to a number of conclusions regarding the relationship of evangelicalism and antislavery in the United States.

The importance of circumstances in the relationship
between evangelicalism and antislavery should not be underestimated. The location of Lane Seminary, only two miles
from Cincinnati, is significant. During the 1830's Cincinnati
was characterized by rapid growth in population, industry,
and trade. The city was tied to the South by its geography,
trade, and the antecedents of many of its citizens. Further,
most Cincinnatians distrusted, suppressed, and attempted to
eliminate--through enforcement of Ohio's oppressive Black
Laws--the city's relatively small black population. Cincinnati's growth and economic prosperity, its pro-Southern attitude, and its anti-black bias all had an impact on the events
which transpired at Lane Seminary in 1834.

In addition, the religious situation in Cincinnati affected
the fortunes of Lane Seminary. Presbyterian ministers and
lay people held prominent positions in the city's political and
economic life, and in its benevolent organizations, and therefore were well-attuned to Cincinnati's character. The issues
disrupting the Presbyterian Church in the 1830's, such as
theology, revivalism, church polity, and control of missions,
were argued heatedly in Cincinnati, and helped to create a
climate of tension, divisiveness, distrust, and animosity.

Lane Seminary was founded within this climate. The roles of Joshua L. Wilson, Ebenezer Lane, and Elnathan Kemper in Lane's establishment demonstrate the Seminary's involvement in numerous controversies from the very beginning. The many conflicts, and their intensity, help to explain, in part, why the trustees acted to restrict the antislavery activities of Lane's students.

The early attempts to secure funds and faculty for the Seminary exacerbated the local situation in the Presbyterian Church, and led to the withdrawal of support from and opposition to the school by Wilson and the Old School faction of the Presbyterian Church. This forced Lane to rely on a smaller base of support. Thus, with fewer sources of aid available, Lane could not afford to alienate any more of its supporters on issues perceived as extraneous to the Seminary's essential purposes. The eventual appointment of Lyman Beecher as Lane's President helped guarantee the Seminary's existence and helped define Lane as a nationally known, unique reform undertaking. It also introduced another group of supporters whose concerns regarding slavery conflicted with those of the trustees in Cincinnati.

Although circumstances did not determine the course of events regarding evangelicalism's role in the formation of antislavery at Lane, they did supply the context from which conflict arose.

Sources: The Lane Debate and Charles G. Finney

Within the context of a pro-Southern and anti-black community, of religious conflict, and of national attention, the Lane debate about slavery took place. The students who planned, participated in, and listened to the discussions were mature, talented, active, self-reliant, evangelical, and united. The Seminary's location near Kentucky, the discussions about slavery in the Cincinnati Journal, the existence of a local branch of the American Colonization Society, the religious context in which slavery was discussed, and the beginning of a movement for immediate emancipation were all additional factors which made the Lane debate possible and controversial. One very important element was the leadership of Theodore Weld.

Weld's role in the Lane debate was central, although, despite the assertions of historians to the contrary, he was not the first nor the major speaker at the debate. [1*] Weld's contributions were his abilities to raise the issue of slavery, to organize and hold the debate over faculty opposition, and to work for the endorsement of immediate emancipation and the condemnation of colonization. The course and content of the debate indicate that Weld was not only an antislavery catalyst, but also a conduit of a particular type of antislavery. Through Weld the participants of the Lane debate received a religiously-inspired form of antislavery based on the revivalistic evangelicalism of Charles G. Finney.

Clearly the course of the debate and the methods employed by Weld and his colleagues to convince their fellow students of the rightness of immediatism were appropriated from the "new measures" revivalism of Finney. Indeed, Finney's significance to the antislavery cause in this respect has been asserted ever since George F. Wright's biography of the revivalist was published in 1891. [2] Although writers since Gilbert H. Barnes have noted routinely the similarity of Finney's revivals and the Lane debate, most of the discussion has dealt only with Finney's techniques of revivalism, and has either ignored or discounted the content of what he was preaching. The substance of Finney's evangelicalism has been overshadowed by the impact of his style. In addition, Finney's relationship to antislavery has been slighted because he refused to make the antislavery cause his major concern, and he criticized it for diverting attention from what he considered to be the more important goal of converting men and women to the "whole gospel."

However, a close examination of Finney's theology in 1834, his early condemnation of slavery, Weld's appropriation of Finney's theology, and the Lane students' antecedents, environment, religious concerns, and evangelical theological perspective reveals that Finney was central to the antislavery of the Lane rebels. [3] To assert that evangelicalism was so pervasive in American society in the 1800's that the Lane students could have appropriated it through the "spirit of the times," and that their antislavery could only have been expressed in the evangelical forms available to them begs the questions of why and how evangelicalism, and, indeed, what type of evangelicalism, was appropriated and used as a foundation for the antislavery of the Lane rebels. [4] Finney supplied the theological framework and moral impulse on which

---

*Notes to Chapter VI begin on page 237.

the Lane rebels based their actions and by which they focused their concerns. That this process came about without Finney's explicit endorsement does not limit his contribution and his significance.

The immediate effects of the Lane debate proved to be more disruptive than the debate itself because they raised the issues of the function of theological education and the proper response of individuals to slavery. Students formed an antislavery society, taught in schools in the black sections of Cincinnati, disseminated antislavery propaganda, and may have aided fugitive slaves. The students were criticized publicly for their apparent self-righteous interference in affairs in which they had no expertise or investment, and for their insistence on treating blacks as social equals. The faculty, concerned with maintaining the Seminary, also criticized the students, and tried to minimize possible damage to the Seminary's reputation by encouraging the formation of a colonization society among the students and by speaking in favor of the American Colonization Society. Beecher misjudged the local situation and journeyed to the East to raise funds for Lane. He left behind many students, who intended to continue their antislavery work, and also the trustees, who were already disturbed by the students' activities.

The Lane debate was significant in two respects. It emphasized the fact that American slavery was a national issue which was not confined to the South or to supporters of the colonization movement. The work of Seminary students in the black community and for antislavery indicated their belief that some response to the sin of slavery, in which everyone was involved, could not be avoided. The debate was important also because it illuminated why the students responded as they did. The revivalistic evangelicalism of Finney provided the basis and impulse from which they acted for antislavery.

Manifestation: The Lane Rebellion

Between July and October, 1834, the trustees' apprehensions increased because of their concern for Cincinnati's prosperity, their fear of mob violence like that which had occurred in New York, their objections in principle to the students' antislavery, and the influence of Professor Biggs, who had a personal dislike for the students. The apprehensions of the trustees, combined with reports of the students' continued antislavery actions, led the Executive Committee to recommend strict measures to control every aspect of Seminary life, including students' extracurricular activities.

Beecher was kept informed of the Executive Committee's actions and, although he urged caution and discretion, endorsed the publication of the Committee's recommendations after it had occurred. Further, he attempted to unite colonizationists and abolitionists in one movement, and have the New York abolitionists lure Weld quietly away from the Seminary. Beecher wanted to avoid confrontation and controversy, but he failed to achieve either of his goals. The situation was further complicated by Beecher's hesitancy to return to Cincinnati when urged to do so, and by his equivocal assertions that he would support both the trustees' actions to control the students and also the students' rights to speak and act freely.

Before Beecher returned the entire Board of Trustees met, accepted the recommendations of the Executive Committee, and passed regulations which put the recommendations into effect. These regulations forbade student extracurricular activities which did not have faculty approval. More important, the Board gave the Executive Committee the power to expel any student without cause. All of the faculty members, after their return to the Seminary, endorsed the new regulations.

When the term commenced, nearly all of the students chose to leave rather than submit to the new regulations. A total of seventy-five out of one hundred and three did not re-enter the Seminary, and have been known since then as the Lane rebels. [5]

Although most of the rebels returned to their homes or went to other schools, over a dozen moved to Cumminsville and continued their studies and their work in the black community. Several of these men aided Weld, who had begun his agency for the American Anti-Slavery Society, in the preparation of the Statement of Reasons. This document explained and defended the students' actions, criticized the trustees and faculty for theirs, and asserted the right of free discussion regarding slavery. Significantly, in the Statement of Reasons, the arguments for free speech and antislavery action were based on an evangelical theological foundation appropriated from Finney, and emphasized particularly his stress on the responsibility of the moral agent to act in total commitment in God's work. [6]

To offset the damage caused by the students' withdrawal, Beecher and Stowe convinced the trustees to amend the oppressive regulations, recruited new students, issued a statement to explain and justify their actions, and defended Lane's course in the press. The "Statement of the Faculty" contained the faculty's reasons for having endorsed the trustees' regulations. It criticized the students for their lack of discretion and refusal to recognize the damage their actions would have on the Seminary's fortunes. The faculty's and the trustees' major concern was the prosperity of the Seminary, and, in their view, antislavery advocacy could only lead to harm.

The students and the faculty and trustees were separated by their respective priorities. Fueled by the "energizing" influence of Finney, the students demanded unconditional and immediate rejection of the sin of slavery. Inspired by the ideal of the reformation of the world from all sin, the faculty and trustees emphasized the importance of Lane as a training center for ministers who would convert the West and the nation to God.

The students' withdrawal generated controversy in Cincinnati and in the East. The extent of the controversy is indicated by the number of newspapers which printed comments and articles about it. Locally, the students were condemned by nearly all of the papers. In the East, papers such as the Boston Recorder asserted that the controversy between students and the faculty and trustees was not about slavery at all, but rather about the control of the Seminary. On the other hand, the trustees and faculty were accused of despotism and duplicity by editors such as Joshua Leavitt, of the New York Evangelist (a paper founded to publicize Finney's views). Besides comments in the press, individuals connected with the Seminary applauded or condemned one side or the other, usually depending on their respective views of the proper attitude towards slavery.

The Lane conflict was significant for the antislavery movement. First, it demonstrated the extent to which the problem of slavery had insinuated itself into the major institutions of American society. Second, it preceded and provided a point of reference for most of the antislavery controversies which occurred in other schools. Third, the rebellion placed antislavery within the context of a Finney-inspired evangelicalism which demanded immediate emancipation. Fourth, it produced a large number of talented and dedicated antislavery advocates who took part in and led various types of antislavery activities. Finally, the antislavery careers of those students who left Lane in the fall of 1834 provided examples of the power--and limitations--of antislavery evangelicalism.

Variations: The Lane Rebels

Of the fifty-four Lane rebels for whom there is some information, at least forty-two engaged in antislavery activities after the end of 1834. [7] At least forty-eight became ordained ministers and many of these worked for antislavery as part of their ministerial duties. The facts that so many were ordained and that most remained evangelicals all their lives indicate the basis from which they supported antislavery.

About one-third of the Lane rebels became students under Finney, who had come west to train a "new race" of revival ministers, at Oberlin Collegiate Institute. At Oberlin there occurred a dispute between Finney, the advocate of revivalism and the "whole gospel," and Weld, the advocate of full-time antislavery action. This conflict illustrates the tensions in the relationship between evangelicalism and antislavery. Finney considered slavery a sin, but asserted that there should be no "diversion of the public mind" from the task of converting people and inculcating their minds with the "whole gospel." In addition, he believed that racial prejudice was not a sin, and that advocating "amalgamation" contradicted the goal of "benevolence," diverted public attention from the very real sin of slaveholding, led to attacks on free blacks, and disrupted the churches. When Finney learned that antislavery advocates would not moderate their actions or rhetoric, he decided to oppose them. Abolitionists, on the other hand, considered the sin of slavery to be "Omnipresent." They believed that the demand for immediate emancipation could not be refuted, nor deferred by any other consideration.

Because of what he considered to be the radicalization of antislavery to evangelicalism's detriment, Finney became estranged from antislavery. This action forced the Lane rebels at Oberlin to choose evangelicalism or antislavery. Finney would have preferred to incorporate antislavery into evangelicalism, and this was the eventual position of most of the rebels. To reach this position it was necessary to make a transition from antislavery to evangelicalism. This transition is best illustrated in the careers of the Lane rebels who were agents for antislavery societies. During the 1830's and 1840's the zeal of these rebels for the antislavery cause continued, but the extent of their activities declined. There were several reasons for this decline, such as the decentralization of the antislavery movement. However, it appears that a resurgence of evangelicalism displaced antislavery as the major focus of many of the rebels' concerns. Thus, evangelicalism itself must be taken into account to help explain the decline of the rebels' full-time antislavery activities. This is especially evident in an examination of the careers of James A. Thome and Edward Weed, both of whom were representative of the Lane rebels who were full-time antislavery advocates. Evangelicalism had supplied the groundwork and impetus for the antislavery of the Lane rebels, but it also limited continued extensive antislavery endeavors by making its own demands.

Nearly all of the Lane rebels for whom there is information eventually emphasized an evangelicalism of which antislavery was a part. The degree to which antislavery was asserted as a part of evangelicalism differed greatly, and was mirrored in the varieties of antislavery activities of the rebels after the 1830's. The extent and character of the part-time antislavery work of the Lane rebels are illustrated in the careers of Christopher C. Cadwell and Uriah T. Chamberlain. Cadwell is representative of those rebels whose careers included a minimal amount of work for antislavery, while Chamberlain was one of those who performed extensive antislavery labors within the context of his evangelical ministry.

Most of the rebels maintained the relationship between evangelicalism and antislavery. There were some, however, who were unable or unwilling to cement or maintain this relationship. Some did nothing for antislavery after 1834; instead they became home or foreign missionaries, or engaged in other religious or secular pursuits. A few left the antislavery movement in discouragement and were pessimistic of its possible success. In various degrees, Marius R. Robinson, William T. Allan, and Theodore D. Weld rejected aspects of evangelicalism because of its appropriation by the churches, which were perceived to be corrupt institutions because of their failure to condemn slavery. In the rejection of the doctrines of evangelicalism, these three paralleled the experience of William Lloyd Garrison. [8] Weld not only moved away from evangelicalism but also from the antislavery and reform which it had precipitated.

An examination of the antislavery careers of the Lane

rebels illustrates the changes in the relationship between evangelicalism and antislavery over a period of time. It also illustrates some of the complexities of the antislavery movement, and helps to explain why people sometimes left the movement. Ironically, the evangelicalism which was responsible for the antislavery of the Lane rebels was also a force in restricting the same antislavery by making its own demands. Taken as a whole, the Lane rebels present a microcosm of evangelical America in its attempts to end the complex and frustrating problem of slavery, and to secure human rights in an unrighteous world.

In the 1870's and 1880's, Theodore Weld occasionally wrote to his fellow Lane rebels, and asked them for their pictures and their reminiscences about Lane Seminary, the debate and the rebellion. His old friends were understandably nostalgic about the events which had occurred on Walnut Hills so many years before. John T. Pierce remembered his "conversion" to immediatism under Weld's influence, and sent along to Weld letters written during the time of the debate and rebellion.[9] George Clark, living in retirement in Oberlin, clearly recalled the speakers and issues discussed at the debate, and his own decision, on learning of the trustees' regulations to forbid student involvement in antislavery, "to take my dismission whoever else might consent to wear a chain."[10] Sereno W. Streeter wrote Weld a description of Cincinnati and Lane Seminary as he had viewed them on a visit in 1874. The city had encroached on the Seminary's grounds, Streeter said, and much had changed in forty years. However, he wrote, "The hall which was completed while we were there and in which we studied, recited, and discussed, still stands in good state of repair." While at the Seminary, Streeter reflected on the events which had taken place in that hall, and their effects, and said, "I thought I could trace a hand overruling events then transpiring, to effect high and holy purposes all his own, and intimately connected with the highest welfare of our race." In turning towards the future, Streeter "could see none of the original Lane Seminary students among the living," but he "could not but hope that some of their works would abide."[11]

Notes

1. See above, pp. 79-84.

2. Wright, Charles Grandison Finney, pp. 151-52.

3. See above, pp. 82-88.

4. Ronald G. Walters has asserted that historians should look at the context in which antislavery arose, and give up the search for sources of motivation of the reformers. His approach is summed up in the following: "As we ought to expect from men and women belonging to a larger culture, defenders of slavery, Northern anti-abolitionists and abolitionists frequently played in an identical key, yet disharmoniously. We should be as intrigued by that particular key as by why some chose to play it one way, others another, and the majority not at all." The Antislavery Appeal: American Abolitionism after 1830 (Baltimore: The Johns Hopkins University Press, 1976), p. 149. A concern with context should not lead, however, to a disregard of the reformers themselves, their interactions, and specific ideas.

5. See above, pp. 132, 157 n. 2.

6. See above, pp. 135-36.

7. See above, pp. 167, 199 n. 2.

8. See William L. Van Deburg, "William Lloyd Garrison and the 'Pro-Slavery Priesthood': The Changing Beliefs of an Evangelical Reformer, 1830-1840," Journal of the American Academy of Religion 43 (June 1975): 224-37.

9. John T. Pierce to Theodore D. Weld, 12 September 1884, Weld-Grimké Papers, Box 16, WLCL.

10. George Clark to Theodore D. Weld, 10 October 1884, Weld-Grimké Papers, Box 16, WLCL.

11. Sereno W. Streeter to Theodore D. Weld, 18 August 1875, Weld-Grimké Papers, Box 15, WLCL.

SELECTED BIBLIOGRAPHY

PRIMARY SOURCES

Manuscripts, Archival Materials, and
Records

Ann Arbor, Mich. University of Michigan. William L.
Clements Library. James Gillespie Birney Papers.

_____. Theodore Dwight Weld, Angelina Grimké Weld,
and Sarah Grimké Papers.

Boston, Mass. Boston Public Library. Amos A. Phelps
Papers.

Chicago, Ill. McCormick Theological Seminary. Lane Theological Seminary Papers.

Cincinnati, Ohio. Cincinnati Historical Society. ALS from
Mrs. William H. Beecher to Mr. and Mrs. Thomas
Perkins, 3 November 1834.

_____. Female Association for the Benefit of Africans.
Constitution, Members, Proceedings, Reports, 1817-1825.

_____. Kemper Family. Collection of Letters, Documents
and Miscellanea of Many Members of the Kemper Family.

_____. Lane Seminary Papers.

_____. Vine Street Congregational Church. Minutes of
the Board of Trustees, 1831-1926.

_____. Nathaniel Wright Diary, Journal & Miscellaneous
Papers.

_____. Wright, Smithson E. , comp. "Obituaries of Cin-
cinnatians" (Scrapbook).

Cincinnati, Ohio. Lane Theological Seminary. Office of the Treasurer. Lane Seminary. Formal Minutes of Meetings of the Board of Trustees, 1828-1838.

_____. Lane Seminary. Minutes of the Meetings of the Faculty, 1833-1879.

Cleveland, Ohio. Western Reserve Historical Society. Marius Racine Robinson Papers.

_____. Vertical File.

_____. Western Anti-Slavery Society. Minute Book, 1857-1864.

Columbus, Ohio. Ohio Historical Society. Wilbur H. Siebert Papers.

London, U. K. London Missionary Society. Candidates Answers to Printed Questions.

New Orleans, La. Dillard University. Amistad Research Center. American Home Missionary Society Papers. Glen Rock, N. J.: Microfilming Corporation of America, 601112, 1975.

_____. American Missionary Association Archives (Microfilm).

New York, N. Y. New York Historical Society. Slavery Manuscripts, Box 2.

Oberlin, Ohio. Oberlin College. Alumni Records Office. Files on Students and Faculty, 1836-1840.

Oberlin, Ohio. Oberlin College. Oberlin College Archives. Henry Cowles Papers.

_____. James H. Fairchild Papers.

_____. File 16/5.

_____. Charles Grandison Finney Papers. Cleveland: Recordak Corporation for Oberlin College, 1958.

_____. Charles Grandison Finney Correspondence, 1830-1875 (Microfilm).

_____. Robert S. Fletcher Papers.

_____. Letters Received by Oberlin College, 1822-1866 (Microfilm).

_____. Morgan-Hopkins Correspondence.

_____. John J. Shipherd Papers.

_____. [Weld, Theodore D.] "The Oberlin Institute" (Typed copy).

Philadelphia, Pa. Presbyterian Historical Society. ALS from Eliza and Henry Spalding to Lorena Hart, 31 March 1834.

Springfield, Ill. Illinois State Historical Society Library. Allan, James. "Autobiography of One of County's Original Settlers" (Undated newspaper clipping).

Washington, D. C. Library of Congress. James G. Birney Papers.

_____. Lewis Tappan Papers (Microfilm).

_____. Elizur Wright Papers.

_____. Nathaniel Wright Papers.

Books and Pamphlets

Barnes, Gilbert H., and Dumond, Dwight L., eds. Letters of Theodore Dwight Weld, Angelina Grimké Weld and Sarah Grimké, 1822-1844. 2 vols. New York: D. Appleton-Century Co., 1934; reprint ed., Gloucester, Mass.: Peter Smith, 1965.

Beecher, Lyman. Beecher's Works. Vol. 2: Sermons, Delivered on Various Occasions. Boston: John P. Jewett & Co., 1852; Cleveland: Jewett, Proctor & Worthington, 1852.

_____. A Plea for Colleges. 2d edition. Cincinnati: Truman & Smith, 1836.

Brainerd, M. Life of Rev. Thomas Brainerd, D. D., for

Thirty Years Pastor of Old Pine Street Church, Philadelphia. Philadelphia: J. B. Lippincott & Co., 1870.

Bristol, Sherlock. The Pioneer Preacher: An Autobiography. Introduction by J. H. Fairchild. New York: Fleming H. Revell, 1887.

The Cincinnati Directory for the Year 1834. Cincinnati: E. Deming, 1834.

Cross, Barbara M., ed. The Autobiography of Lyman Beecher. 2 vols. Cambridge: Harvard University Press, The Belknap Press, 1961.

Crothers, Samuel; Dickey, James H.; and Graham, William. An Address to the Churches on the Subject of Slavery. Georgetown, Ohio: D. Ammen & Co., 1831.

Debate at the Lane Seminary, Cincinnati. Speech of James A. Thome, of Kentucky, Delivered at the Annual Meeting of the American Anti-Slavery Society, May 6, 1834. Letter of the Rev. Dr. Samuel H. Cox, against the American Colonization Society. Boston: Garrison & Knapp, 1834.

Dresser, Amos. The Bible Against War. Oberlin: Published for the Author, 1849.

_____. The Narrative of Amos Dresser, with Stone's Letters from Natchez,--An Obituary Notice of the Writer, and Two Letters from Tallahassee, Relating to the Treatment of Slaves. New York: American Anti-Slavery Society, 1836.

Dumond, Dwight L., ed. Letters of James Gillespie Birney, 1831-1857. 2 vols. New York: D. Appleton-Century Co., 1938.

Executive Committee of the Ohio Anti-Slavery Society. Narrative of the Late Riotous Proceedings against the Liberty of the Press, in Cincinnati. With Remarks and Historical Notices, Relating to Emancipation. Cincinnati: n.p., 1836.

Finney, Charles G. Charles G. Finney: An Autobiography. Specially Prepared for English Readers. London: Hodder & Stoughton, 1882.

_____. Lectures on Revivals of Religion. Edited with an Introduction by William G. McLoughlin. Cambridge: Harvard University Press, Belknap Press, 1960.

_____. Lectures on Systematic Theology, Embracing Moral Government, the Atonement, Moral and Physical Depravity, Natural, Moral, and Gracious Ability, Repentance, Faith, Justification, Sanctification, &c. Edited and revised with an Introduction by George Redford. London: William Tegg & Co., 1851.

_____. Lectures to Professing Christians. Delivered in the City of New-York, in the Years 1836 and 1837. New York: John S. Taylor, 1837.

_____. Memoirs of Charles G. Finney. Written by Himself. New York: A. S. Barnes & Co., 1876.

_____. Sermons on Important Subjects. 3d edition. New York: John S. Taylor, 1836.

Jenkins, Warren. The Ohio Gazetteer, and Travelers Guide. Rev. ed. Columbus: Isaac N. Whiting, 1837.

Johnson, Oliver. William Lloyd Garrison and His Times; or, Sketches of the Anti-Slavery Movement in America, and of the Man Who Was Its Founder and Moral Leader. Introduction by John G. Whittier. New, rev. & enl. ed. Boston: Houghton Mifflin & Co., 1881.

Lane Seminary. Laws of the Cincinnati Lane Seminary. n.p., [1833].

[Lillie, James]. Faith and Works: or the Life of Edward Weed, Minister of the Gospel. New York: C. W. Benedict, 1853.

Mahan, Asa. Autobiography: Intellectual, Moral, and Spiritual. London: T. Woolmer for the Author, 1882.

_____. Out of Darkness into Light, or the Hidden Life Made Manifest through Facts of Observation and Experience: Facts Elucidated by the Word of God. New York: Willard Tract Respository, 1876.

Marryat, Frederick. A Diary in America; with Remarks on Its Institutions. Edited with Notes and Introduction by Sydney Jackman. New York: Alfred A. Knopf, 1962.

May, Samuel J. Some Recollections of Our Antislavery Conflict. Boston: Fields, Osgood, & Co., 1869; reprint ed., New York: Arno Press & the New York Times, 1969.

Pillsbury, Parker. Acts of the Anti-Slavery Apostles. Boston: Cupples, Upham & Co., 1884.

Reminiscences of Rev. Charles G. Finney. Speeches and Sketches at the Gathering of His Friends and Pupils, in Oberlin, July 28th, 1876. Together with President Fairchild's Memorial Sermon, Delivered before the Graduating Classes, July 30, 1876. Oberlin: E. J. Goodrich, 1876.

Ruchames, Louis, and Merrill, Walter, eds. The Letters of William Lloyd Garrison. Vol. 2: A House Dividing Against Itself, 1836-1840. Edited by Louis Ruchames. Cambridge: Harvard University Press, The Belknap Press, 1971.

Sherwood, Elisha B. Fifty Years on the Skirmish Line. Chicago: Fleming H. Revel Co., 1893.

Stanton, Henry B. Random Recollections. 2d ed. New York: MacGowan & Slipper, 1886.

A Statement of the Reasons which Induced the Students of Lane Seminary, to Dissolve Their Connection with that Institution. Cincinnati: n.p., 1834.

Sweet, William Warren, ed. Religion on the American Frontier. Vol. 2: The Presbyterians, 1783-1840: A Collection of Source Materials. New York: Harper & Bros., 1936.

[Tappan, Lewis]. The Life of Arthur Tappan. New York: Hurd & Houghton, 1871.

Taylor, Nathaniel William. Practical Sermons. New York: Clark, Austin & Smith, 1858.

Thome, James A. Prayer for the Oppressed. A Premium Tract. Boston: American Tract Society, [1859].

Thome, James A., and Kimball, J. Horace. Emancipation in the West Indies. A Six Month's Tour in Antigua, Barbadoes, and Jamaica, in the Year 1837. New York: American Anti-Slavery Society, 1838.

[Weld, Theodore D.]. American Slavery as It Is: Testimony of a Thousand Witnesses. New York: American Anti-Slavery Society, 1839; reprint ed., New York: Arno Press & The New York Times, 1968.

[Weld, Theodore D., with the assistance of Thome, James A.]. Slavery and the Internal Slave Trade in the United States of North America; Being Replies to Questions Transmitted by the Committee of the British and Foreign Anti-Slavery Society, for the Abolition of Slavery and the Slave Trade throughout the World. Presented to the General Anti-Slavery Convention, Held in London, June, 1840. London: Thomas Ward & Co., 1841.

Wright, Elizur, Jr. The Sin of Slavery, and Its Remedy; Containing Some Reflections on the Moral Influence of African Colonization. New York: Printed for the Author, 1833.

Wright, Nathaniel. Memorial Address Delivered before the Second Presbyterian Church and Society of Cincinnati. Sunday Evening, April 28, 1872. Cincinnati: Robert Clarke & Co., 1873.

Articles

[Beecher, Lyman]. "Union of Colonizationists and Abolitionists." Spirit of the Pilgrims 6 (July 1833): 396-402.

Clark, George. "Remarks of Rev. George Clark of Oberlin." In Reminiscences of Rev. Charles G. Finney. Speeches and Sketches at the Gathering of His Friends and Pupils, in Oberlin, July 28th, 1876. Together with President Fairchild's Memorial Sermon, Delivered before the Graduating Classes, July 30, 1876, pp. 49-50. Oberlin: E. J. Goodrich, 1876.

Dickore, Marie, ed. "The Elnathan Kemper Account Book, 1829-1843." Bulletin of the Historical and Philosophical Society of Ohio 17 (January 1959): 69-73.

Donald, David, ed. "The Autobiography of James Hall, Western Literary Pioneer." Ohio State Archaeological and Historical Quarterly 56 (July 1947): 295-304.

[Drake, Benjamin]. "Cincinnati at the Close of 1835. "
Western Monthly Magazine 5 (January 1836): 26-31.

[Hall, James]. "Education and Slavery. " Western Monthly
Magazine 2 (May 1834): 266-73.

Jewett, Isaac Appleton. " 'Cincinnati is a Delightful Place: '
Letters of a Law Clerk, 1831-34. " Edited by James
T. Dunn. Bulletin of the Historical and Philosophical
Society of Ohio 10 (October 1952): 257-77.

Lyman, Huntington. "Lane Seminary Rebels. " In Oberlin
Jubilee, 1833-1883, pp. 60-69. Edited by William Gay
Ballantine. Oberlin: E. J. Goodrich, 1884.

Stanton, Robert L. "Remarks of Rev. R. L. Stanton, D. D. ,
of Cincinnati. " In Reminiscences of Rev. Charles G.
Finney. Speeches and Sketches at the Gathering of His
Friends and Pupils, in Oberlin, July 28th, 1876. Together with President Fairchild's Memorial Sermon, Delivered before the Graduating Classes, July 30, 1876,
pp. 25-28. Oberlin: E. J. Goodrich, 1876.

Stowe, Calvin E. "Sketches and Recollections of Dr. Beecher. " Congregational Quarterly 6 (July 1864): 221-35.

Tappan, Lewis [William Penn]. " 'Union of Colonizationists
and Abolitionists. ' " Spirit of the Pilgrims 6 (October
1833): 569-78.

Thome, James A. "Come-outism and Come-outers. " Oberlin Quarterly Review 2 (November 1846): 158-88.

Weed, Edward. "Report on Anti-Slavery Memorials, Adopted
by the American Board of Commissioners for Foreign
Missions, September, 1845. " Oberlin Quarterly Review
1 (February 1846): 279-317.

White, J. C. "Reminiscences of Lane Seminary. " In Pamphlet Souvenir of the Sixtieth Anniversary in the History
of Lane Theological Seminary, Containing Papers Read
before the Lane Club, pp. 5-15. Edited by Howard A.
Johnston, John H. Walter, and Nelson A. Shedd. Cincinnati: Elm Street Printing Co. , 1890.

Newspapers and Periodicals

African Repository, 1833-1835.

Anti-Slavery Record, 1835-1837.

Boston Recorder, 1831-1835.

Cincinnati Baptist Weekly Journal, 1835.

Cincinnati Catholic Telegraph, 1834-1835.

Cincinnati Chronicle and Literary Gazette, 1834-35.

Cincinnati Daily Gazette, 1834.

Cincinnati Journal (earlier called the Pandect, and then the Cincinnati Christian Journal and Religious Intelligencer), 1828-1835.

Cincinnati Standard, 1833-1834.

Emancipator, 1833-1850.

Friend of Man, 1836-1837.

Genius of Universal Emancipation, 1838-1839.

Hudson Ohio Observer, 1833-1835.

Liberator, 1831-1861.

New York Evangelist, 1833-1835.

Oberlin Evangelist, 1838-1862.

Oberlin Quarterly Review, 1845-1849.

Philanthropist, 1836-1843.

Salem (Ohio) Anti-Slavery Bugle, 1851-1859.

Spirit of the Pilgrims, 1833-1835.

Union Missionary, 1844-1846.

Western Monthly Magazine, 1833-1836.

Published Proceedings and Reports

American and Foreign Anti-Slavery Society. Annual Reports.
1840-1854.

American Anti-Slavery Society. Annual Reports. 1834-1840,
1855-1861.

_____. Proceedings of the Anti-Slavery Convention, As-
sembled at Philadelphia, December 4, 5, and 6, 1833.
New York: Dorr & Butterfield for the American Anti-
Slavery Society, 1833.

American Missionary Association. Annual Reports. 1847-
1865.

_____. Proceedings of the Second Convention for Bible
Missions, Held in Albany September Second and Third,
MDCCCXLVI: With the Address of the Executive Com-
mittee, of the American Missionary Association, &c.
&c. &c. New York: J. H. Tobitt for the American
Missionary Association, 1846.

American Union for the Relief and Improvement of the Colored
Race. Report of the Executive Committee of the American Union, at the Annual Meeting of the Society, May 25,
1836. Boston: Perkins & Marvin for the American Union
for the Relief and Improvement of the Colored Race, 1836.

Christian Anti-Slavery Convention. Minutes. 1850-1851.

Lane Seminary. Annual Reports. 1834-1835.

New York Anti-Slavery Society. Proceedings of the First
Annual Meeting of the New-York Anti-Slavery Society,
Convened at Utica, October 19, 1836. Utica: New York
Anti-Slavery Society, 1836.

Ohio Anti-Slavery Society. Annual Reports. 1836-1840.

_____. Proceedings of the Ohio Anti-Slavery Convention.
Held at Putnam, on the Twenty-second, Twenty-third, and
Twenty-fourth of April, 1835. n. p. : Beaumont & Wallace
for the Ohio Anti-Slavery Society, [1835].

Ohio State Christian Anti-Slavery Convention. Proceedings of
the Ohio State Christian Anti-Slavery Convention, Held at
Columbus, August 10th and 11th, 1859. n. p. , [1859].

Presbyterian Church in the United States of America. Minutes of the General Assembly of the Presbyterian Church in the United States of America from A. D. 1821 to A. D. 1837 Inclusive. Philadelphia: Presbyterian Board of Publication and Sabbath-School Work, n. d.

Rail Road Proceedings and Address of Fulton and Vicinity, to the People of Ohio. Cincinnati: Kendall & Henry, 1835.

SECONDARY SOURCES

Books

[Adams, John Q. , and Hinke, William J.] General Biographical Catalogue of Auburn Theological Seminary, 1818-1918. Auburn, N. Y. : Auburn Seminary Press, 1918.

Addresses and Proceedings at Lane Theological Seminary, December 18, 1879. Cincinnati: Elm Street Printing Co. , 1879.

Ahlstrom, Sydney E. A Religious History of the American People. New Haven: Yale University Press, 1972.

Allen, D. Howe. The Life and Services of Rev. Lyman Beecher, D. D. as President and Professor of Theology in Lane Seminary. A Commemorative Discourse, Delivered at the Anniversary, May 7th, 1863. Cincinnati: Johnson, Stephens & Co. , 1863.

Baird, Robert. Religion in America; or, an Account of the Origin, Relation to the State, and Present Condition of the Evangelical Churches in the United States. With Notices of the Unevangelical Denominations. New ed. New York: Harper & Bros. , 1856.

Baird, Samuel John. A History of the Early Policy of the Presbyterian Church in the Training of Her Ministry; and of the First Years of the Board of Education. Philadelphia: Presbyterian Board of Education, 1865.

Ballantine, W. G. , ed. The Oberlin Jubilee, 1833-1883. Oberlin: E. J. Goodrich, 1883.

Barnes, Gilbert Hobbs. The Antislavery Impulse, 1830-1844. Introduction by William G. McLoughlin. New York: D.

Appleton-Century Co. , 1933; reprint ed. , Gloucester, Mass. : Peter Smith, 1973.

Beard, Augustus Field. A Crusade of Brotherhood: A History of the American Missionary Association. Boston: Pilgrim Press, 1909.

Birney, Catherine H. The Grimké Sisters: Sarah and Angelina Grimk[é]; the First American Women Advocates of Abolition and Woman's Rights. Boston: Lee & Shepard, 1885; New York: C. T. Dillingham, 1885; reprint ed. , New York: Haskell House, 1970.

Birney, William. James G. Birney and His Times: The Genesis of the Republican Party with Some Account of the Abolition Movements in the South before 1828. New York: D. Appleton & Co. , 1890.

Centre College. General Catalogue of the Centre College of Kentucky. 1890. Danville: Kentucky Advocate Printing Co. , 1890.

Clark, Calvin Montague. American Slavery and Maine Congregationalists: A Chapter in the History of the Development of Anti-Slavery Sentiment in the Protestant Churches of the North. Bangor, Maine: Published by the Author, 1940.

Cole, Charles C. The Social Ideas of the Northern Evangelists, 1826-1860. New York: Columbia University Press, 1954.

Cutler, Carroll. A History of Western Reserve College, during Its First Half Century, 1826-1876. Cleveland: Crocker's Publishing House, 1876.

Dabney, Wendell Phillips. Cincinnati's Colored Citizens: Historical, Sociological, and Biographical. Cincinnati: Dabney Publishing Co. , 1926; reprint ed. , New York: Negro Universities Press, 1970.

Davis, David Brion. The Problem of Slavery in the Age of Revolution, 1770-1823. Ithaca: Cornell University Press, 1975.

Dayton, Donald W. Discovering an Evangelical Heritage. New York: Harper & Row, 1976.

Donald, David. Charles Sumner and the Coming of the Civil War. New York: Alfred A. Knopf, 1960.

Drury, Clifford Merrill. Presbyterian Panorama: One Hundred Years of National Missions History. Philadelphia: Board of Christian Education, 1952.

Dumond, Dwight L. Antislavery: The Crusade for Freedom in America. Ann Arbor: University of Michigan Press, 1961.

_____. Antislavery Origins of the Civil War in the United States. Ann Arbor: University of Michigan Press, 1939.

Fairchild, James H. Oberlin: The Colony and the College. Oberlin: E. J. Goodrich, 1883.

Feuer, Lewis S. The Conflict of Generations: The Character and Significance of Student Movements. New York: Basic Books, 1969.

Filler, Louis. The Crusade Against Slavery, 1830-1860. New American Nation Series. New York: Harper Torchbooks, 1963.

Fletcher, Robert Samuel. A History of Oberlin College: From Its Foundation through the Civil War. 2 vols. Oberlin: Oberlin College, 1943.

Foster, Charles I. An Errand of Mercy: The Evangelical United Front, 1790-1837. Chapel Hill: University of North Carolina Press, 1960.

Fowler, P. H. Historical Sketch of Presbyterianism Within the Bounds of the Synod of Central New York. Prepared and Published at the Request of the Synod. Utica: Curtiss & Childs, 1877.

Galbraith, R. C. The History of the Chillicothe Presbytery, from Its Organization in 1799 to 1889. Prepared in Accordance with the Order of Presbytery. Chillicothe, Ohio: H. W. Guthrie, Hugh Bell, & Peter Platter, 1889.

Gillett, E. H. History of the Presbyterian Church in the United States of America. 2 vols. Rev. ed. Philadelphia: Presbyterian Board of Publication and Sabbath-School Work, 1864.

Goss, Charles Frederick. Cincinnati: The Queen City: 1788, 1912. 4 vols. Cincinnati: S. J. Clarke Publishing Co., 1912.

Greve, Charles Theodore. Centennial History of Cincinnati and Representative Citizens. 2 vols. Chicago: Biographical Publishing Co., 1904.

Griffin, Clifford S. Their Brothers' Keepers: Moral Stewardship in the United States, 1800-1865. New Brunswick, N.J.: Rutgers University Press, 1960.

Handy, Robert T. A Christian America: Protestant Hopes and Historical Realities. New York: Oxford University Press, 1971.

Hart, Albert Bushnell. Salmon Portland Chase. American Statesmen. Boston: Houghton Mifflin & Co., 1899.

_____. Slavery and Abolition, 1831-1841. American Nation: A History, vol. 16. New York: Harper & Bros., 1906.

Henry, Stuart C. Unvanquished Puritan: A Portrait of Lyman Beecher. Grand Rapids, Mich.: William B. Eerdmans Publishing Co., 1973.

Herbert, John A., ed. History of Cumminsville, 1792-1914. n.p.: Raisbeck & Co., [1914].

Hibben, Paxton. Henry Ward Beecher: An American Portrait. New York: George H. Doran Co., 1927.

History of Cincinnati and Hamilton County, Ohio. Cincinnati: S. B. Nelson & Co., 1894.

History of the Foundation and Endowment, Catalogue, and Trustees, Alumni, and Students of the Lane Theological Seminary. Cincinnati: Ben Franklin Printing Press, 1848.

Horvath, David G., ed. A Guide to the Microfilm Edition of the Papers of the American Home Missionary Society, 1816 (1826-1894) 1936. Glen Rock, N.J.: Microfilming Corporation of America, 1975.

Hudson, Winthrop S. Religion in America. New York: Charles Scribner's Sons, 1965.

Johnston, Howard A.; Walter, John H.; and Shedd, Nelson A., eds. Pamphlet Souvenir of the Sixtieth Anniversary in the History of Lane Theological Seminary, Containing Papers Read Before the Lane Club. Cincinnati: Elm Street Printing Co., 1890.

Kennedy, W. S. The Plan of Union: or a History of the Presbyterian and Congregational Churches of the Western Reserve; with Biographical Sketches of the Early Missionaries. Hudson, Ohio: Pentagon Steam Press, 1856.

Kraditor, Aileen S. Means and Ends in American Abolitionism: Garrison and His Critics on Strategy and Tactics, 1834-1850. New York: Random House, Pantheon Books, 1969.

Lane Theological Seminary General Catalogue, 1829-1899. Cincinnati: Elm Street Printing Works, 1899.

Leonard, Delavan L. The Story of Oberlin: The Institution, the Community, the Idea, the Movement. Boston: Pilgrim Press, 1898.

McLoughlin, William G., Jr. Modern Revivalism: Charles Grandison Finney to Billy Graham. New York: Ronald Press Co., 1959.

_____, ed. The American Evangelicals, 1800-1900: An Anthology. New York: Harper Torchbooks, 1968.

Macy, Jesse. The Anti-Slavery Crusade: A Chronicle of the Gathering Storm. Chronicles of America Series, vol. 28. New Haven: Yale University Press, 1919.

Marsden, George M. The Evangelical Mind and the New School Experience: A Case Study of Thought and Theology in Nineteenth-Century America. New Haven: Yale University Press, 1970.

Mead, Sidney Earl. Nathaniel William Taylor, 1786-1858: A Connecticut Liberal. Chicago: University of Chicago Press, 1942.

Memorial Association. In Memoriam. Cincinnati 1881. Containing Proceedings of the Memorial Association, Eulogies at Music Hall, and Biographical Sketches of Many Distinguished Citizens of Cincinnati. Cincinnati: A. E. Jones, 1881.

Muelder, Hermann R. Fighters for Freedom: The History of Anti-Slavery Activities of Men and Women Associated with Knox College. New York: Columbia University Press, 1959.

[North, Earl R. , ed.]. One Hundred and Fifty Years of Presbyterianism in the Ohio Valley, 1790-1940. Cincinnati: Presbytery of Cincinnati, 1941.

Norton, A. T. History of the Presbyterian Church, in the State of Illinois. St. Louis: W. S. Bryan, 1879.

Nye, Russel B. Fettered Freedom: Civil Liberties and the Slavery Controversy, 1830-1860. East Lansing: Michigan State College Press, 1949.

Oberlin College. General Catalogue of Oberlin College, 1833-1908. Seventy-Fifth Anniversary. Including an Account of the Principal Events in the History of the College, with Illustrations of the College Buildings. Oberlin: Oberlin College, 1909.

Osthaus, Carl R. Freedmen, Philanthropy, and Fraud: A History of the Freedman's Savings Bank. Urbana: University of Illinois Press, 1976.

Peet, Stephen. History of the Presbyterian and Congregational Churches and Ministers in Wisconsin. Including an Account of the Organization of the Convention, and the Plan of Union. Milwaukee: Silas Chapman, 1851.

Portrait and Biographical Album of Henry County, Illinois, Containing Full-page Portraits and Biographical Sketches of Prominent and Representative Citizens of the County. Together with Portraits and Biographies of All the Governors of Illinois, and of the Presidents of the United States. Also Containing a History of the County, from Its Earliest Settlement to the Present Time. Chicago: Biographical Publishing Co. , 1885.

Quillin, Frank. The Color Line in Ohio: A History of Race Prejudice in a Typical Northern State. Ann Arbor: George Wahr, 1913.

Rice, C. Duncan. The Rise and Fall of Black Slavery. New York: Harper & Row, 1975.

Scheiber, Harry N. Ohio Canal Era: A Case Study of Government and the Economy, 1820-1861. Athens: Ohio University Press, 1969.

Scott, Donald M. Pastors and Providence: Changing Ministerial Styles in Nineteenth-Century America. The 1975 M. Dwight Johnson Lecture in Church History. Evanston, Ill. : Seabury-Western Theological Seminary, [1975].

Shotwell, John B. A History of the Schools of Cincinnati. Cincinnati: School Life Co. , 1902.

Shumway, A. L. , and Brower, C. DeW. Oberliniana. A Jubilee Volume of Semi-Historical Anecdotes Connected with the Past and Present of Oberlin College, 1833-1883. Cleveland: Home Publishing Co. , [1883].

Smith, H. Shelton; Handy, Robert T. ; and Loetscher, Lefferts A. American Christianity: An Historical Interpretation with Representative Documents. 2 vols. New York: Charles Scribner's Sons, 1960-1963.

Staudenraus, P. J. The African Colonization Movement, 1816-1865. New York: Columbia University Press, 1961.

Stephens, John Vant. The Story of the Founding of Lane: Address Delivered at the Centennial of Lane Theological Seminary, June 25, 1929. Cincinnati: n. p. , 1929.

Tewksbury, Donald G. The Founding of American Colleges and Universities before the Civil War; with Particular Reference to the Religious Influences Bearing upon the College Movement. New York: Bureau of Publications, Teachers College, Columbia University, 1932.

Thomas, Benjamin P. Theodore Weld: Crusader for Freedom. New Brunswick, N. J. : Rutgers University Press, 1950.

United Presbyterian Synod of Ohio. Buckeye Presbyterianism: An Account of the Seven Presbyterian Denominations with Their Twenty-One Synods and More than Sixty Presbyteries which at One Time or Another Have Functioned Wholly or in Large Part within the State of Ohio. n. p. : United Presbyterian Synod of Ohio, 1968.

United States. Department of Commerce. Bureau of the

Census. Tenth Census of the United States, 1880. Vol. 19, Report on the Social Statistics of Cities, pt. 2.

Waite, Frederick Clayton. Western Reserve University: The Hudson Era. A History of Western Reserve College and Academy at Hudson, Ohio, from 1826 to 1882. Cleveland: Western Reserve University Press, 1943.

Walters, Ronald G. The Antislavery Appeal: American Abolitionism After 1830. Baltimore: The Johns Hopkins University Press, 1976.

Weisberger, Bernard A. They Gathered at the River: The Story of the Great Revivalists and Their Impact upon Religion in America. Boston: Little, Brown & Co., 1958.

Wilson, Henry. History of the Rise and Fall of the Slave Power in America. 3 vols. Boston: Houghton Mifflin & Co., 1872-1877; reprint ed., New York: Negro Universities Press, 1969.

Wright, George Frederick. Charles Grandison Finney. American Religious Leaders. Boston: Houghton Mifflin & Co., 1891.

Wyatt-Brown, Bertram. Lewis Tappan and the Evangelical War Against Slavery. Cleveland: Press of Case Western Reserve University, 1969.

Yale University. Eighth General Catalogue of the Yale Divinity School, Centennial Issue, 1822-1922. New Haven: Yale University Press, 1922.

Articles

Adams, James Luther. "The Voluntary Principle in the Forming of American Religion." In The Religion of the Republic, pp. 217-46. Edited by Elwyn A. Smith. Philadelphia: Fortress, 1971.

Ahlstrom, Sydney E. "Theology in America: A Historical Survey." In Religion in American Life. 3 vols. Edited by James Ward Smith and A. Leland Jamison. Princeton Studies in American Civilization, no. 5. Vol. 1: The Shaping of American Religion, pp. 232-321. Princeton: Princeton University Press, 1961.

An Alabama Man. "Account of Mrs. Beecher Stowe and Her Family." In Uncle Sam's Emancipation; Earthly Care, a Heavenly Discipline; and Other Sketches. With a Sketch of Mrs. Stowe's Family, pp. 5-29. By Harriet Beecher Stowe. Philadelphia: Willis P. Hazard, 1853.

Banner, L. W. "Religion and Reform in the Early Republic: The Role of Youth." American Quarterly 23 (December 1971): 677-95.

Conteur. "Interesting Facts Concerning a Prominent Family in Early Cincinnati." Cincinnati Enquirer, 9 September 1923.

Evans, L. J. "In Memoriam--Calvin Ellis Stowe, D. D." In Pamphlet Souvenir of the Sixtieth Anniversary in the History of Lane Theological Seminary, Containing Papers Read before the Lane Club, pp. 56-82. Edited by Howard A. Johnston, John H. Walter, and Nelson A. Shedd. Cincinnati: Elm Street Printing Co. , 1890.

_____. "The Faculty." In Addresses and Proceedings at Lane Theological Seminary, December 18, 1879, Cincinnati, pp. 24-31. Cincinnati: Elm Street Printing Co. , 1879.

Felter, H. W. "History of Cumminsville, 1811-1873." In History of Cumminsville, 1792-1914. Edited by John A. Herbert. n. p. : Raisbeck & Co. , [1914].

Hammond, J. L. "Revival Religion and Antislavery Politics." American Sociological Review 39 (April 1974): 175-86.

Harrold, Stanley C. , Jr. "The Perspective of a Cincinnati Abolitionist: Gamaliel Bailey on Social Reform in America." Cincinnati Historical Society Bulletin 35 (Fall 1975): 173-90.

Henry, S. C. "The Lane Rebels: A Twentieth Century Look." Journal of Presbyterian History 49 (Spring 1971): 1-14.

Hightower, Raymond L. "Joshua L. Wilson: Frontier Controversialist." Church History 3 (December 1934): 300-316.

Hildreth, William H. "Mrs. Trollope in Porkopolis." Ohio

Archeological and Historical Quarterly 58 (January 1949): 35-51.

Johnson, James E. "Charles G. Finney and a Theology of Revivalism." Church History 38 (September 1969): 338-58.

Johnson, Jesse. "Early Theological Education West of the Alleghanies." Papers of the American Society of Church History, 2d ser., 5 (1917): 119-31.

Keagy, Walter R. "The Lane Seminary Rebellion." Bulletin of the Historical and Philosophical Society of Ohio 9 (April 1951): 141-60.

Loveland, Anne C. "Evangelicalism and 'Immediate Emancipation' in American Antislavery Thought." Journal of Southern History 32 (1966): 172-88.

Mabry, William Alexander. "Ante-Bellum Cincinnati and Its Southern Trade." In American Studies in Honor of William Kenneth Boyd by Members of the Americana Club of Duke University, pp. 60-85. Edited by David Kelly Jackson. Durham, N.C.: Duke University Press, 1940.

Maxwell, G. M. "Early History." In Addresses and Proceedings at the Lane Theological Seminary, December 18, 1879, pp. 18-22. Cincinnati: Elm Street Printing Co., 1879.

Miller, Edward A. "The History of Educational Legislation in Ohio from 1803 to 1850." Ohio State Archaeological and Historical Quarterly 27 (1919): 1-271.

Morris, Edward D. "Leaves from the Early History of Lane." In Thirty Years in Lane and Other Lane Papers, pp. 50-71. n.p., [1896].

Morse, O. E. "Sketch of the Life and Works of Augustus Wattles." Collections of the Kansas Historical Society 17 (1928): 290-98.

Myers, John L. "Antislavery Activities of Five Lane Seminary Boys in 1835-36." Bulletin of the Historical and Philosophical Society of Ohio 21 (April 1963): 95-111.

Nicolai, Edna Ritzi. "Groesbeck, Ohio: The Olive Branch

Church Cemetery. " Bulletin of the Historical and Philosophical Society of Ohio 21 (April 1958): 179-86.

Nye, Russel B. "Marius Robinson, A Forgotten Abolitionist Leader. " Ohio State Archeological and Historical Quarterly 55 (April-June 1946): 138-54.

Pease, Jane H. , and Pease, William H. "The Clerical Do-Gooder: Hiram Wilson. " In Bound with Them in Chains: A Biographical History of the Antislavery Movement, pp. 115-39. Contributions in American History, no. 18. Westport, Conn. : Greenwood Press, 1972.

Reilly, Timothy F. "Robert L. Stanton, Abolitionist of the Old South. " Journal of Presbyterian History 53 (Spring 1975): 33-50.

Steward, T. G. "The Banishment of the People of Colour from Cincinnati. " Journal of Negro History 8 (July 1923): 331-32.

Strong, Sidney. "The Exodus of Students from Lane Seminary to Oberlin in 1834. " Papers of the Ohio Church History Society 4 (1893): 1-16.

Sweet, Leonard I. "The View of Man Inherent in New Measures Revivalism. " Church History 45 (June 1976): 206-21.

Sweet, William Warren. "The Rise of Theological Schools in America. " Church History 6 (September 1937): 260-73.

Tenney, Henry M. "The History of the First Congregational Church of Cleveland. " Papers of the Ohio Church History Society 2 (1892): 26-44.

Thalheimer, M. E. "History of the Vine Street Congregational Church of Cincinnati. " Papers of the Ohio Church History Society 9 (1898): 41-56.

Van Deburg, William L. "William Lloyd Garrison and the 'Pro-Slavery Priesthood': The Changing Beliefs of an Evangelical Reformer, 1830-1840. " Journal of the American Academy of Religion 43 (June 1975): 224-37.

Wade, Richard C. "The Negro in Cincinnati, 1800-1830. " Journal of Negro History 39 (January 1954): 43-57.

Walters, Ronald G. "The Erotic South: Civilization and Sexuality in American Abolitionism. " American Quarterly 25 (May 1973): 177-201.

Welsh, E. B. "The Presbyterian Church in the U. S. A. : Their [sic] Old Synod of Ohio, 1814-1837. " In Buckeye Presbyterianism: An Account of the Seven Presbyterian Denominations with Their Twenty-One Synods and More than Sixty Presbyteries which at One Time or Another Have Functioned Wholly or in Large Part within the State of Ohio. By the United Presbyterian Synod of Ohio. n. p. : United Presbyterian Synod of Ohio, 1968.

Wolf, Richard C. "Charles Grandison Finney: Mr. Oberlin, 1835-1875. " Oberlin Alumni Magazine 71 (September-October 1975): 2-14.

Woodson, Carter G. "The Negroes of Cincinnati Prior to the Civil War. " Journal of Negro History 1 (January 1916): 1-22.

Zorbaugh, Charles L. "From Lane to Oberlin--An Exodus Extraordinary. " Ohio Presbyterian Historical Society Proceedings 2 (June 1940): 30-47.

Unpublished Materials

Abzug, Robert Henry. "Theodore Dwight Weld: A Biography. " Ph. D. dissertation, University of California, Berkeley, 1977.

Corcoran, Thomas Bryant. "The Lane Seminary Rebellion: Its Causes and Consequences. " M. A. thesis, University of Cincinnati, 1962.

Dillon, Merton L. "The Antislavery Movement in Illinois: 1809-1844. " Ph. D. dissertation, University of Michigan, 1951.

Finnie, Gordon Esley. "The Antislavery Movement in the South, 1787-1836: Its Rise and Decline and Its Contribution to Abolitionism in the West. " Ph. D. dissertation, Duke University, 1962.

Harding, Vincent. "Lyman Beecher and the Transformation of American Protestantism, 1775-1863. " Ph. D. dissertation, University of Chicago, 1965.

Hightower, Raymond Lee. "Joshua L. Wilson: Frontier Controversialist. " Ph. D. dissertation, University of Chicago, 1933.

Johnson, Clifton Herman. "The American Missionary Association, 1846-1861: A Study of Christian Abolitionism. " Ph. D. dissertation, University of North Carolina, Chapel Hill, 1958.

Johnson, James E. "The Life of Charles Grandison Finney. " Ph. D. dissertation, Syracuse University, 1959.

Kuhns, Frederick Irving. "Operations of the American Home Missionary Society in the Old Northwest: 1826-1861. " Ph. D. dissertation, University of Chicago, 1947.

Lodwick, Robert Clare. "The Anti-Slavery Controversy in Lane Seminary. " Typewritten paper, McCormick Theological Seminary, 1951.

Myers, John Lytle. "The Agency System of the Anti-slavery Movement, 1832-1837, and Its Antecedents in Other Benevolent and Reform Societies. " Ph. D. dissertation, University of Michigan, 1961.

O'Dell, Richard Frederick. "The Early Antislavery Movement in Ohio. " Ph. D. dissertation, University of Michigan, 1948.

Rice, Arthur Harry. "Henry B. Stanton as a Political Abolitionist. " Ed. D. dissertation, Columbia University, 1968.

Schwalm, Vernon Franklin. "The Historical Development of the Denominational Colleges in the Old Northwest in 1870. " Ph. D. dissertation, University of Chicago, 1926.

Scott, Donald Moore. "Watchmen on the Walls of Zion: Evangelicals and American Society, 1800-1860. " Ph. D. dissertation, University of Wisconsin, 1968.

Vulgamore, Melvin L. "Social Reform in the Theology of Charles Grandison Finney. " Ph. D. dissertation, Boston University, 1963.

Warford, Malcolm Lyle. "Piety, Politics, and Pedagogy: An Evangelical Protestant Tradition in Higher Education at Lane, Oberlin, and Berea, 1834-1904. " Ed. D. dissertation, Columbia University, 1973.

Wyatt-Brown, Bertram. "Partners in Piety: Lewis and Arthur Tappan, Evangelical Abolitionists, 1828-1841." Ph. D. dissertation, The Johns Hopkins University, 1963.

Zikmund, Barbara Brown. "Asa Mahan and Oberlin Perfectionism." Ph. D. dissertation, Duke University, 1969.